THAT GUY IN OUR WOMEN'S STUDIES CLASS

"When Derek Hunter moves to Los Alamos from Valdosta, Georgia, in eighth grade, he is bullied mercilessly. A tall, thin boy with glasses, who likes to wear stovepipe pants and slicked-back hair instead of bell-bottoms and long tresses (this is 1974), he embraces nonconformism mostly because he has nothing in common with boys his age.

"What he knows about boys is "ribald and crude" and a "constant undercurrent of threat." He favors the company of girls, who are more accepting and physically attractive. Boys he begins to think of as "them," as the enemy. And they return the favor in terms of verbal and physical bullying.

"In this tortured litany of harassment mostly set in Northern New Mexico, author Hunter, who lived in New Mexico until the mid-1980s, before moving to New York to become an activist in gender theory, presents a coming-of-age novel of ambivalent identity that the protagonist ultimately figures out on his own."
—María Dolores Gonzales, *Taos News*

Sunstone books may be purchased for educational, business, or sales promotional use.
For information please write: Special Markets Department, Sunstone Press,
P.O. Box 2321, Santa Fe, New Mexico 87504-2321.
Printed on acid-free paper
∞
eBook 978-1-61139-658-4

––––––––––––––––––––

Library of Congress Cataloging-in-Publication Data

Names: Hunter, Allan D., 1959- author.
Title: That guy in our women's studies class : a novel / by Allan D.
    Hunter.
Description: Santa Fe : Sunstone Press, [2022] | Summary: "A personal
    memoir of a genderqueer male seeking a political platform within
    collegiate women's studies programs in the era before modern
    gender-identity politics"-- Provided by publisher.
Identifiers: LCCN 2022001491 | ISBN 9781632933751 (paperback) | ISBN
    9781611396584 (epub)
Subjects: LCSH: Hunter, Allan D., 1959- | Gender-nonconforming
    people--Biography.
Classification: LCC HQ77.8 .H86 2022 | DDC 362.897092--dc23
LC record available at https://lccn.loc.gov/2022001491

––––––––––––––––––––

WWW.SUNSTONEPRESS.COM
SUNSTONE PRESS / POST OFFICE BOX 2321 / SANTA FE, NM 87504-2321 /USA
(505) 988-4418

THAT GUY IN OUR WOMEN'S STUDIES CLASS

ALLAN D. HUNTER

SUNSTONE
PRESS

SANTA FE

The people and events described in this memoir were all quite real, but to streamline and optimize the narrative flow, I have sometimes combined several characters into one composite character, so as to not have to develop so many characters; and on occasions I've also condensed multiple similar events and described them as single events.

The names have all been changed.

DEDICATION

To my professors: Rosalyn Baxandall, Elizabeth Ewen, Naomi Rosenthal, Laura Anker, Deborah D'Amico-Saunders, Charshee McIntyre, Hedva Lewittes, Tom DelGiudice, Luis Camnitzer, Judy Walsh, Eileen Landy, and others whose names escape me, Thank you.

CONTENTS

PREFACE

In 1980, at the age of 21, I came out as a sissy. I was reclaiming the term the same way that proud lesbians referred to themselves as "dykes" or the way that many gay folks were reclaiming the word "queer."

"Sissy" comes from the word "sister" and so it seemed like the right word: a sisterlike, i.e., feminine or girlish, male person.

1980 may seem like the distant past, but the Stonewall riots were already ten years behind us then. We had gay rights activists. We even had trans activists. A lot of people didn't understand why I was using a new and different term. But I wasn't trans. It was something else.

Trans women, both back then and today, tend to say "Don't see me as a trans woman. See me as a woman." That wasn't me. I didn't consider myself female. I considered myself femme. I had been one of the girls when I was a child, and I had not been ashamed of it and hadn't tried to hide it. But until now, I hadn't made a point of telling the world I was *proud* of it. Until now, I hadn't fully realized how much of the world's not-very-warm reaction to me was all about this—that having difficulty making friends, being taunted and bullied and harassed, and being left out from consideration as a romantic or sexual possibility were all strongly predicted by me being a sissy femme.

An identity as a male femme, as opposed to an identity as transgender woman, existed in our culture, but only as a gay male identity. I didn't identify with the gay rights movement: my sexuality wasn't same-sex attraction and I saw a need to untangle gender from either physical sex *or* sexual orientation.

The activists I identified with the most were feminists. They were the ones who said having different behavioral standards and polarized social roles for the sexes was sexist.

So I headed off to the university to major in women's studies.

That Guy in our Women's Studies Class is a rare thing in the world of memoirs: a sequel. In March 2020, my book *GenderQueer: A Story From a Different Closet* was published by Sunstone Press (Santa Fe, New Mexico).

GenderQueer tells the coming-of-age and coming-out story of realizing I had a different gender identity and of giving it a name. At the end of it, I vow to confront the world about how sissy males are treated. In *That Guy in our Women's Studies Class*, I set out to do exactly that, choosing the world of academic women's studies as my platform.

I am a blogger and a theorist, writing about gender, the experience of writing and trying to get published, and other relevant subjects. My theory papers are available on my web site, https://www.genderkitten. com, along with reviews of my books; the blog posts are available in identical form on these platforms:

LiveJournal: https://ahunter3.livejournal.com
WordPress: https://genderkitten.wordpress.com
DreamWidth: https://ahunter3.dreamwidth.org

I can also be reached by email: ahunter3@earthlink.net

I want to express my fond gratitude to Cassandra Lems for reading over two million words' worth of the original autobiography from which the two books were condensed, for finding many of my errors and inconsistencies, and for being very patient with my self-immersion throughout this process. I'd also like to thank my publicist John Sherman for his assistance in getting these words in front of people, and Alice Klugherz for her encouragement and her participation in creating the cover art.

—Allan Hunter, 2021

PART ONE: COMMUTER STUDENT

FALL SEMESTER 1985

I had to find Professor Baxwood and get her okay for me to be in her Women's Studies course.

The course catalog entry for Intro to Women's Studies listed a required prerequisite: "instructor approval." That could be a problem. What if she didn't allow males in her classroom? It wouldn't even have to be anti-male sentiment. It could simply be that the department felt that women needed a space of their own to discuss things as women, which wasn't exactly a rare perspective among feminists.

I hoped not. I'd come a long way to get to this point and already I'd encountered barriers to my plans to become a women's studies major; although so far none of those had been feminist barriers, just pragmatic and procedural difficulties. Would I have to plead my case at this point to be allowed in?

I am one of those male people who always got tagged by other people as being more like a girl than like the other boys. One of the ones who, instead of butching up defensively, said "Yeah, so? The girls are doing it right!"

Five years ago, after being plagued and tormented by questions about my sexual identity and trying to sort out who I was and who I wasn't, I had finally come out. What I had come out *as* was something entirely different from anything or anyone I'd ever heard or read about: a "heterosexual sissy." I had declared that my male body was not wrong but neither was my feminine nature. I had made my first attempts to communicate all that to people. I wasn't a regular straight guy but neither was I gay or transsexual; it was something else.

After several years of frustration it had finally occurred to me that if I wanted to have conversations about such things, women's studies was probably a good place for it. They would be used to talking about sexist expectations and oppressive rules and social roles.

Corridors of white brick, with fliers and posters every twenty yards stapled to corkboards advertising upcoming theatrical events, concerts, handlettered requests for rides or someone selling a camera or a guest speaker to discuss the violations of Native American sovereignty as covered in American history. The busy clatter of shoes, the babble of conversation as students pass en route between class periods. A cluster of young people in bright colors in a sunken semicircle gathered around a boom box cassette player. This was Academic Village, the main building for both classrooms and faculty offices.

I followed the signs for American Studies, which was the home of the Women's Studies program. A young black woman with beautiful textured braids sat at the departmental receptionist desk, typing on an IBM Selectric from handwritten notes attached to a clipboard stand. "Hello, may I help you?" I nodded and asked if Professor Baxwood was available. "I think she's in her office. Down that hall and up the stairs where it says 'Tower One,'" she told me.

I found her door, standing open. The luxuriously dark smell of good coffee greeted me. Professor Baxwood had a square jaw, brick-red hair. On her wall was a poster declaring that equality is not when a female genius can do as well as a male genius; equality is when a female nebbish can get by as easily as a male nebbish. Baxwood was reading from a book and scribbling something on a typed paper next to it. I knocked gently on the doorframe and she looked up and waved me in.

"Hi, I'm Derek Turner," I said, introducing myself. "I am interested in feminism and I want to take this course, 'Intro to Women's Studies.' It says here in the course catalog that the instructor's permission is required."

"It does?" she asked, reaching for the class listing I held out to her. "They must have made a mistake when they typed these up, I don't know how that got in there."

"So it's okay for me to sign up for the course? Good! I'm looking forward to it!"

"Yes, definitely, it's an intro course and I wish it was a required course for all incoming students, especially men. We're certainly not trying to keep people out of it!"

Fantastic! "Oh, and I've also been told that I need an academic advisor, that I'm supposed to select a professor who is in my intended major field. Professor Baxwood, I came to this school in order to major in women's studies."

She nodded. "Yes, I'd be happy to be your advisor. Do you have the card for me to sign? Let's see what else you're taking for your first semester. Hmm...American People, that's the required core course, good...Intro to Anthropology, that's with Cofield, you'll like him, he's a great teacher...Vocal Music, nice. We like to see students getting a diverse education and exploring many interests." She scrawled her signature on the line marked Advisor and handed it back to me. "See you Tuesday!"

I thanked her again and headed back down the Tower One steps. I was in! I was in! I was actually going to be a women's studies student!

Due to the bus schedule, I was early and had hovered in the hallway outside the classroom, imagining informal pre-class discussions of feminist issues among my impending classmates. Three quiet and very young looking black women arrived shortly afterwards, each standing apart, one reading from a magazine. An older white woman came and checked the course listing on the door and nodded to herself. A more confident-looking black woman came around the corner and headed for the pay phone and after a moment or two, from her end of the conversation I gathered that she was Nzuma and was speaking with someone back in New York City: "Yeah, they got us out here all right. 'Old Brookville,' huh! We're out in the middle of fucking *nowhere*. I don't know. I don't know what the hell I'm supposed to do for fun out here in East Bubblefuck. Yeah right. Well you come out and see me. I'm gonna be so bored you wouldn't believe it."

A different conversation to my left became louder and more emphatic and redirected my attention. A black guy with a fade cut was making sharp gestures with his hand and scowling at a white woman in old-fashioned-looking cats-eye glasses; she faced him armed with a brochure or flier of some sort, saying "But it's not fair that all the student activities that get funded are for resident students. We pay the same student fees the same as you do."

"No one says commuter students can't attend," he retorted. "They aren't, as you put it, 'only for resident students.' Why don't you try coming to some functions instead of trying to make this into an 'us versus them' fight?"

She of the cat's-eye spectacles turned in my direction and with a hand-wave included me and a couple others standing nearby and said, "You guys, are all of you commuter students too? Tell me, do you ever go to things like...," she paused to read from a nearby corkboard, "...'hip hop house dance night at the treehouse'?"

The boy next to me shook his head and said, "I just come for classes."

I answered, "Probably not that one, so much, but I saw a flier about a lecture on how Native American treaties are taught and I'd probably go to that if I had a way of getting to it."

Guy with the fade replied, "See? Stuff that happens here isn't just for resident students."

His opponent sighed and turned away, but a moment later was at my elbow. "Listen, I don't know if you realize it or not, but those lectures are sponsored by the faculty, mostly. I'm talking about the student government events, and I don't want to sound prejudiced or anything but most of the resident students are black and, well, I don't mean they shouldn't have their events and things they care about from their culture, because they definitely should, but student government is always run by the resident students and, well, I'm not saying there's no overlap either but a lot of what they put on, what they spend our student fees for, is going toward things that, if you're a...if you're not a part of... black culture, they're not...going to have a lot of appeal to you is what I'm saying. I just want things to be more even-handed."

I shrugged. "What kind of things did you have in mind? Do you want to see the student government sponsor an evening of hard rock and country or something?"

"No, I don't think commuter students want to hang out on campus for things all that much, really. But how about commuter parking spaces reserved for students so we don't have to park way down by the gym, for instance? And a commuter lounge for us to use between classes."

"Well, in my case I ride the bus so I don't need parking spaces, but I see your point, it might benefit other commuters. But why do commuter students need their own lounge?"

She indicated the open half-circle with its chairs and benches off to the side of the hallway. "Well, if you're comfortable hanging around out here between classes...I just think it's easier to study if there's a quieter place without loud music and conversation, that's all. I'm Tracy Marshall by the way, and I'm running for student government president."

"Derek Turner. First year student, for the third time around."

I pulled the signal cord on the bus two full blocks before the entrance to Creedmoor Psychiatric Hospital. I'd learned that it was a good idea to do so because the N22 tended to pick up a lot of speed after crossing over into Queens and the drivers didn't expect many people to get off here.

I came into the front foyer and signed my name and the time in the sign-in sheet. "Where you been off to, huh?" challenged Tony, the security guard at the desk. "You missed lunch, homeboy. That'll teach you to mess around all day."

Pompous self-important jerk. "I have school," I told him, wearing the absence of any facial expression like a shield.

I strode down the linoleum corridor and into the dining room. "Hey, Cowboy!" I called out. "Hi Mary!" My friends waved me over to their table. "Hang on, let me get my lunch first."

I walked into the cafeteria food line, where I was fended off with the immediate statement "We're closed!"

"Yeah, I know, but you're supposed to have a lunch saved for me there in the refrigerator. I have school. It's been cleared with my case manager."

"I don't know anything about it. I don't got nothing in here," the cafeteria worker stated dismissively, thumb pointed at the fridge.

I stalked back out to Cowboy and Mary's table. "They didn't hold lunch for me. Big surprise."

"I have some tuna fish and crackers in my room, if you want," Mary told me.

"Naah, I'll just wait for supper. I'm not all that hungry, it's the principle of the thing."

"Hey," interrupted Cowboy. "We found a cat! She doesn't have a collar but she's been well taken care of before, and I bet somebody lost her."

"We made posters and put them up around the neighborhood," Mary added. "But if no one claims her, we're going to keep her."

"We've named her 'Suzy,'" Cowboy continued. "Come on down and meet her!"

"Hello, Turner residence."

"Hi Mama! It's Derek, calling from New York! I started classes this week, and even though things are just getting started, I'm enjoying it so far."

"Oh, I'm glad to hear it. Your Dad and I are very proud of you. I'm sorry if we let you down when you said you wanted to go there, but we were worried about you and concerned that you were involved with... well, there's no point in bringing that up now, I guess. We always knew you would do well in college if you applied yourself. Now don't get sidetracked by hanging out with the wrong people..."

"I didn't get sidetracked in Albuquerque, and I wasn't hanging out with the 'wrong people.' I got on the right track and figured out what I wanted to do with my life, and I wish you'd quit thinking of that as a bad time. It wasn't."

"Well...as I said before, I shouldn't bring that up, I didn't mean to try to start an argument. We're both very proud of you and glad that you want to be in school, and that you're liking it so far. We'd like to do something for you. I know you said you don't need help with tuition or anything like that but we've been discussing it and...we'd like to buy you a word processor. You can write your papers on it and save them to edit later on. Would that be something that you'd accept from us?"

I was happy to hear what I was hearing. My parents had come a long way from the days when they were declaring that I was mentally ill and a loser who never finished what I started and that I was never going to make anything of myself and that it was all because I got involved with drugs and drug users. This was ninety five percent of the way to being a full apology and they wanted to make reparations. "It sounds really nice," I said truthfully. "I've never used one but I need a typewriter or something of that sort. I'm a little concerned that it will get stolen here is the only thing. But I'll think of something."

Baxwood was having us go around the room and each introduce ourselves and say something about what we had heard or thought about feminism. In the first row of students, a woman who identified herself as Jodi diPietro said she supported women's equality but that she wasn't a bra-burner, and another, Shantay Solomon, also proclaimed that she hadn't burned her bra.

"Does anyone in here know where the term 'bra burner' came from?" Baxwood asked the class. After a moment's pause, she continued, "Back in the late sixties, I was in a New York group, we originally called ourselves 'New York Radical Women' and then we changed our name to 'Redstockings.' This was an era where women couldn't get credit in our own name at the banks; the newspaper job ads had separate listings, 'jobs for men' and 'jobs for women.' Guess which jobs paid more?

"Well, every year at Atlantic City, there was a major media extravaganza where they'd crown the girl who was the best at what women were supposed to be good at, the best at what girls are for. Do you know what event I'm referring to? We still have it. The Miss America Pageant. We felt like we were being told that it wasn't important if we were smart, or could...plan an agenda, invent a new product, sink a basket from the free throw line, suggest a policy...because we were girls and it didn't *matter* if we were any good at any of those things, it wasn't *valued* in us. What was important was to look pretty in a bikini.

"As proponents of women's liberation we had been talking about not getting equal pay, and sex discrimination in hiring, and the news media was basically ignoring us, but they'd televise the Miss America pageant and tell the whole country that this was what was important to American women.

"So we decided to go down and, as long as the media was there to cover the event, see if we could get some attention to our issues. And we set up a huge barrel and called it the Freedom Trash Can, and we threw away spike heel shoes and garter belts and girdles and lipstick tubes, it was a media stunt to get the press to cover us and interview us, and it worked. There was no fire though, nothing got burned. But someone on the television news described us as 'bra burners' and the term stuck."

In the hallway after class, I saw the same guy with the fade haircut going around campaigning to be student government president. "I'm Omar Mason," he told us, "and I want to be your voice and protect your interests." He turned his attention to one of the students who had been in the next row over from me in the classroom. "Hey lovely lady, I must say you're looking fine, it is a privilege to say hello to such a pretty lady, have you decided how to cast your vote?"

She scowled at him in exasperation. "Don't you have any more sense than to address a woman coming out of a women's studies classroom and call her 'pretty lady'? I don't see where your ability to objectify women you don't even know makes you qualified to hold office."

"Whoa, sister, I didn't mean any insult to you, I was just saying how pretty you were and I intended it as a compliment."

I laughed. "You may as well quit while you're behind, because you're digging yourself in deeper."

Omar rolled his eyes. "You think you're going to impress the women by acting like you agree with that shit, you go right ahead, but I don't think that's going to fly."

"At least he's listening to what we have to say," retorted the student he'd singled out for his attention.

Omar Mason shook his head, smiling, and then turned and walked off down the hall, presumably to speak with other students more likely to give him their support.

"Hi, I'm Sharon Solerno," she said, and offered me a handshake. I nodded, taking it.

"Derek Turner. Nice to meet you."

"The way you jumped right in and came to my rescue...that was really something."

I intercepted my own reply before it was off my tongue. Replayed what she had just said again inside my head. Started again. "Umm...I didn't mean to come off that way, like I was some kind of hero. You were doing fine on your own."

Sharon shrugged. "I wasn't really setting a trap for you, but...good catch. In fact, to be honest, okay, maybe I was, a little bit."

I nodded. "I might actually have been preening just a bit."

She gave me a rather wry smile. "I wondered what it would be like if it turned out there were men in the class, how I'd feel about it. I think I was thinking about it in oversimplified terms. Lately I've come to think that for a lot of things, the simple answer isn't the best one after all. Well, I think it's going to be an interesting year. See you Wednesday."

When next I saw Sharon Solerno, she was already seated in Baxwood's class and Tracy Marshall was berating her: "Oh come on, you can't be serious! I'm proud to call myself a feminist, but Andrea Dworkin and her war on porn is an embarrassment. She *is* anti-sex! Have you read some of her articles?"

Sharon faced her, determination in her face, gesturing with her hands. "Doesn't it ever bother you that the moment any feminist says things that criticize the sexuality status quo, she's immediately called anti-sex?" She repositioned herself in her red plastic desk chair. "There are a lot of things that get called sex, or sexual, or sexy or whatever, that when you get right down to it are all about objectification and doing stuff to women or children without their consent. As far as I'm concerned, that's not sex, it's rape. Or the things that get called sex are actually rape. Dworkin is one of the few people brave enough and blunt enough to say so."

I was formulating my own thoughts, considering whether to insert myself into the conversation or remain a spectator. I could talk about the way the sexes are polarized by sexual initiative and why that was political.

Nzuma was apparently also thinking about injecting herself into the discussion, and she beat me to it. "There's more going on in what gets said to be sexy than whether or not there's violence. Maybe you white women don't look at that so much, because the standards are white standards, but you look at who gets violence pointed to them the most, it's often women who don't measure up as beautiful. I hear what you're sayin' about porn, but let me ask you this, you ever look at black porn? A black woman in porn is more often degraded, violence and shit but also disgust like eww bitch you aren't woman enough to be passin' as beautiful, so you deserve this, and suck this, and you're just a whore and black ass is cheap." She shook her head, making her intricate braids toss around her shoulders.

I was shyer about intruding into the conversation now that it was about race as well as gender. I watched and listened instead. Jodi diPietro said the point was that porn was made for men and men felt more powerful if women were having insulting things done to them; Shantay Solomon said that as a black woman she felt like lots of time black women did it to themselves, being nasty to other black women if they were darker or didn't match a stereotype of what a black woman was supposed to look like; Tracy Marshall said this was true for white women too, and was why women needed to bond together.

I was enjoying the conversation even if I wasn't an active participant. These were the kinds of things I wanted to talk about. And my own gender issues, the things I'd come here to discuss, would fit in with the rest of this stuff.

I was also thinking more about race than I was accustomed to. I had noticed that there was an attitude among some white students about the residential campus students, as if the residents were nearly all black and that white students were therefore some kind of endangered minority or something. It was kind of silly because white residential students were actually at least as large a minority among the residential students here as black people were in the New York metropolitan region in general. And yet instead of trying to learn from that, like "Oh, I guess this is what black peoples' lives are like everywhere else," white students often act like they've got to circle the wagons or something.

I wasn't always perfectly at ease among black folks myself; I was sometimes self-conscious about the prospect of saying something that would tag me as a racist or an idiot. I'd grown up in the South as a young child, but then we'd moved to New Mexico when I was thirteen, and although there had been tension and issues between the Anglos and the Spanish, I spent those years out of the company of black people, and that's the way it had been up until I came to the New York area.

But in the last year and a half since I'd come to New York, I'd been in a white-minority situation a few times myself and it hadn't been a threat or anything. I was thinking of moving onto campus and becoming a residential student myself, if things continued to work out.

While searching the library for some extra readings that Dr. Baxwood had mentioned, I ran into Tracy Marshall, who was there for the same purpose. I gave her a short wave, and she nodded. We checked out our books and exited out into the corridor.

"So how's electioneering going?" I asked, displaying my usual skills at small talk. "Do you think you're in the lead, or Omar?"

Marshall laughed. "Neither one of us. We're both going to get whomped. Jim Dortman is a shoe-in for reelection. He's the current prez and this is his senior year and he's popular. He's done a great job. Me and Omar are both doing this as warm-up for next year, when it counts."

"Wow," I responded. "You folks take your student politics seriously. Which is great, but kind of unusual, isn't it?"

"Well, this is a very political campus. The important thing about taking a political stance is you've got to market it, you've got to sell people on the idea you've got something to say. Otherwise, you can have all kinds of political ideas but no one's going to hear them."

Back at the residential facility at Creedmoor, there was a notice pinned up in the entrance foyer for everyone to see, stating that our curfew was being changed from 10 PM to 9:30 PM, effective Monday.

I scowled and muttered darkly about this latest breach of their original promise to us here, to include us in decision-making that affected us, and to treat us with dignity and respect.

I dumped my schoolbooks and things in my room and locked it, then went looking for my friends.

Mary was drinking coffee in the cafeteria, so I headed over to her table. "Did you see that they're locking us in at nine-thirty?" I asked.

"I know, Cowboy told me about it. He's going to meet with his friend Jay, and find out if they can do that. Jay says they're breaking so many regulations and laws that the place could get shut down. Also, there's some kind of thing he wants us to go to in Albany where we can testify about the shit that they pull on us here!" She reached into her worn black handbag and pulled out a flier and handed it over to me. It stated that the New York Commission on the Quality of Care was hosting a two-day event for the community to discuss the housing initiatives called Residential Care Centers for Adults, or RCCAs. That's what ours was, an RCCA, operating in an old building on Creedmoor grounds. The event was open to the public and anyone could read prepared comments. I found it telling that our cheerful little residential facility had posted the note about our curfew but hadn't bothered to publicize this event.

"I need to go upstairs and get something out of my room," Mary told me. "If you'd go up with me just to be a witness...I've been waiting for Cowboy to get back because Jerry Durst has been after me to sign some piece of paper that says I broke the rules, and Cowboy says if I sign it they'll use it against me to try and put me out. Last week he got between me and the elevator and wouldn't let me go anywhere if I didn't sign, and I'm thinking he'd try that again if I went up alone. Cowboy doesn't let him get away with that bullshit."

I rode up with her on the rattly, graffiti-stained elevator to the women's floor. In the little foyer by the elevator, the residence building's notorious lesbian gang was clustered at a formica table. "Hey Leese, hey Moby," Mary greeted them, "is Durst hanging around anywhere?" Moby, the broad-shouldered leader wearing the beret cap, shook her head and indicated that the coast was clear. Mary told me, "Derek, you better stay here or someone will spread rumors that I'm bringing men into my room." She went down the hall toward her quarters.

"Hey, Derek," Moby said, smirking. "We're collecting donations. Do you want to contribute for Jerry's kids?"

The willowy Lisette bent her arms awkwardly at the elbow and shuffled around as if impaired, grinning. "Sorry, I'm all tapped out," I said, laughing.

Queenie was there, hanging out with them. Queenie, like me, was designated male and neither of us was supposed to be on the women's floor. But Queenie, currently adorned in a blonde wig and sporting eyeliner and rouge and lipstick, wasn't seen by staff as a threat to the women's safety and privacy. As if to underline that, Gary Prito came down the hall, clipboard in his right hand, calling out, "Hey, you better not be bothering...oh...I don't guess either of you two would be bothering these ladies, huh?"

Moby laughed and strutted. "There nobody gonna bother any of us here. Cuz I would fuck them up!"

Prito glanced at Lisette and the other women and seemed satisfied that the consensus was that they were fine with us being there, and nodded and walked away.

"You like Cowboy, huh?" Lisette asked insinuatingly. "I seen you two together a lot. I know."

"Not the way you mean," I replied. "I'm a sissy femme but I'm not actually gay. I like Cowboy but we're not a couple."

"Yeah, you just don't want anyone to know. You be liking his ass, you just like the rest of us here."

I saw Queenie again later and came over to talk. "I always hear your friends say 'she' and 'her' when they're speaking about you," I began, "and I wanted to ask you some stuff, if that's okay."

Queenie smiled with a graceful gesture: sure, continue.

"Well, I also hear black people call each other 'my nigga' and stuff, but that doesn't mean I ought to go calling them that."

"Oh no, that surely wouldn't go over, you got that right."

"So I didn't know how you felt about other people saying 'she' to mean you, if it was like 'only if you're one of us' or you'd like it if everyone did."

"You know, that's real sweet of you to ask that, you're a nice boy. Not many people around here would ask such a thing, and I want you to know I do appreciate it, I surely do."

I smiled back and Queenie clasped my hands in his. Hers. I still didn't specifically know. I continued with my train of thought. "Sometimes around gay guys, there's somebody that the others say 'she' about, who doesn't dress all feminine, and I got to wondering if saying 'she' is about being gay or if it's about a person being more like a girl than a boy. What would you say people mostly mean by saying 'she' about a person?"

"Well I always knew when I was growing up that I was this way, and everybody else, they going yeah, this one, he one of them. Everybody know about them people, some people be all nasty and mean about it, but honey I don't care, this is who I am."

"I guess what I mean is...well, I always was more like one of the girls myself, and people thought the same thing about me, but I was attracted to girls and not to boys and that wasn't what they thought about me. So when someone like you gets called 'she' I get to wondering if it's about who you get hot for or if it's about being more like a girl than a guy."

But Queenie didn't understand the distinction I was trying to make, and kept repeating that there were people who were of a type that everyone knew about, and she was recognized as one of that type.

Queenie's perspective seemed to be mostly formed around belonging to an already-existing category that people knew about, while mine on the other hand was all wrapped up in theory, describing myself as belonging to a hypothetical group that I then had to describe.

If I was understanding correctly, all the gay males that Queenie had grown up knowing about painted their nails, wore dresses and skirts and high heels, did their hair, carried handbags and purses, and referred to each other with female pronouns. Or at least except for the ones trying to keep it hidden. That was how you did gay. It wasn't a thing separate from doing femme.

Queenie reminded me strongly of a person with similar personality and behavior that I'd met shortly after I'd arrived in New York last year. And contemplating that got me reminiscing about the sequence of events that had led me to my current situation, living as a college student by day and as one of New York's infamous homeless mentally ill by night.

IGNITION POINT

My teenage years had not been easy; I hit puberty like the Titanic hit the iceberg. Being sexually attracted to girls while also being a boy who was more like a girl *himself* was complicated, and I had had no role model, no socially shared notion of a heterosexual sissy male to identify with and emulate.

I came out on campus at the University of New Mexico in 1980 as a heterosexual sissy, after a long and harrowing fall semester of self-doubt and self-examination. That coming-out venture had its own Titanic-and-iceberg characteristics, too: although I was mostly optimistic and excited about having figured out my peculiar sense of identity, the immediate result of me going public about it was that I was removed from campus and put in a psychiatric facility because I was saying things that people didn't understand and was being rather intensely fervent about it.

I didn't stay locked up for long; there wasn't anything wrong with me, and I knew it, and didn't let medical labels or the suggestion that there must be something wrong with my head dissuade me. But the psychiatric incarceration interrupted my college semester so my parents withdrew me to keep me from being assigned failing grades.

When I extracted myself from the facility a couple weeks later, I wasn't sure what to do next, or how. I had said to myself, "I am going to find a way to grab the world and give it a good hard shake and tell everyone about this gender identity. The world is going to make room for sissy heterosexual males whether it's ready for that or not. I'm going to raise social awareness." But it wasn't at all obvious to me how to go about doing that.

Over the course of the next three years, I took odd jobs and traveled around the country quite a bit, looking for my people, others who had had similar insights or reached similar conclusions, mostly to no avail.

And I wrote. I wrote copiously, trying to put my thoughts into words that would make sense to other people. Toward the end of 1981, I had a 49 page essay. By 1983, I was toting around a 140 page manuscript I called *The Amazon's Brother*, a book that combined descriptions of my personal experience with academic-style social theory. But for the most part my writings went unread.

In the summer of 1984, I was living in Los Alamos, New Mexico, where my parents resided and where I'd attended high school. My former boss at Precision Body Repair, Darrel Mason, had rehired me full-time to do a mixture of janitorial clean-up and random auto mechanic work, with the promise that he would teach me how to do automotive body work. That was the theory, at least. But he kept sending me home early when there wasn't much that needed doing around the shop. "Derek," he'd say, "hey, why don't you empty those trash cans in the paint booth and do a spiffy on those back bays and then you can call it a day." He'd say it like he was offering me a reprieve from unpleasant work, but it meant I wasn't logging enough hours to stay financially independent.

As we moved into the last week of August I paid my September rent with a wince. Darrel was sending me home early more days than not and things were getting tight. I didn't understand what was going on. I hadn't been trained to do anything that would make me a body repair expert, and now, when the shop was quiet, seemed like an ideal time to show me things, teach me the techniques I needed to learn. I was impatient for the day when he'd have me mask up and show me how to paint. And the grunt-work looked kind of fun, too, pulling dents and whatnot. Was he somehow possibly waiting for me to come in on my unpaid off-hours time to learn these things? That didn't seem at all fair; my wages were low, entry-level; how was I supposed to make ends meet if he was taking me off the clock and expecting me to apprentice myself to learn the body repair work for free?

I lived in an efficiency apartment down the block from the shop, so in theory I could stay as late as I wanted and still stumble home and get enough sleep for the next day. I said to Darrel, "If you want, I could hang out if you think I could pick up some techniques or you wanted to put me on a project to learn how...."

"Naaw, that's okay, Derek, there's not much happening here to tell you the truth. Why don't you go catch a meal and relax and we'll see you in the morning?"

It would be easier to catch a meal if I felt like I could afford food. I spent my evenings revising my book instead.

My mom had called me on the phone to let me know that some mail addressed to me had been sent to their place, and she mentioned that a newspaper reporter from out of town would be dropping in in the evening to interview her and my Dad. Some kind of feature story about what it was like to live in Los Alamos. So I went down to White Rock to my parents' house. My mail turned out to be a delayed income tax refund check of close to a thousand dollars, arriving just when I needed it.

The newspaper reporter came in and introduced herself, Vivian Gornick, for *Mother Jones* Magazine. She was an intense-looking woman with an angular face, wide perceptive-seeming eyes, and a crop of short wavy hair. "The magazine wants a story about Los Alamos, what it's like to live here and work here, in the town that was the birthplace of the atomic bomb," she explained.

My dad shook her hand. "Yes, we spoke on the phone, come on in. This is my wife Lee, my son Derek ...did you have any difficulty finding the place?"

She sat down and began with small talk with my parents while I sat there, thinking, trying to make the memory come, something was familiar, something was definitely familiar...

"Vivian Gornick?" I said suddenly. She looked over at me. "... Gornick and Moran?"

She raised her eyebrows and moved her head back a couple inches. I'd surprised her. "Oh, so you read that?" she asked. I nodded. My dad asked what this interplay was all about. "Your son recognized my name from a women's movement compendium I coedited with Barbara Moran fifteen years ago called *Woman in Sexist Society*. It was a popular resource and sold a lot of copies at the time, but it's kind of unusual for anyone to associate my name with it nowadays."

I sat there on the couch with my mind racing. Vivian Gornick, right here in our house! A no-kidding published feminist, one of the people who'd been involved in the ground-breaking early years of the second wave, and from New York at that!

I had to speak with her, I had to! I waited until she had finished her questions of my parents and then asked if I could talk with her briefly before she left. She said she'd have more time tomorrow when she'd be back for some follow-up questions and would definitely make time to speak with me for half an hour or so.

I returned the following night and waited while she asked my parents things about how they came to Los Alamos and what sort of activities they participated in socially and recreationally and so forth.

I stepped out onto the front porch with her when she was ready to leave and began talking excitedly. "I've been reading feminist theory and I've even done some of my own writing. I'm so desperate to find people I can talk to about these things! I hate the social expectations and people's notions and stuff about what I'm like just because I'm male, and I see how it's part of larger stuff, not just personal choices and things."

"Well, you need to be in a big city, a more metropolitan environment. Lots of people move to the cities to find social activities and political movements that you don't find in small towns."

"Yeah, I was thinking the same thing, that I should either go to the west coast or to New York City. California is closer but lately I've been thinking more about New York, that it's more political instead of being all about lifestyles, like being vegetarian or something."

"Well, I may be biased because I come from New York, but I think you're more likely to find what you're looking for there."

I would have enjoyed talking about feminism, about sexual appetite and being a sex object and what heterosexuality might be like if it weren't so polarized, and a host of other things I spent time thinking about. But I worried that Vivian Gornick didn't necessarily feel like spending a couple more hours chatting with some interview subject's son. She did say it was good to see that guys were reading feminism and taking it seriously.

"Oh, go to New York, definitely," she repeated. "People are *not* all the same no matter where you go. People are always saying that, but it's not true. You're more likely to find people who share your interests in New York." Then she said that as an outgrowth of the project she was doing, she had met and interviewed a Los Alamos expatriate now living in Manhattan. His name was David Moskowitz and she could give me his address. She was confident that he would receive me and give me advice and maybe help me get established there if I got in touch with him.

And then she turned the tables and surprised me. "Look me up if you get to New York, too. Here's my address." And she wrote it down for me.

I was in the public library the following Saturday, reading more feminist theory. The piece I was reading was discussing some campus issue facing the academic program at the author's college, and that's when it hit me. In the course of my theory-starved readings I had come across it before—several times, in fact—so instead of being an entirely new notion it felt like it had been there all along, right under my nose. Now I looked at the same paragraph over and over, just staring at the words and seeing an answer to my communication problems.

Yes, here was an ideal means by which I could "join the feminists" and I would not be left out because I was a guy. I'd be able to discuss theory with interesting intellectual women. Hell, I'd be able to submit my *own* theory writings and expect *them* to be discussed. I'd be among radical women, the ones who wanted to actually change society. In fact it sounded like the most satisfying and most fulfilling thing I could imagine. Excited, I went to the reference librarian's desk and explained what I was looking for, and she generated a list for me. My hands were practically trembling as I read over it, and one entry really leaped out at me as particularly promising.

I hitched a ride to my parents' house in White Rock and went enthusiastically bounding into the room where my mom was sitting. "Hi, Mama! Got a minute? I want to talk with you about my living situation, and, well, what I want to do with my life. You know I came back to Los Alamos because Precision Body offered to teach me the body repair trade, but that doesn't seem to be working out..."

"You have to give these things time. I know you're impatient but it takes a while to learn a new skill."

"I know, but he has less and less work for me and I'm not earning enough to be stable. But that's not the main thing I want to talk about, actually. You know that I've been interested in social issues and feminist theory in particular for several years now. And I know you and Daddy always wanted me to go to college. Well, I think I've finally decided what I want to study and major in. I want to enroll in women's studies!"

I had had the reference librarian do a search for colleges with women's studies programs that were near fairly large cities. "Look at these listings for the State University of New York! That's just *perfect*! I want to go to one of these campuses."

My mom looked at me and slowly shook her head. "We've spent a lot of money trying to send you to school and you didn't do well either time. I don't think you're ever going to do well in college. In fact, we're pretty well reconciled to the idea that you're either mentally ill or brain damaged from the drugs you took, and we're going to have to take care of you for the rest of your life. We might consider paying for you to try the community college here in Los Alamos. But we're not wasting any more money on full tuition for you at some out of state college, that's for sure."

I was angry and frustrated. Sending me to college the other times had not been my idea but theirs. Now that it *was* my idea I wasn't going to get any support? I had been so excited about it and now it was a notion that was very hard to put down and give up on.

At this point, I felt like if I expressed what I was feeling it was just going to feed into her sense of me as a spoiled self-centered immature person. I was an adult and my parents legitimately didn't owe me anything, and if they weren't excited to send me to college again, I couldn't claim they owed it to me—not while asserting my independence. And getting upset in front of her would make her feel that much more convinced that she knew better than I did what was in my best interests. I stifled what I felt. I'd become pretty good at that over the years. Being a sissy male teaches you to not always display what you're feeling.

I woke up in my Iris Street apartment the next morning, showered and dressed and walked to work, absorbed in my thoughts. This time I didn't even make it to midday: Darrel said "Oh hi, Derek, hey, things are slow this week, so, tell you what, if you'll just sweep up the bays and roll up the air hoses and do the trash cans, you can sign out and call it quits for the day." I dawdled and poked my way through the tasks but there was no way to drag things out beyond eleven o'clock. On top of how my week was already unfolding, this was really the last straw!

"Hi, Daddy, hi Mama. Listen, I've got something to tell you. Can you sit down and join me?" I waited for them to take seats on the couch in the living room, my mom in particular looking wary of what kind of news I might be delivering.

I continued. "I gave notice at Precision yesterday. I offered to work two more weeks but Darrel said he didn't really need me to do that. And I told the landlord I was moving out."

My mom couldn't keep from interrupting. "What did you do that for? I can't believe you did that! You're so irresponsible! So now you have no job and no place to live, are you just going to give up everything? And you must be thinking you can just live here in your old bedroom and not work!"

"No, actually. I'm going to New York. It's where I belong. And instead of sticking around here until my income tax refund is all spent, I'm taking it with me and I'll use it to rent a place to live while I look for a job."

My mom started to speak but came to a dead stop before she'd said anything. I guessed she realized I had become somewhat adept at getting around without my parents' help and that there wasn't a whole lot they could do to stop me. And also that she couldn't have it both ways.

"I'll call you or write to you when I've gotten myself established," I added.

I boxed up my dishes and kitchenware and sheets and towels from my apartment and brought everything down to my parents' house and stored it in the basement for whenever I might need it again. Then I went to the sports equipment store and bought myself a voluminous new backpack. I packed up clothing, my favorite feminist theory books, my sleeping bag, and a skinny notebook containing some New York contacts. I had several people I could connect with once I got there: Vivian Gornick; David Moskowitz; my one-time babysitter Susan Atwater who now happened to be living in Manhattan as an apparel designer with her boyfriend Steve Vincent; and a student at New York University, Ronald Lewis, whom I'd met a couple years earlier on the University of New Mexico campus lawn, who had told me I should look him up if I ever came to New York.

I oiled my hiking boots to make them supple and rain-repellent for the coming winter, and double-checked my packing list. I had my hitchhiking sign already made out -- "New York" in big thick magic marker on white cardboard. I had a copy of *The Amazon's Brother*, of course, typed up and enclosed in a three-ring notebook.

It was Fall of 1984; I may have been temporarily thwarted in my impulse to be a women's studies student but I was 25 years old and tired of wasting time and, college or no college, I was headed for the city.

I stood out on the shoulder of the interstate heading out of Albuquerque, backpack on my back, "New York" sign held in my hand. I didn't explicitly need a jacket yet but it was late enough in the year that it wasn't too warm to wear it and it was one less thing to have to pack. The jacket in question was a standard Levis denim jacket, but I had personalized it, embroidering designs on patches of cloth and then sewing them onto the jacket. One patch held the male and female interlocked signs, but inverted vertically: the crosspiece of the female sign, the part that looks like a plus sign, was above the circle instead of below it; and the arrow from the male sign was at the bottom instead of at the top. It was a symbol I'd designed when I first came out. *Gender inverted*. A second patch, done in red cloth with bright yellow lettering, spelled out the words "Radical Feminist." This fragment of cloth curved in an arch over one corner of the main symbol.

The whole works, the combo of jeans jacket with these custom patches applied to it, was deliberately reminiscent of the Boy Scout uniform I'd once worn with pride. In Boy Scouts, such patches refer to rank or to knowledge that one has gained from experience. So in a similar fashion, I was claiming the authority of personal experience. And advertising political intent. I was *in uniform*. Derek Turner, on official activist business, self-identified political radical, headed for New York.

INTO THE CITY

I caught a ride that took me east out of Albuquerque and into Amarillo, Texas, and then ended up walking through Amarillo and out the other side before catching my next ride. The folks who stopped for me next were a pair of guys about my age wearing baseball caps, in a car with Oklahoma plates. "Where ya *from*?" the driver asked me as I clambered into the back seat. I told him about being from Los Alamos and explained that I was bound for New York. "Well we're from T town," he informed me. "Tulsa, you know."

From the front passenger's seat the other guy in the car explained, "Tulsa is dry. You can't buy no liquor anywhere in the county, nor beer or nothin'! Same with the next county over, so we have to drive all the way to fuckin' *Texas* ever' time we want some Beam or some Bud." He offered me my choice of beer, Jim Beam, or vodka.

My hosts had obviously had a good head start on enjoying the proceeds of their trip. The land was as flat as a kitchen table and the road didn't curve or swerve, but I was nevertheless getting worried about how the driver was driving. He could still manage to attack a telephone pole or question the right of oncoming traffic, such as it was, to occupy the left lane, either of which seemed like a probable occurrence, the more so the longer I stayed in the car with them. "Someone should make a public service ad featuring these two," I thought. "Your liquor policy in action. This is the effect of your dry county law."

I was spared the necessity of making a decision, and potentially having to argue with my new companions about setting me out, when the car started slowing down of its own accord.

Eventually, the shotgun-seat passenger noticed, too. "Hey, wharr you slowin' down for?"

"I ain't, it's slowin' it *self* down, and it ain't the gas, I got a mostly full tank, I don't know what this cuntmobile's problem is!"

I smelled a hot metallic smell that also smelled vaguely like blood, and I had a suspicion about what the situation was, from my experiences doing auto mechanic work. Sure enough, once they'd pulled onto the shoulder and yanked up the hood, there was a lot of nasty smelling smoke rising from the oil fill cap and the radiator overflow spout was violently hurling up surges of boiling green radiator water. The whole engine compartment was radiating heat like a blast furnace.

"You might want to get a reading on your oil level," I suggested, pointing.

The driver of the car seemed obsessed with removing the radiator cap, first trying to grab it bare-handed—"Gawww, fuck, give me a towel from in back, shit that hurts..."—then, with a dirty towel in hand, got it loose, which resulted in a geyser of the remaining coolant splashing out. But I repeated my suggestion and he finally pulled out the dipstick and wiped it on the towel and did a check. The stick came back out completely dry: no oil.

"Well that ain't good is it?" commented the driver's buddy.

"I think the engine light is done burned out. Aww fuck me, man!"

I took my backpack and sign from the back seat and asked them if they wanted me to stop at a service station in the next town and send someone for them. They didn't really acknowledge me, as they'd started yelling at each other and bewailing their fate. The last I saw of them, they were passing one of their liquor bottles back and forth and drinking big gulps of whatever was in it.

I was maybe three miles past where they had broken down when a Volkswagen bus stopped to pick me up. "Hey, how's it going? You're trying to get to New York? That's where we're going. Can you chip in some for gas?"

"Yeah, sure. If you're cool with taking me all the way in, the next tank is on me, and we can alternate."

"Sweet! Well hop in. You can crash in the back seat if you want, or we were going to light up a doobie if you'd rather sit up and hang out. I'm Judy, and this cutie sitting behind the steering wheel is Hank."

I made good on my offer to buy a tank of gas, and then took them up on the offer to doze for a while. Later, when I was awake again, we got to talking. "So do you originally come from New York?" Hank asked. "Or are you going to visit someone?"

"No, I wanted to attend a college in the area, then when that didn't turn out to be possible I decided I'd still like to live there. I think I belong in a big city. I'm tired of small town America and folks not knowing what I'm talking about if I bring up ideas that question society."

"I hear you. So you saying you never been there before?"

"That's right, this will be my first time in New York."

"Oh you're in for a treat. You're gonna like it, I can tell. There's people from all over, from other countries, from all kinds of backgrounds, and nobody expects you to be like everyone else."

"Yeah, I can hardly wait to be back," Judy chimed in. "There's no other place like it." She said she lived on the lower east side of Manhattan, on a block where a lot of Hell's Angels lived, and older European Jewish families and some political militants, and that it was all kind of crazy, and that you could do anything you want.

Hank was from East Orange in New Jersey, which was pretty close to the city, he said, but so boring; he had been hanging out in downtown New York most of the time since he was a teenager, and had been a squatter in an abandoned apartment building for several months before this road trip.

Later, they asked me if I could drive a stick shift. "Sure, I drove a VW bus once before. They got that weird slant to the shift pattern, right?" Judy nodded.

"The way I figure it," Hank said, "if we each took turns driving we could drive straight on through and be in New York by noon. We want to get back so we can score some drugs." Judy nodded emphatically. She rolled a joint and lit it and passed it around, and I took a hit off it when it came my way.

They kept a cassette player loaded with one tape after another, and when we weren't talking we just listened to music and flowed down the highway. I had the van to myself in Tennessee and the beginning of the Carolinas, with the others both asleep, her in the back seat and him sprawled against the passenger side window with a blanket over him. I traded seats with her as the sun was rising, took the back seat and covered myself and soon was sleeping soundly.

When I woke up, Hank was at the wheel and we were in Maryland or northern Virginia, thereabouts. We stopped for food at a delicatessen, getting cold cuts and chips and hard rolls and cheese, and made ourselves sandwiches which we ate while passing around another doobie. I asked Hank if he wanted me to take the wheel for a bit and he agreed and we rotated seats again.

I came up through Pennsylvania and began to see occasional mentions of New York on various signs. I became one car-particle within rush hour traffic for a while and drove along in bumper to bumper traffic for several hours, and when it began to thin out I had crossed over into New Jersey and was on the Turnpike, a toll road. Judy said not to worry, that we didn't have to pay until the end. Somehow I'd always thought of New Jersey as industrial, ecologically ruined, immersed in the urban sprawl centered around New York, but instead we were passing through absolutely gorgeous red and orange and yellow and gold trees in autumn. Judy said they were changing early this year for some reason but that the trees in general looked like this every fall. I wasn't used to deciduous forests like this, and could not believe the spray of incredible colors in the trees. New Mexico had had aspens, which turn bright yellow-gold, but no other color. This was spectacular, like 4th of July fireworks. Being stoned made me especially receptive to the experience.

Within seventy miles or so of the city, Judy took over the driving. Hank was fully awake. I was sitting up, alert and far too excited to have any interest in sleeping.

"Hey, what did you get in this lane for? C'mon, pay attention, now we're stuck behind these people trying to merge!" Hank criticized.

"There was a poky-ass trailer in the left lane! If you want to be useful, look back and tell me when I can pull around!" Judy sniped back. "Aww, you bastard, stay in your lane, learn how to drive," she muttered, cursing traffic.

Judy and Hank seemed to be oddly irritable; they hadn't been, throughout our trip so far, but they were now. They seemed quite obsessed about buying drugs, which they said was the first order of business as soon as we got into the city. I thought they'd been remarkably free and easy with the joints for folks so concerned about running out.

"Who are you going to meet up with first?" Judy asked me.

"Well, I kind of stormed out and didn't make any specific arrangement," I confessed. "My parents wouldn't send me to school like

I wanted and my employer was cutting my hours back and I just decided split-second to go now and quit wasting time. I have some people I'm going to try to drop in on, but they don't really know I'm coming."

We were now in a blighted and ruined part of town, with lots of windows boarded up with plywood panels and scrawly black graffiti painted all over everything. There were broken beer bottles and cars without tires, some of them without window glass, and there were empty paper bags and trash everywhere. A cop was directing traffic at an intersection and pointed at Judy and made motions for her to roll down her window. "Hey you! What's your business here?"

Judy shouted back, "I'm just driving through on my way to the Bronx."

"Get out of here! Turn around and drive off, I don't want to see you in these parts!"

"We got as much right as anybody to drive where we want," Hank yelled at him from the other window. "You can't tell us where we can go!"

"Oh yeah?" snarled the police officer, "you want me to arrest you? I'm telling you get your ass out of here, now!"

I was outraged, too, that a police officer, a pig, *The Man*, would think he had the authority to tell citizens what neighborhoods they could go into.

Judy make a couple of turns and continued in our original direction from one block over. Hank turned to me. "Listen, I don't think we should leave you in the van, I'm sorry, but would you be okay coming upstairs with us while we do the drug buy? Are you gonna be all right with that, you're sure?"

I said, "Sure, no problem." I was thinking maybe if they had some acid I might want to score some myself as long as we were here. I mean, what the heck.

Judy drove around the block and came back one street over and finally found a parking space. We got out and started climbing rusty metal steps. At the next landing, we were intercepted by guys who patted us down as if they were police officers, checking for weapons. We were waved onward and allowed into an apartment.

I followed Hank and Judy. They began talking quietly with a guy wearing a red fedora hat. On either side of me, sitting on the floor, were people with stretchy rubber tubes tied around their arms above the elbow, and they were using needles. Shooting up. *Holy fuck. Holy fuck. Heroin. This is heroin.* Hank and Judy came back and embraced each other lovingly, affectionately, while Hank held a lighter under a bent metal spoon that Judy positioned over the flame, melting some of the drug they had bought. Then Hank drew the bubbling liquid up into a hypodermic needle. He did her first, tying her off. She glanced at me and asked me if I was okay and I said I was. It was sweet, she was worried that they were exposing me to stuff I perhaps needed to be kept insulated from. As if it were going to corrupt me or something. Admittedly I *was* rather freaked out, but I was damned if I was going to let on to that. *Nope, I'm cool.*

Hank slipped the business end of the needle into her vein and injected it slowly. She made sighing sounds and then tied him off and reciprocated the process. Now I understood about the irritability and the impatience to get back to New York. They were nice people, these two, the first heroin addicts I'd ever known. *Holy fucking shit. Welcome to New York. I'm in a goddam heroin den.*

Afterwards, they drove me to the address I said was the best one to try first. They waited while I knocked on the door. I had picked Susan Atwater's address. No answer. They asked if I wanted to try another. I selected Vivian Gornick's apartment building and we went there and there was a doorman at the desk. He buzzed and said no one was picking up.

"If you could leave me off somewhere that I can get a sandwich or something, I can take it from here. I'll wait a while and then go back and try again later and see if someone's home."

They took me to a 24-hour diner that Judy recommended. "Okay," she said, "well...be safe, and take care of yourself. It was nice meeting you."

I must have been aware that Manhattan is an island, and that therefore the cityscape of phenomenally tall buildings that lay in front of me was limited to that island's narrow scope. At the moment, though, I was high on Hank and Judy's pot and a bit discombobulated by the shooting den visit, and so I momentarily forgot what I knew. And in my forgetfulness I visualized a city that extended like this in every direction for miles and miles and miles, farther than I could walk in a day, a place so immense in all of its glorious dimensions that I would never be able to get out of it now that I was here. I was feeling more than a little overwhelmed in this imposingly vertical cityland, and my heart started beating more rapidly and my breath got shallow.

I had contact people, and some money (although not a lot of it) but I hadn't thought to bring maps and I had no idea how to get to the addresses that I had in my notebook. I hadn't done any homework. In a somewhat flouncy fit of pique I had relocated myself to the largest city in the United States without bothering to make any preparations. I hadn't even brought a map. I didn't know how to get back to Susan Atwater's apartment where Hank and Judy had taken me earlier.

The diner where I sat right now was on West Ninth Street. Susan's address was on East Eighth Street. In Albuquerque, Tenth Street Southeast was in a completely different quadrant of the city than Tenth Street Northeast. So if New York was the same way, they could have one set of numbered streets on the east side and a completely different set on the west side and who knows how many hundreds of blocks of other streets in between. Great.

I sat there and the immensity of the city enveloped me and then I took a deep breath and thought about it all. The city is big, *very* big. So if there are people like me *anywhere*, if there are *any* people who have these same thoughts and ideas about being a different gender, the city will have some of them. In other words, if I can't make it here I won't be able to make it anywhere else.

So this is it. Make or break time. I sensed all the people, the immense clustered population of New York, and I reached out to them in my head and I embraced them collectively and relaxed a bit and said to myself, "This is home now. I don't *need* to leave. I am not *going* to leave. I will find what I am looking for here. I am here, I got myself here. I didn't get here in order to turn around and leave. This is my home now."

I got the attention of one of the people waiting tables and ordered a cup of coffee, and when she brought it to my table, I asked about East Eighth Street. "Well, this is Ninth, so you go back a block," she said, pointing, "and then across town to the east side."

Yeah, I'm going to make this work.

The apartment that Susan Atwater and Steve Vincent lived in was on the third floor of an apartment building with a narrow stairway.

Again, no one answered when I knocked. I sat down in the stairwell landing and waited for a while. When I saw another tenant I asked if he knew Susan or Steve and had any idea if they were out of town or anything but he just shook his head.

After a while I left and decided to try Vivian Gornick. I walked to her street (the grid arrangement of New York's streets seemed ridiculously easy; I don't know why it had seemed intimidating earlier) and when I got there once again asked the doorman if Vivian Gornick in apartment 6F was in. He pushed a button and waited and then said apparently not. I asked if the building lobby was available to sit and wait and he said they'd prefer I didn't. I asked if I could leave a note, and he said that would be fine, and provided me with writing paper and a pen. I left a note reminding her of our conversation on the doorstep of my parents' house in Los Alamos.

The other contact people I had available to me were David Moskowitz, whose address was on some place called West End Avenue, and I didn't know where that was; and Ronald Lewis, in an NY University dorm on Fourth Street. These were both people that I had less of a connection to. David Moskowitz was someone I only knew *of*, via Vivian Gornick, and Ronald Lewis was someone I'd talked with a long time ago on the UNM front lawn. 1 was less comfortable about showing up this late on the doorstep of either of them than doing so at Vivian Gornick's or Susan Atwater's.

I decided that I was best off toughing the night through and trying to catch my contacts the next day. I walked back in the direction of Susan's apartment. Many of those apartment buildings had concrete stairs that went *down*, below sidewalk level, to little narrow spaces that looked like utility and trash areas. I didn't think they had any apartments down there, below ground. So no one would have to walk past me to get into or out of their apartment, and folks walking by on the sidewalk probably wouldn't notice me either. I examined several and finally saw one where there were some pasteboard boxes in a stack, and no bulging plastic trash bags, and climbed down and fitted myself behind the pasteboard boxes, which pretty well hid me from view unless someone looked carefully. Then I put on some extra layers of clothes, draped my sleeping bag over me like a blanket, and leaned back against my backpack using it as a pillow and after a while managed to fall asleep.

The next morning I went searching for a place to get some breakfast food before trying my contacts again. I discovered a busy establishment, a delicatessen, processing a lot of people's food orders quickly; people gave their orders and waited around briefly then received the food in a paper bag, paid for it, and left to eat their food elsewhere. Nearly all the orders were for some variation on "egg on a roll"; some folks wanted cheese, some wanted bacon or sausage, some specified how the egg was to be cooked. A fair number of the customers seemed to be known by the guy behind the counter and didn't have to order at all—he apparently already knew their order. Coffee and orange juice were fairly standard accessories. Sounded good.

I got on line and when he asked "Yeah?" I said I'd like an egg on a roll with bacon and cheese, and orange juice and coffee. "Regular?" he asked. I certainly didn't want decaf so I said yes. He was fast; I paid up and took my bag of food out to a nearby bench to eat.

The egg sandwich was quite nice. When I got to the coffee, though, it had cream and sugar in it, which I hadn't ordered, so I went back inside. It took a while to get his attention and then he was somewhat irritable about it. "I thought you said 'regular.'"   "Yeah, regular, not decaf."

He looked at me oddly and asked how did I want it. "Just black," I said.

"Sugar?" he asked.

"No!" I said, getting a bit irritable myself at this point. "Just coffee, black coffee, nothing in it, just coffee by itself. Ordinary normal coffee. Don't put cream or dill pickles or tomato juice or anything else in it." He glared and poured me a cup and handed it to me sourly. I didn't care. It tasted good and it was hot.

Before 9:30 I had checked and verified that neither Susan Atwater nor Vivian Gornick were in. I decided to try Ronald Lewis at NYU. I walked west. I somehow ended up at a weird intersection where 4th Street crossed 8th Street, which seemed like a mistake but that's what the sign said. I finally found the right address and knocked on the door, and a sleepy-looking guy in a hooded jacket opened it. I asked, "Is this where Ronald Lewis lives?"

"Oh, yeah, but he's not in at the moment." He rubbed his eyes and added, "I don't know when he's gonna be back, sorry, I don't know what to tell you."

"Do you know where West End Avenue is?'

"West End...I think that's way uptown somewhere, it doesn't exist down here. Like it belongs to another reality, you know? Maybe try the subway and see if you can find it on the subway map." He gave me directions to a nearby subway station.

On the way there, I walked past a newspaper dispenser that had free classifieds, and I glanced at it and saw that it listed rooms available. I hadn't thought about renting a room, but a single room would certainly be cheaper than an apartment. I folded it up and took it with me.

I stared at the subway map. I was able to figure out my current location, and with the clue that West End Avenue was "way uptown" I found that as well, and saw that a train called the "AA" would take me there from where I was. A token to ride the subway cost me ninety cents; I bought one at the token booth and entered the subway system for the first time.

David and Barbara Moskowitz invited me up, after the doorman at their building had relayed the fact that I was from Los Alamos, New Mexico and that Vivian Gornick had given me David's name. I had caught them on a day when they were headed out for the afternoon; a family friend was coming over to watch the baby, Christopher. They asked how I was faring so far and they were both friendly and welcoming. The baby was cute and I was enchanted. The three of them made a pleasant and warm contrast to some of the harshness of the previous day.

I felt awkward about explaining my full situation, so I shaded the truth a little bit and said that I had other contacts and that I was looking for an inexpensive room and did not explain that I hadn't managed to actually contact any of those other contacts and had no place to spend the night. They said they'd keep an eye out for any possibilities for a room I could rent, and encouraged me to try them again later in the week when they'd have more time. When I left, I was in a more cheerful mood.

I read the free newspaper's classified ads in a nearby coffee shop and circled a few listed as available for immediate occupancy. From a pay phone I called one of the phone numbers and got no answer; tried another and reached an answering machine; but eventually a call resulted in a conversation with a guy who confirmed that the room was available and said I should come out and look at it quickly because he would rent it to the first person who laid down money for it. The apartment was in the Bronx, which he said was fairly close to where I was at West End Avenue. He gave me directions. I took the 1 train and rode for a pretty long time before reaching the stop, which was out in the open air instead of underground.

I rang the doorbell. The metal door buzzed and I opened it and came into the foyer and rode the tiny little elevator to the second floor. A man with tufts of sand-colored hair smiled and waved me toward the doorway where he waited. "You came to see the room I advertised, didn't you? I, umm...well, I may as well tell you what the situation is. I rented it to somebody. It's a very nice room. Would you like to see it?"

Confused, I looked back at him, then replied, "You mean...it was rented previously...and they left?"

"I mean it's not...well I can't rent it to you, you see, because, well, earlier today, earlier this afternoon, I rented it to somebody else. So it's taken, for now. But things could change. I'd like to show it to you, it's a very nice room."

"I...I don't understand, why would I want to look at a room that's not available?"

"Well, maybe you wouldn't. But you traveled all this way. I'm just sitting down to dinner. Would you join me? I am having a very good chicken cordon bleu with mashed potatoes and I have some wine. Do you like white wine?"

"Yes, I *did* travel all this way, because you said you had a room to rent! Are you telling me you rented it to someone else in the time it took for me to get here?"

The man dropped his eyes for a moment. "Don't be angry with me. Please, come, sit with me, won't you?"

The food he had described sounded appetizing, but the situation did not. I wasn't enjoying the conversation so far and the idea of sitting at a table with this person for the duration of a meal repulsed me. I shook my head.

"Oh, I suppose you have better places to go. Because you are a very busy and important person, you are!"

"I have places I need to go because I need to find a place to rent and you don't have one!" I said back.

"Go. Go on then. Some day you won't be so young yourself and you'll see how it feels when nobody will spend time with you!" He made a dramatic wave with his hand, glaring at me, then stomped back in and slammed the door.

In the hallway, as I was waiting for the tiny little elevator to come, another door opened farther down the hall. Someone stepped out, an individual with long dangly earrings, dusky rose lipstick, and a purple kimono, black, svelte, most likely male although I wasn't really sure about that part.

"Is he still pretending to be renting rooms?"

I nodded and smiled a wry smile.

"He's a nasty act, honey, I'm telling you, I said so to him more than once, why he has to be that way, it's rude, sure as I'm breathing. Look, are you actually trying to find a place to stay? No, don't worry hon, I'm not trying to take you home with me. I know a place, though."

I nodded. "I need a place to stay but it would be nice if it didn't include expectations about sharing my bed. I can pay, but it has to be cheap, I don't have a lot of money."

"No, I didn't think you would. You seem nice. This place I know, the old fag who runs it, he's trying to get young guys off the street. You don't have to pay and you don't have to *pay*, if you know what I mean. It's for young gay men, so don't be telling anyone there that you aren't gay if you're not. Stay a couple weeks, stay longer, it's indoors with a bed. You're sweet. You shouldn't ought to be out there on the streets, honey, you take care of yourself now." He wrote down the address and instructions on how to get there. It wasn't far away. As my visit with the Lazarus's had, the kindness of this compassionate guy who had just seen me in the hallway warmed me and made up for the oily creepiness of the other guy.

There were a lot of guys my age, give or take a few years, standing around, leaning against the cast iron trellis or sitting on the porch railing, some smoking cigarettes. I hung out as unobtrusively as possible. They seemed relaxed and I didn't pick up on any vibes that made me uncomfortable. After a while I summoned up the courage to approach one of them, a redhead with large gold hoop earrings. "Hi, I met someone while I was looking for a room and I was pointed in this direction. Do you know of anyone here or around here who has a space available?"

He immediately confirmed that there was a sprawlingly large apartment that many of the guys here were staying in and that I could join them and stay for no charge, pending the okay of the older guy who owned the apartment; I'd have to meet him for a brief inspection. When some of the guys finished their cigarettes and went into the foyer to go inside, he went with them and waved me to come along.

Theoretically I was surrounded by gay guys. I had no reason to doubt it, but at the same time I could not have told you that any of them were gay. It was an assessment that I seldom made of people anyway. It had annoyed and outraged me over the years that so many people had been inclined to categorize me without asking, leaving me to kick against the assumptions. So I'd developed a sort of militant attitude that unless someone told me or at least hinted at it, I didn't know their sexual orientation; and that was on top of being pretty oblivious anyway.

"You look like you're new in town," one of the guys said. "Where are you from?"

"I just hitched here from New Mexico."

"What do you think of New York so far?"

"Well, it's amazingly tall, but not as complicated as I was expecting. I've never seen so many taxicabs in all my life, that's definitely different. I thought I was a fairly sophisticated guy, not uptight or anything, but when the folks I got a ride from said they were going to stop off to score some drugs, I thought they meant marijuana and maybe LSD. It was kind of freaky to suddenly find myself surrounded by people tying off at the elbow and shooting up all around me."

After a little while, the guy with the hoop earrings asked me to follow him to be scrutinized by the guy running the place. I asked for advice: "How is he, is there anything I should do or say, or anything to *not* do or say?"

He replied, "Oh...she's a bit of a real queen, just be nice and be polite, she'll like you."

Oh, like a drag queen, or female-identified, femme...? I wonder, will I have stuff in common with a gay male who gets called she?

But no. He wasn't feminine, or not as I would think of it . The man who stepped forward to meet me was a short, nearly bald red-faced middle-aged man who came out looking disgusted about something. He didn't have on any remotely female accoutrements and didn't mince or prance or whatever they call it with the really stylized gestures. Even around the eyes his skin was red, like a rabbit in a dust-storm. And I didn't feel any sense of sisterly connection or anything.

The red-eyed man interrogated me. "How did you hear about this place? Who brought you here?"

"I met someone where I went to look at a room to rent and...well that didn't work out and we got to talking and he said he knew about a place and sent me here."

He made a kind of "go-away" gesture with his hands. "So I guess I'm like Holiday Inn now." He shrugged and then turned and walked away from me. Interview over, I guess.

The guy who'd brought me up there pointed to indicate we should go back down.

"Did that go okay? I can stay?" I asked.

"Yeah, if the old queen hadn't wanted you here she'd have said so. Don't worry about it, you're cool."

But less than an hour later, a tall guy wearing a knit cap came over to me looking agitated and said, "You're going to have to leave. You know earlier, when you were talking about going to that drug den. Some of the guys here are in recovery and one of them got very upset. We can't have that stuff here. This is a place for people who are trying to get on their feet and leave that kind of stuff behind."

I said, "Oh, well *I* wasn't shooting up, I don't do any kind of IV drug. I went there with the folks who gave me a ride, not knowing that's what they meant by wanting to pick up some drugs. I thought they meant they were going to buy a bag of weed."

He shook his head. "You can't stay here. You got a lot of people upset."

I was frustrated and angry to have a safe place stripped from me so shortly after I'd found it. I tried to talk him out of it, to ask for some sort of confrontation or meeting to talk it out with everyone but he was implacable. I was a disruption they did not need. "I have no place to stay. Do you have any idea where I can find a room? I can pay, but I haven't had any luck yet finding a room I can rent."

He didn't.

After getting something to eat at a coffee shop, I rode the subway back the way I'd come and again went to Susan Atwater's apartment. It was still unresponsive to knocks, so I checked with the doorman at Vivian Gornick's building, where she also wasn't in and had not left any message for me.

I read the job postings section of the little free newspaper I'd taken. Several ads mentioned employment services that would find you a job, and quite a few of those had addresses on 14th Street. That was just a few blocks away from where I was and I could walk from one to the next. It seemed like a real possibility, whereas trying to reply to a typical job ad presented logistical problems: how could an employer contact me until I had an address and a phone number? So I made my way to 14th Street.

I found myself on a block with employment agencies in a cluster. Those were the only businesses on the entire long block except for little delicatessens and magazine and newspaper stores and whatnot. However, it was now late enough that they were all closed. I'd have to come back tomorrow. Well, at least I knew where they were now.

I still had no place to sleep, dammit! Also, I'd been on the road and slept in my clothes and spent one night laying down against concrete where folks put their trash bags. I needed to get cleaned up or nobody was going to want to help me or employ me. I had a decently large supply of clean clothes in my backpack, if I could find a likely bathroom where I could wash up.

I obtained a plastic bag at the cash register of one of the local businesses, which I could use to stuff the dirty clothes in for the time being. I examined the facilities at a diner I came to, but it was a multiple occupancy bathroom with no way to bar the door and I wanted to take my clothes off and wash up good before putting on fresh clothes. A neighborhood bar had a single person bathroom but had loud patrons and the bathroom wasn't very clean and I decided against it. On the next block I came to a neighborhood medical clinic of some sort, a small place with rows of comfortable chairs in the waiting room and brochures about rape trauma and STD prevention and fliers taped up on the wall.

I approached the guy behind the desk, who appeared to be making entries in a stack of medical charts. "Hey, do you mind if I use your bathroom?" He pointed down the hall and then went back to whatever he was working on.

It was indeed a single person bathroom, just what I was hoping for, with a sink and a liquid soap dispenser. I took my time, using an extra t-shirt as a washrag and patting myself dry with a paper towel. I put on fresh clothes, and packed away the ones I'd been wearing to wash later. No one knocked at the door or called out to me. I thought about asking them if they had any advice about a place to stay.

To my surprise, when I stepped out of the bathroom, most of the lights were out and the front desk was empty. I investigated quietly and determined that the little office rooms in back were all unoccupied and the front door was locked from the inside. I guessed that the guy who'd been at the front desk had assumed I'd left without him noticing or had just forgotten about me. I was indoors and there was an actual couch among the chairs in the waiting room and I was clean and in fresh clothes. Nice! I made a pillow out of some rolled-up jeans and fell asleep on their couch.

INTO THE STREETS

The next morning I slipped out early before anyone returned to the clinic. I was soon back on 14th Street at one of the employment service offices. I was asked to fill out paperwork, various forms listing my employment record. I wrote down Precision Body Repair, the Albuquerque hospice home care service I'd worked at before that, included my experience washing dishes and waiting tables at Redbird's Bagel & Broth even farther back, and listed as many places as I could recall from my days in Rangely, Colorado, when I'd done a lot of outdoors day work.

The interviewer waved me to a chair and flipped though the form I'd filled out, then shook his head. "Oh. No, man, listen up, this agency for people who have experience doing your maintenance work in your residential buildings. Each agency, it got a different focus, you gotta go to one where they be wanting a person who gots your skill set, y'see? That one there, across the hall, they sometimes lookin' for short order cook, you could try them. What you need, you gotta find a place that want the personnel for doing the food service. I see you got bussing tables and washing dishes what you done before, that your best bet."

I kept my paperwork with my job info on it and began walking from building to building, and within each of those from one office to another, since three or four agencies would be in the same building— across the hall or up the stairs from each other. I told people I'd worked kitchens as a dishwasher and had done work as a home attendant and was looking for an agency that handled that kind of work.

Finally I found one. I was called into a small office and interviewed by a woman who introduced herself as Marta Kassas. She confirmed that they placed people with experience in kitchen work and ancillary nursing or home attendant type services, mostly in institutional settings.

As I was filling out the forms she hailed a colleague and introduced me to him, Mr. Bikel, known as "Bike." Sometimes I would be working with him, sometimes with her, but they'd both try to place me in a position. Because I had no home, they suggested I take a job where I would be expected to sleep in, which was typical of many of the institutional job settings they dealt with.

It turned out they had an immediate opening. I would pay a $95 fee for the referral, but after that would draw full salary from the employer. The job would include room and board. It was one train ride away on a train called the Metro North, in a town called Katonah. A private boarding school for boys. I would be working in the kitchen. Marta described where to go to catch the Metro North train and explained that a limousine would be waiting to take me from the Katonah station to the school. She spoke for a while on the telephone to the person who would be my supervisor at the school, then asked me if I was comfortable with working for a black woman as my supervisor. I said, "Sure, why wouldn't I be?"

Living outside of New York hadn't really been my intention, but I'd be nearby, and I'd have days off each week. And with room and board covered I could save my money and pursue my other plans later on down the line. It was a reasonable solution to both employment and a place to live. I signed the document, paid the fee, and thanked her.

The Metro North would depart from Grand Central Station, which I found on the subway line map easily. I bought my ticket and located my departure track. I had several hours before the specified late afternoon train to Katonah, but I didn't want to go very far and risk underestimating travel time back to Grand Central, so I bought lunch and got myself a book to read and sat drinking coffee and reading for a while. Later, still having time to kill, I went into a nearby laundromat and washed my small bundle of dirty clothes.

As promised, I was met at the Katonah station by a chauffered limousine and taken to the school. It was a small sprawl of old-fashioned buildings. I followed the driver and was handed off to a small black woman at a desk on the second floor.

She explained my schedule, which days I'd be working and what my starting time would be, where to show up to start my day, and so on. She warned me not to ever use the front entrance, nor to go onto any of the halls and floors used by the students. She called one of the other employees and asked him to show me my quarters; after that, I could come down and eat at the employees' cafeteria and relax for the rest of the evening.

My bed was an old wooden frame bed, not fancy but solid-looking. I had a shelf and a drawer to put my belongings in. Looked nice. I followed the other employee down to the cafeteria and ordered a soup and main course and a cup of coffee, which were provided to me as take-out, to be eaten either at one of the handful of tables or back in my room if I preferred; I was warned not to go into the students' cafeteria area behind the double doors.

I found the food decent. I disposed of my trash and took my coffee with me since I hadn't finished my second cup, and walked back down the hall toward my room. By the time I'd reached the end of the second floor hallway where my room was, my coffee cup was empty so I looked for a trash can to dispose of it. They didn't seem to have any in the hallway. I saw a room with the door open so I glanced in and saw a trash can there next to the door. I stepped in and threw away my cup, then belatedly realized the room was occupied with a couple dozen people sitting at a long table, many of whom had looked up when I'd come in. I nodded then retreated back out into the hallway and went to my room.

A couple hours later I was asked to go to the supervisor's office. When I arrived there, she told me she could not keep me on because the Board of Directors had complained that I'd barged in on their meeting and it was my first day there and it just wasn't a good beginning. I explained what had happened, that I hadn't even realized the room was occupied and had gone in because I'd needed a trash can. "I can't help that," she said. "I have no choice. They asked who you were and when they found out this was your first day here they said to dismiss you. It's beyond my control."

Apparently beyond mine as well. This whole situation was spiraling in that direction. I felt panicky but also as if dissolving into panic was a luxury I couldn't afford; I had to endure and cope.

I was taken back to the train station and was on the sidewalks of

New York City late that same evening, having not even gotten a night's sleep out of the arrangement. I selected a five-floor apartment building with a stairwell and climbed the stairs past the top floor, and curled up as best I could on the landing below the rooftop exit, hoping no one would accost me there. Eventually I fell asleep.

I failed to turn my situation around, and the days began to blur together.

Twice more I paid Marta and Bike a placement fee for a job only to have it evaporate out from under me before I could really get started. They sent me as general kitchen help to a senior citizen's nursing facility, but the crabby hateful man running it was so horribly abusive to the residents.

"On table seven, Mrs. Goldberg, she doesn't get the hamburger patty or the fruit, got it?"

"Dietary restriction, right?"

"Dietary restriction my ass. Her family doesn't pay shit, so she doesn't get any extras on her plate. And dinner is at six. At six oh one, you lock that door, no one else eats, don't fall for their tricks. Teach 'em to get down here on time, I can't wait around for them."

My disgust toward him showed on my face and he said I'd be on the bus back to the city the next morning. I didn't regret losing that one.

But another sleepover job I was sent to in New Jersey failed because the previous worker, whom I was being hired to replace, had decided to keep their job after all. Or so I was told.

I went to look at unfurnished rooms and apartment-share situations, attempting to rent space to stay in. I didn't need anything fancy, just a place to be indoors at night! But I would go to locations and meet someone and they would not finalize the arrangement, or the room was available only to someone who would perform sexual favors.

I finally thought I had identified a good situation—a shared room with two beds, partly furnished, cheap, and immediately available—but I came back to find the locks had been changed and discovered that the person I'd paid the money to didn't have any right to live there himself; and that, furthermore, he had stolen my backpack and sleeping bag while I was out.

I kept on going back to Vivian Gornick's building and Susan Atwater's building but not catching them in. I had better luck visiting the Moskowitz family and Ronald Lewis at NYU, but there was a limited amount that I could reasonably ask of them. David and Barbara Moskowitz hired me to babysit Christopher once, and said I could give people their telephone number as a way of contacting me about jobs or rooms to rent, which were both very nice gestures.

Eventually I did connect with Vivian Gornick but by then I was spending my days scavenging for free food and then scouting around for a place I could spend the night safely, and I often went entire days without speaking to anyone.

And one day in mid-November I drew out the last two dollar bills I had to my name and decided to ceremonially mark my transition to street person in a suitable and appropriate fashion, and bought a forty ounce bottle of beer in a paper bag and drank it in a nearby park.

A month later I got a sinus infection and was feeling pretty rotten with it. I had post-nasal drip and my throat was raw and sore and it hurt fierce to swallow. I went to a community medical services office to ask if I could get some lidocaine samples for my throat, and that's when I was told about the shelters for homeless people.

"Take your shoes off at night and put the rails of your bed down into them," the clinic doctor advised. "That will keep people from being able to steal your shoes while you sleep. It's not a good place, I'll be honest, but you need to be indoors in a heated environment at least until you get over being sick."

Once in the shelter system, I discovered they had social workers, and I made an appointment to see what my options were.

"Have you ever received psychiatric care?" was one of the questions asked. I was suspicious of the relevancy and asked why the social worker wanted to know.

"The newspapers and TV stations are constantly talking about the 'homeless mentally ill,' and the city administration is setting up programs to address that. The programs need success stories, so the mayor can say they put people back on their feet and got them off the streets. So those programs have more resources than the shelter system in general."

"I don't have any interest in being on a locked ward again, or people trying to put me on psychiatric drugs," I warned.

"I can give you a letter and they'll interview you. They aren't equipped to lock people up, that much I can tell you. You'll have to navigate the system and figure out your risks and watch out for your interests, but you seem to me like you're capable of doing that. You'll have a stable situation, your own room, and if they can take credit for you getting out of the system and becoming independent, they'll help you get yourself set up."

And that's how I ended up in a halfway house for people designated homeless mentally ill, on Creedmoor Hospital grounds.

We were all supposed to pick a *program,* a structured activity that would let us work toward our own rehabilitation. I had now been living without income and without a benefactor long enough that I qualified for a full ride on financial aid, so I found my way to the SUNY Brookville campus and applied to attend college. That was my designated *program.*

I hadn't exactly done it the easy way but I'd done it. By day I was a women's studies major attending classes. The place where I ate and slept was RCCA, Building 4, Creedmoor Psychiatric Hospital. At least for now.

CLASSROOMS

The heavy stone fortress that constituted Creedmoor Building 4 was no doubt intended to convey a sense of security—to the surrounding community, not to the people kept within its walls. The interior space had been split: large communal spaces where residents could be observed by staff, small offices with massive steel doors, and long aggregate sleeping quarters with iron bars on the windows. The folks who had refurbished it for use as the Residential Care Center for Adults had carved out two-person bedrooms from the long sleeping rooms and thoughtfully removed the locks from our window bars, but it was still a dismally institutional facility. My footsteps echoed off the thickly painted brick walls of the corridor as I headed for my room.

At my desk, I spun the combination on my master lock and removed the bicycle chain from the hole I had carefully drilled in the Smith-Corona word processor my folks had bought for me. Then I flipped the power switch and watched as the daisy wheel spun and the carriage positioned itself for action. Our assignment was to write a three-four page paper describing when we had first learned about menstruation, at what age, from whom, how it had been described, and what sorts of attitudes and messages we had learned about it.

On the way home on the N-22 bus, I'd been reminiscing about when I was maybe five or six. My parent and grandparents had been impatiently waiting for me to get dressed in my Sunday best in order to go to church; I was being cranky about the dress pants and tie, which I hated. "It could be so much worse," my dad's father had said. "Girls have to wear a girdle when they get older. Be glad you're a boy, a tie and slacks aren't so bad."

My own dad had added, with a conspiratorial look at his father, "Yes, a girdle and worse things. You would have to spend a lot of extra time tending to things in the bathroom that as a boy you are fortunate that you don't need to worry about."

It wasn't the first time there had been vague allusions to odd things that women had to deal with, different merchandise that they kept in the bathroom. In the bathroom that my grandmother used I had seen a rubber bag with a hose on one end and a filler cap on the other; I'd wondered if this was what they were hinting at, but I couldn't imagine what the secret function was, what they did with it and why.

Now I thought about how I could describe that long-ago conversation. I hadn't known about menstruation back then, didn't learn about it until years later; but it seemed like this had been a hint of such things, secret female things to be kept hidden from little boys, so if I could get it down effectively in a paragraph, maybe I would start my paper off with this memory.

I stretched and stood up from my desk and decided to take a break and go socialize with Cowboy and Mary for a while.

Cowboy and Mary tended to hang out in the first floor television lounge; they were both fond of old science fiction movies and cartoons, and the TV lounge gave them more privacy than they had in the cafeteria or the day room. By convention and per the preference of the dedicated TV watchers, the lights were always off.

I stood blinking in the doorway of the unlit lounge, smelling the scent of tepid coffee and milk and stale cigarette smoke. I saw motion from one of the cheap plastic couches; Mary was waving me over. "Suzy wants to say hello," she informed me, lifting the purring cat, who raised her head for skritching. "Hey, I gotta tell you something you are not going to believe. Guess who brought cat treats for Suzy to play with, you'll never in a million years. Tony Blaine, the security guard! I would've figured he'd be one to try to throw her out, or throw us out for having a pet."

"That is surprising," I agreed. "Well, Suzy, you manage to make friends out of just about anybody, don't you?"

Cowboy said there was a classic horror film fest starting in ten minutes. We sat together for the duration of the first movie, and then I decided I should go back and finish my homework.

The assigned reading for Baxwood's class had included a selection from Susan Brownmiller's *Against Our Will* and a short analysis that stated that rape is not a sexual behavior, but instead an expression of power and privilege. She said that the reason men rape is that they can, that they are in a social position where they have the opportunity with relatively little real risk to themselves, and that the only reason it's illegal at all is because of men's property interests in their wives and daughters.

Now we were having a lively discussion in the classroom. Jodi diPietro had her hand up and got called on. "This is the kind of exaggerated statement that makes lots of women not want to call themselves feminists. Rape is a very real problem, and I think it's important to speak up about it, but to go around acting like all men are rapists, or would be if they thought they could get away with it, that's not helping the cause."

Nzuma Randolph didn't wait for Professor Baxwood to recognize her, just jumped in. "You're missing the point. All the men get their situation as the folks in charge kind of like shored up, you know, reinforced, by a few men raping now and then. It's not something that happens because they too horny to stop themselves, it's about 'Girl, don't you go out doing whatever you want, or something happen to you'. It's about power and keeping us in our place."

This prompted Shantay Solomon to shake her head while Tracy Marshall nodded emphatically behind her. Shantay got her licks in first, sliding around in her seat to face Nzuma across the aisle. "I get the whole thing about how rape is about power and not a crime of passion, but that doesn't mean every man is all about that power and would do that kind of thing. The ones that do, they ruin everything so we aren't safe, but I don't think most guys want to be rapists. And I agree with Jodi, there's nice men in the world and they probably don't appreciate being told that all men are like that."

That looked like a good opening so I jumped into it. "The way I look at it, if you're gonna posit that the reason rape exists is because someone has the opportunity, as if anyone would want to have power over other people any time they get the chance, then you're effectively saying that *you* would rape, that you'd be a rapist if you were in the situation where you could. And if that's the case, we've got a problem, not just for rape but for the whole thing about power over, oppression, because if it's so appealing to oppress people that the opportunity to do it is enough to explain why it happens, there's *always* going to be someone somewhere with an opportunity.

"What seems more useful to me is to think about the way that patriarchy polarizes the sexes and makes women into sexual commodities and paints sex itself as a conquest. Our society makes men conquering women the definition of erotic, so all that sexual energy gets shaped toward men getting power over women, and I think that's it, more than power being what people started off having the hots for in the first place."

Professor Baxwood interjected, "Let's not get too far afield. These are all interesting points but I think the main takeaway is that if you start examining issues like rape with the awareness of women's social position as your starting point, you see how they contribute to the power imbalance between men and women."

As class was letting out, Baxwood caught my eye and beckoned me with a finger. "I wanted to let you know I think you've got quite a grasp of these issues and you always have something interesting to say...but most of the people in this class aren't at a place where they can follow that kind of complicated argument. I interrupted because I was afraid it would be confusing to some of the students. I'm trying to get them to the point of using the question '*who benefits?*' as a starting point. I don't mean to shut you down, you make a lot of good contributions in this class."

She handed me back my paper "Period Piece," the one about menstruation. "You have a gift for writing," she said. "I enjoyed reading your paper."

Baxwood must have been burning the proverbial midnight oil to grade our papers: she hadn't just noted that yes we had turned them in, nor had she just skimmed them and given them an overall grade. She also took the time to write long comments in the margins. At the bottom of the last page was this rather lengthy comment and grade:

A. Thank you.

This is beautifully written. You have a fine flair for writing & capture your feeling at all ages extremely well. Have you ever thought of writing an autobiography? Have you read any of the literature on Men's Liberation, Joseph Plec?. I think you might take some creative writing courses as you really have a talent, or even journalism.

Sharon Solerno was waiting in the hallway and approached me while I was basking in the teacher's praise. "I like some of what you said in class, and I remember something you said last week about Andrea Dworkin and pornography. I'm going to go to this conference," she said, pulling out a flier to show me, "and I thought maybe you'd want to attend too." The conference was titled *Sexual Liberalism versus Feminism?* and it promised a critical examination of the sexual revolution. Dworkin would be a speaker, as would Mary Daly. I nodded and took out a pen to scribble down the information, but Sharon handed it to me. "I have another copy in my bag," she said, tilting her head toward her green canvas tote. She stared at me for a moment, then added, "You're interesting. I don't always agree with you and sometimes you're just plain wrong, but you make me think." Then, having made that pronouncement, she spun on her heels and headed off down the hall.

John Fanshaw was my assigned social worker; it was through him that I had arranged that attending college would constitute my rehabilitation "program," which served the dual purpose of getting RCCA to supply me with transportation money to travel to and from school and staved off any pressure for me to attend some other kind of programming.

I waited until he finished up with the resident in his office, Robert Scarborough, and then as Robert left, nodding to me as he passed, I went in and sat down in the empty chair.

"Hey there, how's the world been treating you?" John greeted, jotting down an entry in his log book. "Everything going good at the school?"

I nodded. "The world and I have at least arrived at a cease-fire, and we're in negotiations. And school is good, quite good. I'm liking it very much and I seem to be off to a good start."

"Glad to hear it."

Fanshaw was a genuinely supportive staffer. Generally speaking, the RCCA personnel came in three broad types. There were plenty of self-important true believers who thought themselves to be doing good things for the homeless mentally ill, and were horribly condescending to all the residents and questioned our judgment on each and every little thing, but weren't malicious about it. There were the sadistic ones like Jerry Durst and Tony the security guard, people who got a jolt of pleasure from dehumanizing and humiliating people, who had probably gravitated toward these kind of situations because of the perpetual supply of powerless victims. And then there were people like John Fanshaw, who were mildly cynical about the world, its institutions, and the fairness of things, who enjoyed helping people where they could and didn't see the residents as entirely different from themselves, but rather as people in a complicated and unfortunate situation or two.

"I have a couple of conferences that I'd like to attend," I told him. "Commission on the Quality of Care is doing one in Albany, about care centers like this one...and there's one in the city about sexuality and feminism and sexual objectification and stuff like that, which is relevant to my coursework. I want to put in for transportation."

Fanshaw took down the dates and costs. "I can't predict what they'll say, but I can put in a request."

I went bounding into the TV lounge and plopped down next to Cowboy and Mary. "I just got back that paper I was working on last week. Check it out!"

"Hey," said Mary. "You got an A! Gimme five!"

"Yeah, but not just that. Read the comments she wrote on the back page."

Mary and Cowboy dutifully passed the paper back and forth and read what Baxwood had scribbled below where the typing ended.

"Wow, I never had a teacher do anything more than give me a grade," Mary said.

Cowboy was taking time to go back and read the actual paper I'd turned in, or at least he was skimming it. "This reminds me of things in Wicca," he commented after a moment. "Women's bodies being sacred and things that are natural not being treated like they're shameful. It's the Catholic Church, or, rather, the Christian Church, that turned everything that's got to do with sex into something dirty that has to be kept hidden."

I nodded. I didn't formally identify with Wicca, but it definitely had feminist overtones and overlap. "Speaking of sex and such things," I said, "it looks like I'll actually be attending *two* conferences in the next few weeks. In addition to going with you to Quality of Care in Albany, I've been invited to go to a conference in the city, about feminism and pornography and sex and things like that."

"Don't let the Christians find out about that," Cowboy warned with a grin. "They'd have a stroke, just to think about feminism and pornography coming together."

"Well, they're not precisely coming together. There's a lot of feminist critique of pornography and sexualized portrayals of women, you know, that whole thing about being treated as a sex object. I think this conference is mostly focused on feminists speaking out against how sex tends to be represented in society."

"Being as how a lot of porn has been made by men, I guess I can see they've got a point, but lots of women are making their own porn now and I think it's a whole lot better for women. And lots of women like porn. Mary likes porn."

"Well, sometimes," Mary piped up. She shrugged. "I think some of it's pretty disgusting, but I gotta admit, if you find something that you like, it can really get you going, if you know what I mean." She nudged Cowboy with an elbow and winked at him.

Mary turned her attention back to me. "That reminds me, we gotta find you a girlfriend. It's not right that you don't have anyone to be with. C'mon now, who do you think is cute here at RCCA? I seen you looking at Debbie, do you like how she looks? You should tell her!"

"Well first of all it's not just about how someone looks. I'm very picky...or well not so much that I'm picky but it's complicated with me so my gears don't mesh with just anyone, and that's the hard part, finding someone who would be, you know, compatible with how I am."

"But you aren't going to find out if you don't ask anyone to go out with you," Mary retorted.

"Part of the problem is that I need to be found sexually desirable in an equal way to how I find her desirable, whoever she is. Because otherwise it's unequal, it's not a stable situation. It's important to me that when I get with someone, she's just as interested in me sexually as I am in her. And the world is full of men always being the sexual initiators, the ones to get things started, and I don't want to do that."

"Okay, but you may be waiting for a long time. It may not be fair but I'm just sayin'."

CONFERENCES

There was a welcoming speech by Clarence Sundram, head of the Commission on the Quality of Care, and then a short presentation on what the RCCA programs were supposed to be and how they were supposed to operate. The relevant keywords and key phrases were "warehousing" (ending it), "neglected" (our needs as homeless mentally ill people), "program management" (how to run your facility efficiently), and "services provision" (as in, providing us with services). There wasn't much mention of our self-determination or our role in shaping the program from within, but the implication of the recurrent references to "warehousing" was that the shelters for the homeless weren't doing anything to help us get out of our situation, so presumably they felt the RCCA programs' mission was to do so.

Then they opened the mike for various people to come up and speak. Several pompous politicians each droned on for a bit in meaningless polysyllables and buzzwords. Robert Hayes of Coalition for the Homeless spoke for a while and made some good points about the vulnerability of the homeless population and the additional, special vulnerability of the psychiatric population within it. He got in some particularly good shots about how we weren't homeless as a consequence of being mentally ill—instead, psychiatric incarcerations had played a role in causing us to lose our low income housing when there wasn't much low income housing to be had.

I was the first person to stand and identify myself as a resident of an actual RCCA. I talked about the promises originally made to us: that we would be accorded the full dignity of people who were entitled to self-determination, that we would be allowed to self-govern, that no rules would be imposed on us that we had not had a participatory role in creating.

"And let me describe some of the residents. I don't know what kind of preconceptions you may be holding of us in your minds, but on our wing we have a pharmacist, we have a former law student whose education got interrupted when his parents died, and we have enough experienced office workers to staff this floor. There's a veterinarian, several restaurant cooks, a couple of elementary and high school teachers, and a railroad engineer. We were all promised personally tailored programming to help each one of us in ways we would personally and specifically benefit from, but that never materialized. There's been no real effort to help us get up and out of this situation. Most people in the RCCA are pressured into taking psychiatric medication, and most of the so-called rehabilitation programs are never going to lead to anything like independent living. I, for one, feel like I was sold a bill of goods."

Cowboy got up to speak after me and introduced himself. He described anecdotally the treatment he'd seen in the Queens Men's Shelter and the attempts of residents to organize ourselves, and about the RCCA, which was supposed to be different. Over time, though, he said, the treatment was becoming closer and closer to how it had been in the Queens Men's Shelter. Cowboy said this was why we needed to link up via organizations such as Jay Richardson's "Home Grown." He noted that the RCCA had not sent us here, had not advertised this event, and most of the residents had not heard about it unless they had heard about it from him, and he had heard about it only from Jay.

We broke for lunch. Some people came up to me to ask other questions and one person kept posing questions about how Didn't I Think that most of the homeless mentally ill needed paternalistic monitoring and Didn't I Think that the homeless mentally ill population would not really benefit from trying to treat them as if they actually had any hope of independent functioning.

As I was arguing with him, a dark-haired woman suddenly materialized by my side and glared at him thin-lipped and snapped "Don't *you* think opportunity and freedom of choice should not be taken away from people just because someone has stuck a label on them and said they are different? Have we learned any lessons about categorizing people as other? Just what option do you think would be an improvement over letting us choose our own course and take advantage of the same kinds of opportunities that people like you have?"

The questioner backed down quickly and removed himself from

our table. My defender turned to me, serious, intense, offering her hand. "Laura Wahlberg. I'm here with Project Release from New York City. We're a bunch of psychiatric ex-inmates organized against forced treatment and the lies of the psychiatric establishment. Or somewhat organized, at any rate," she added, rolling her eyes. "Are you an 'ex' too, one of us who have been psychiatrized?"

Psychiatrized. I liked that term, and filed it away for future use. I nodded. "I was invited to talk to the nice doctors at the loony bin for behaving in an unmasculine manner on campus, and I didn't know they could just hold me there, so I went over and ended up being kept on a locked ward for a few weeks. That was back in New Mexico." I explained about how the social worker in Manhattan had said I should parlay my psychiatric history to my advantage and use the resources being made available for homeless mentally ill to get off the streets.

Laura gave a single emphatic nod. "My school dropped the net on me too, but I was still in high school," she told me in rapid-fire summary. "The school psychiatrist talked to my parents ahead of time and got them convinced that I was out of control and needed treatment. I didn't know anything about it until they grabbed me in the hallway and took me to South Oaks. The shrink kept asking me all these questions and I said 'I haven't consented to be here and I'm not interested in having this discussion'. So he processed my commitment and told me, 'Now you're going to learn how to act like a lady'. They kept me there for over two years, shot up with drugs the whole time. I refused to talk to anyone except other patients. When I turned eighteen I got a visit from Mental Hygiene Information Services and I got a good attorney who represented me and eventually the judge ordered them to let me out."

She exhaled and switched gears. "Did you come up here with a group?"

"Jay Richardson, one of the people in the homeless shelter system, started a union of homeless people, and a couple of us who live in the RCCA rode up with him."

"So your group is organized around homelessness issues. Do you want to hang out for a while with us lunatics? C'mon, I'll introduce you around. We have extra food in Louise's room, that's where everyone is gathering. There are six of us splitting the hotel room, sleeping on sleeping bags and bedrolls. They should hold this conference in a more affordable location, not everyone has money for a hotel room. The food's vegetarian of course. Are you a veg?" She grinned and added, "Take some haldol or thorazine and you will be."

I grinned back. Laura was like a blue-white star brilliantly burning a few thousand degrees Kelvin hotter than any of the other stars around her. Knifelike quick, clever, cynical, and determined.

I followed Laura Wahlberg through hotel corridors, past the elevators, and down a flight of stairs—"I never saw it as a good tradeoff to consume electrical energy to gamble on my chances of getting stuck in a small box, so I prefer to take the stairs, is that okay with you?"—and she rapped a couple times on a numbered door, which was opened for us. "Hey, Bill, I've brought a new recruit with me. This is Derek, who lives in that RCCA site out in Queens."

The standard residential room's furniture was all piled to one side, and around a dozen people were sitting or lying down on the floor on quilts and shawls and blankets, many of them balancing plates of food on their knees.

"This is Project Release, or at least a large part of it. The room is in Nancy's name, she being one of the few of us madpeople to carry anything so bourgeois as a credit card. Nancy Linderhoff, Derek Turner. He came up with some homeless advocates to talk about being in the RCCA. Nancy does a lot of our protest banners and signs, she's a graphic artist." I nodded and shook hands with Nancy.

"Oh, hey, there you are," said an older woman, beaming at Laura. "I saved you some of the chick pea salad." She turned to me. "Hi there, I'm Louise. Have you eaten? Would you like some babaganoush and some tea? It's chamomile, and that's good for digestion and tension."

Laura gave Louise a brief hug and introduced me yet again, then added, "Louise has been in the group since the beginning. She has to take care of everybody, that's just who she is. Even if we can't make a dent in the psychiatric system, we'll be well-nourished crazies. Project Peasoup."

An hour later, I was sitting cross-legged on the floor eating hummus and pita triangles, comfortably propped up on a mixture of sofa cushions and rolled-up quilts, comparing stories with other people who had been mistreated by the psychiatric system. Louise had been a victim of long-term incarceration, locked up for nearly a decade in the sixties. Sitting next to her was Bill Kenderman, who explained that he had been in psychotherapy, Freudian-style, for years and then come to recognize it as based on a pack of lies and that psychotherapy was an abusive practice along with the rest of psychiatry. Laura introduced me to Allan Markman, who had a regular radio show about psychiatric oppression and our psychiatric patients' liberation movement on WBAI. Yet more people came over and introduced themselves. A woman about my age, Nancy Lindenhurst. An older woman, Ellen Remmers. A woman named Rosary Mariana, who liked the feminist sentiments on my jacket and said she headed up a women's collective for opposing psychiatric oppression.

It was pretty heady stuff, being in a group like this with a shared experience and a shared political attitude about it. I had come to New York precisely in order to be a part of things like this, although I had been thinking in terms of the *heterosexual sissy* stuff and feminism. I hadn't attained this sort of connection and involvement with feminist women yet, and I certainly hadn't found other male people who shared my peculiar sense of identity. I definitely craved that feeling of being a part of it all, of being connected and involved, and now I was getting that experience with the anti-psychiatric activists.

This had also been on my list of hoped-for and desired-for commonalities and now here I was. I had "been" so many movements unto myself, the solitary local manifestation of some radical cause or idea I'd either read about or formulated on my own. To actually be able to be among others who'd reached the same conclusion on one of my issues? Fantastic! The Project Release people told me there were many events I could get involved with if I were so inclined, and I promised that I would.

My eyes were drawn to Laura's; I pretty much just fell into them, and followed her around as much as I could up to the verge of feeling intrusive. I felt shy and at the same time I wanted her to notice me. I liked her wry smile, shot full of humor and dark angers and stubbornness. How cool was this, to have such a person on my side as a political ally?

As I entered the corridors of Academic Village, my attention, yea, even my actual eyeballs, were still focused on the spectacular scenery outside where I'd just come from. The trees were celebrating the end of fall with a spectacular explosion of colors. I still wasn't accustomed to it even after a year here in the northeast. That's how it transpired that I managed to walk headlong into Shantay Solomon—I had my head swiveled around to stare at the trees still visible in the plate glass windows behind me.

"Oops!" I apologized. "Sorry, I'm not always this oblivious to where I'm going. I was distracted by the autumn leaves back there."

"I know, they're really bright this year. Maybe Baxwood will let us take our desks outside, I heard she does that sometimes when the weather is nice."

I smiled and nodded. It *would* be pleasant to do our schoolwork outdoors!

Shantay remarked, "You got the professor figured pretty good, I gotta say. She likes the way you always got your hand up and you always know something smart to say about our readings."

"Oh, umm, do I talk too much in class and act like a know-it-all?"

"No, I don't mean that. Just you got a good sense of the kinds of things the teachers like us to say."

"Wow...so...are there...are you saying there's things you'd want to bring up, things you wish we would discuss, that you don't think Baxwood would be comfortable with?"

She shrugged. "It's just a class to get through. I like them better when they tell you what stuff they want you to learn and you study it and then you put it down on the test. In this kind of class you have to psych out the teacher and figure out what she wants."

"Oh...well, are you taking any more women's studies classes for spring semester? Or are you afraid they'll all be like that?"

"I dunno...'Women in Music and Art' maybe, that's McClendon's class. I like her and it sounds like a more regular kind of class. I'm not really into all this 'women are so oppressed' stuff, I mean I guess things were different when Baxwood was growing up, but there's more important shit to be focused on now."

I shrugged. "I think I'm going to sign up for 'Anthropology of Women,' and maybe 'The Family, Institution in Crisis' if they end up doing it...the schedule has it crossed out."

"God, it really is getting to be that time of year, isn't it? Finals right around the corner!" Shantay gave a mock shudder. "Well, see you..."

It wasn't like Shantay Solomon had an unusual attitude. It felt like most of the women in the classroom didn't really see feminism and women's studies as their movement or consider it to be about them and their lives. There were significant exceptions, like Tracy and Sharon, but still, that did seem to be the trend. I'd noticed the same thing with regards to the professors trying to teach about the working class, too. A lot of the professors had a strong Marxist viewpoint, and I could tell that they wanted to engage with the students and get them involved in discussing their everyday lives and the ways in which the things they were teaching us were true for us personally, but it mostly didn't happen. The students just reacted to it the same way as English grammar or math: take notes and learn it well enough to get good grades in it. The one exception was when a professor would talk about race or ethnicity. That's really the main time you'd hear students using the word "us" when discussing the topics.

The city bus in which I was precariously standing gave a sudden lurch to the right and then came to an abrupt stop, pitching all of us into each other's torsos. I clambered past and somewhat over the other passengers and made my escape. The downtown buildings loomed over me and everything was lit up. I hadn't been back to Manhattan in months. I missed it. There was something about the sense of "things are happening here" that appealed to me on a gut level.

I slithered between slower moving pedestrians on the busy sidewalk for several blocks and found the conference center, and after a few moments of staring at the various entrances, decided on a likely door. Sure enough, there were three lines of people queued up to go in, brandishing credit cards or printed paper receipts.

"Hello, are you here for *Sexual Liberalism versus Feminism*? May I have your name? Aah, okay, I see you're paid. Here's your pass and your program...and thank you for attending."

I browsed the list of events as I ambled down the carpet toward the auditorium doors. Looked like the first speaker was going to be someone named Sheila Jeffries, from the UK.

"Derek, is that you?" I heard from in front of me, amidst the red velvet auditorium chairs. "Oh, I'm glad you decided to come." Sharon Solerno! She waved me over. "This is Renna. Renna, this is Derek, a pro-feminism really cool guy I know from school. Renna and I have been friends off and on since kindergarten. She's a nurse at St. Luke's Hospital."

After the kickoff speaker and introductions were over, the podium was handed over to an anonymous speaker. "Between the ages of eight and nineteen, I was sexually abused by the man who contributed his chromosomes to my mother. I'm not going to call him my father. I spent my childhood with the hand of a person who was supposed to be protecting me, a person who was supposed to care about my well-being, shoved down inside my pants. This was my introduction to that wonderful thing that all the songs are sung about, what the sexual liberal establishment says is our liberation: sex!

"Let me tell you about the joys of sex. Sex is when you learn to hate your body and the way it responds when someone you can't escape from puts their fingers down between your legs and makes you feel things you don't want to feel. I can remember sitting in my room, wanting to run away, wanting to be dead, knowing he was going to come through that door. I can remember praying silently inside my head, 'Please God don't let me like it this time'. Does that sound hot to you? Does it sound like fun, does it sound fulfilling and liberating? I learned to hate my own feelings. They erased who I was and twisted me into something disgusting and foreign."

We broke into small groups to discuss the presentations, gathering around small tables in various small rooms to the side of the main auditorium. I was feeling squirmy and uncomfortable with what I'd just heard, it had been painful to listen to.

"I think there really needs to be a contrasting optimistic vision of how things could be, instead," I complained. "It is truly horrible that predatory sex is like this, that it is so prevalent to the point that it's normative. Don't get me wrong, I don't see anything to celebrate in sex as sex currently exists in society. I don't think this is an unusual case or an exaggeration. But sex would not have to be like that, it's not like this is a characteristic of sex, it's a characteristic of *patriarchal* sex. And I think it's important to conceptualize how it could be different, to have a vision of a feminist future where sex is not about one person having power over another."

A compact olive-skinned woman scowled at me. "This is how it is. This is reality. But you want to talk about fantasies, promises, never-never land. I've listened to enough promises. I don't ever want to hear again about how sex could be this wonderful transcendental thing. I don't care, don't you get it? We don't care. Because this is how sex is for us, for most of us women. Can't we say so for once without some noble male fucking savior piping up to tell us we got it all wrong, sex could could be *oh so wonderful* if we just gave it a chance? Give me a break!"

I shut up.

As we were filing out of the room, Renna, Sharon's nurse friend, said to me, "Hey, I really like your jacket. Is it your sister's?"

I was wearing the denim jacket that had my embroidered patches on it. I proudly tapped the results of my needlework and replied, "No, I made these myself. My designs, my work, my jacket."

"Well, you see, it says 'Radical Feminist,' but you can't be a radical feminist."

"Sure I can! That's my politics!"

"No, you're a man. Men can't be feminists. Men can be supporters, but patriarchy benefits men. The liberation of women is not your fight, all you can do is stand down and try not to contribute to women's oppression more than you can avoid, but you have no business appropriating 'feminist' for yourself."

"Well, I do support the liberation of women, but there's more to radical feminism than that. Patriarchy oppresses me as a sissy, and so I'm an activist against patriarchy for my own reasons, not just chivalrous ones."

"You're not oppressed as a man. If you want to say that heterosexual society oppresses gays and lesbians, you should sew a lambda symbol on your jacket, not a tag that says 'radical feminist'."

"But I'm...I support gay rights but I'm not gay myself."

"Well then, none of this is your concern really, then is it? I'm sure you mean well, but you should take that off your jacket. C'mon, Sharon, let's go before we miss our train."

I was fuming and frustrated; I wanted to argue but I needed time to formulate my thoughts, and Renna seemed to have just dismissed me from consideration.

Sharon gave me a kind if somewhat wry smile and said, "I'll talk to you at school, all right?" and the two of them dashed down the subway corridor together.

As I passed the wire box of *Catalyst* newspapers in the Academic Village hallway, I saw from the headlines that Jim Dortman had won another term as Student Government President. That reminded me of what Tracy Marshall had said to me about marketing ideas to people.

I had come to New York to be in women's studies, to talk about being a sissy heterosexual male. The different set of traits that rendered a man heterosexually eligible, compared to those that made a woman heterosexually eligible, the sexist double standard, all that seemed self-evidently a feminist issue. Self-evident to me. Apparently it was less self-evident to other people, though, and I was going to need to get better at explaining it. And defending it, apparently. I didn't like being waved off as if I had no idea what I was talking about; like it or not, it appeared I was going to have to get used to arguing that I had a right to complain and not let people dismiss what I was saying so readily.

Most of what we discussed in the classroom were the bread and butter issues of feminism: rape and sexual harassment, equal pay for equal work, fair allocation of housework and child care in the household. We also discussed unequal social meanings, like when a man is willful, he's being assertive, a real leader, but when a woman does the same thing she's being aggressive and shrill and bossy -- that kind of thing.

I hadn't had as many opportunities as I would have liked to come out in class and explain my situation and position it within a feminist context. The starting point was the "sauce for the goose is sauce for the gander" stuff, plain old fairness.

Then to get people to realize that masculinity is a "straight jacket"—that if you're male and you're straight, you're supposed to wear it. I figured most people already knew that, but hadn't spent much time pondering the situation of a guy who isn't and didn't want to be, and especially had not thought about it as a social justice issue.

I needed to find the right words from things that were already a part of feminism, words to talk about my way of being in the world and how the patriarchal society's intolerance of people like me meant that I did not benefit from how things are. That I had a stake in feminism, a stake in getting out of this social situation and somehow establishing new social and behavioral norms that would let me, and other people like me, be ourselves.

Our most intellectual and analytical textbook was called *Issues in*

Feminism, by Sheila Ruth. Or it was partly by her and partly edited by her, rather; each section had several pages of her own writing to make her main point and then she'd follow that with several articles by other feminists dealing with that topic.

As early as page four, she wrote, "As feminists we reject attitudes that regard the traditionally masculine characteristics of aggression, power, and competition as good and desirable and the traditionally feminine characteristics of compassion, tenderness, and compromise as weak and ridiculous." And she distinguished between sex and gender a few pages later, saying "*Sex* is a term used by social scientists and biologists to refer to certain biological categories female and male... *Gender*, on the other hand, is a social, not a physiological, concept. Femininity and masculinity, the terms that denote one's gender, refer to a complex set of characteristics and behaviors prescribed for a particular sex by society and learned through the socialization experience."

I was impatient for us to dive into a classroom discussion anchored in these kinds of things as our starting point. And I needed to be ready for it when we did. I was capable of putting my thoughts into words, and in fact I was pretty good at it. But I needed to get better at launching my arguments from points that the people I was trying to convince would already agree with.

That all this material was political was something I had understood for a long time now; but I was just really starting to realize that that meant I needed to become a politician.

Cowboy waved me over from the red overstuffed plastic TV room couch; I plopped down next to him. "Hey, it looks like Suzy has been making the rounds. She's got a boyfriend out there somewhere. We're pretty sure she's pregnant!" He grinned.

Mary smirked. "Suzy knows where to find what she likes. We already have residents asking if they can adopt a kitten when they're born, can you believe it?"

I nodded. "Well, isn't that what RCCA stands for? Residential Cat Care Annex!"

Mary high-fived me.

Cowboy put on his serious authoritative face, raising his finger as he made his point. "As I said to Jay the other day, we need to decide what RCCA *does* stand for. Not leave it to the staff and the administration.

We are RCCA, that's what they promised us. Jay says we should call a residents' grievance meeting."

I nodded. I was totally on board with that. The Quality of Care conference and my interactions with the psychiatric liberation front people had given me new fervor and resolution to confront the institution. "Have you asked around? I'd think Sid Lapidus would be an obvious participant, and Louis Altus. And Manny. And Moby for sure."

Cowboy tipped back his signature western hat, the accessory that had acquired for him his nickname in the shelter system. "I don't know about Sid, I think he's all talk and no action, but we can ask him. You know that Scarborough is gonna come whether we invite him or not. Moby? Are you serious?"

"Moby can be a clown but she's smart. Yeah, I would ask her. And Lisette, too. Oh, and Queenie."

"Yeah, Queenie's a good one, she doesn't complain much but these Catholic workers are always trying to change her or humiliate her."

INTO THE FRAY

L aura Wahlberg had invited me to drop in after college classes so we could catch up and go over some items. She was renting a room in Westbury, so I hopped off the N22 as it made its way through the area and, following the instructions she had given me, found her street and house without too much problem.

"Hey, come in. Don't trip over my detritus. I don't see very well and the most efficient way for me to get projects done is to use the floor like a big work table, and scramble around on all fours putting the pieces together."

Laura guided me through the labyrinth and then indicated that I should sit on my choice of cushions against the wall, and invited me to strip off my socks and shoes, so I did.

"So what have you been doing since I saw you at the conference?" she asked me.

"Cowboy and Mary and I are trying to organize the residents at the RCCA. I think it will be easier now that I can let them know that there's an actual movement, and that we're not alone. I know it makes a huge difference to *me* to not be alone." I held the eye contact, studying her face as I continued. "When I was locked up in New Mexico, I had recently read a newspaper or magazine article about mental patients' liberation front, so I told the other patients about the movement and we declared ourselves to be a chapter of the front, and I'm pretty sure that's what prompted them to boot me out."

Laura handed me a cup of tea and sat down on an adjoining cushion. "Mental Patients' Liberation Front is actually Judi Chamberlin's group, up in Boston. Did you read her book, by any chance?"

"No, it was definitely a newspaper or magazine article. She wrote a book? There's a published book about psychiatric patients' rights and stuff?"

"I'll lend you my copy. You'll have to tell her this story when you meet her. Which you will if you keep going to conferences. Judi's great."

I took a long sip of the tea and smiled at her over the cup rim. "It's nice to read that there's a movement but it's so much more powerful to be in a room full of other people who are with you in that. It's very rare for me to meet someone that I really connect with and who understands so many of the same things."

"Well, I hate to break it to you, but the solidarity is, shall we say, somewhat illusory. Like last fall, we had Bill, Rosary, Louise, Alan, Nancy, and Richard and me to put together a flier so we could hand it out at the housing and civil rights rally. And Nancy was saying 'I don't like this image, can't we find a better one?' and Bill didn't like the wording on the back. So he wrote out a different version and Richard said 'that's awful, they'll say we need to be locked up if they read that,' and Rosary didn't like Nancy's image, and Alan was shouting that we have to finish this in half an hour because he has to leave. Nancy got angry with Richard for saying Bill's text would make us all sound crazy, although he kind of had a point there, to be honest, and Richard stomped out and slammed the door." She pantomimed a huffy pouty face and the motion of flinging a door closed.

She sighed. "A person can get locked up in the looney bin for almost any reason, or even no reason at all, but we do tend to have some characteristics in common. Unfortunately, those characteristics don't include listening well to ideas that disagree with our own, being diplomatic and finding ways of saying things that don't make other folks angry, or staying calm and not getting upset. It's important for us to work together but it doesn't come easy."

I nodded. "I've been telling people for years that what we call sanity assumes that whatever most people think and do is correct and healthy, but it's mostly about conformity, not the quality of the ideas and all that. So the people in touch with actual reality, the people with the best understanding and insights, are often the ones called insane." As I was saying this, I stretched out my bare foot to nudge hers, where she had it extended in front of her own cushion.

"Ehh, stop," Laura said, pulling her foot away. "I don't think you should get all philosophical about the definition of sanity and inverting what's considered pathological and all that. I think we should focus on involuntary treatment. That's easier to explain to people and it's the easiest thing to get all the activist lunatics to agree with and get on board with. That and exposing the lies that the psychiatric establishment tells about psychiatric medication, all that 'chemical imbalances' stuff they like to talk about."

I was ensconced at my typewriter, backspacing through the saved text to make a revision in a few sentences. Behind me, Suzy the cat was kneading my pillows and blankets on my bed. "Mrrow?" I said to her inquisitively. "I don't suppose I could con you into doing that to my shoulders?"

Suzy regarded me and flicked her ears, then did a prolonged kitty-stretch and hopped from my bed into my open wardrobe, a piece of particle-board furniture the RCCA issued us to hang our clothes in.

Tap, tap, tap-a-tap. Cowboy's knock on my door. Time to save my homework-in-progress and go to the residents' meeting. I chained up my word processor and killed the lights and stepped out. "Come on, Suze," I said, beckoning the cat off a pile of my folded shirts.

"I was right," Cowboy bragged. "Sid Lapidus says we won't amount to anything and won't get anything done and he doesn't want to waste his time. But Moby and Lisette are both coming, I wouldn't have expected that."

We walked down the hall. Mary joined us at the TV room and we continued into the lunchroom. Mary said, "You went to hang out with that girl who was at CQC, didn't you? How was it?"

"She's really sharp. I think maybe she would help us organize here. She knows a lot about psychiatric rights and she's spent a lot of time thinking about our issues."

"Uh huh. So...you kind of like her, don't you? C'mon, admit it!"

"I do, very much. I think she's hot, and brilliant, and I like being around her."

"Well, when are you going to ask her out?"

"I have my own way of doing things. I'm afraid she doesn't think of me in that way or doesn't have any interest in going there."

"Oh, what, you made a pass at her?"

"Not my style. But if she'd been thinking salivating thoughts about how cute I was and stuff like that, I gave her an opening, but she kind of closed it."

Cowboy advised, "You shouldn't give up too easily. She may want to see how serious you are about her, and make sure you weren't just throwing her a line."

I sighed. "I'm not exactly giving up, but I'm not going to make a nuisance of myself either. She has to have an interest in me or it's not something I want to pursue. I definitely like her, but it has to be mutual."

"Your problem," Mary pronounced, "is you think too much."

The residents' meeting turned out to be less of an occasion of activist uprising than I'd hoped for. Robert Scarborough showed up and told us all that we had gotten ourselves into this situation in the first place by our misbehaviors and poor judgment, that if we hadn't lived our lives so irresponsibly and gotten involved with drugs and other illicit activities we would not have ended up homeless and diagnosed with psychiatric conditions; and that we were being foolish to sit here talking more juvenile disobedient trash when we should be respecting the institution more and trying to obey the rules more than we did.

It didn't seem like a really good idea for me, a white resident, to call the black Robert an "Uncle Tom," although the phrase certainly crossed my mind. I settled for talking about how any group that gets put down a lot ends up including people who believe what's been said about them and go around putting down their own group. Self-inflicted victim blaming. Several other residents agreed with me and attempted to shout down Scarborough. Eventually we prevailed enough to hold our intended meeting. But most of the residents who spoke up after that related specific stories about specific staff members doing specific things, and for a while it seemed that all we would accomplish would be a gossip and whining session, with no discussion of rights or what we wanted to do about any of it.

Cowboy pushed pretty hard to get people to sign up as members in his friend Jay's advocacy group, and there were people who agreed that Jay was a good person and was probably doing good things.

I kept repeating my litany of broken promises, how we'd been told we would be self-governing, but were constantly being bombarded with new restrictions and regulations, and that the program staff weren't helping any of us get out of this place. Manny the former pharmacist and Louis the artist agreed but both shrugged and said this was how things always were, no point in getting your hopes up and getting upset about it later.

But there was a tentative agreement that those of us who wanted to secure our rights could move forward, trying to get support from advocacy groups or social workers or attorneys, with none of the residents except Robert Scarborough actively opposing us.

I was crossing Academic Village, textbooks under my arms, taking the outside route because the hallways were crowded. One of the buildings I passed had a large placard in the window which caught my eye: PEER COUNSELING.

One of the key issues for the Project Release people, one of the few that focused on what they wanted rather than what they didn't want (such as incarceration and forced psychiatric treatment), was user-run self help. And that was what I had informally set up within Mountain View Psychiatric Facility back in New Mexico, when the university health center had tricked me into signing myself in. It had just seemed natural and self-explanatory at the time: I didn't think anything was wrong with me, nor did the other people locked up along with me on the ward seem impaired. My attitude had been that if I were going to talk to anyone about my concerns, it would be other patients, not the people keeping me locked up and treating me like my brain was damaged goods.

The phrase "peer counseling" struck me as implying the same thing, that instead of turning to professionals and enduring the polarized "I am the therapist and you are the recipient of services" attitudes, students were organizing to provide counseling services on a mutual and equal basis!

The black metal doorknob rattled uncooperatively in my hand. Locked. I peered in the big storefront windows at a deserted room with a couple of desks and telephones and a file cabinet. The lights were off and I didn't see any signs or posters inside providing additional information.

I had some time before my next class started, so I went into the nearest hallway and poked my head into an office. "Hello. Do you know anything about the 'Peer Counseling' center next door down?"

The woman sitting there doing clerical work shook her head. "I don't know whose project that is." She called into the office behind her, "Norma, hey Norma, this student is asking about that Peer Counseling service."

An elegant woman in a mauve scarf came out into the front reception area. "I think that...don't quote me on this but I believe that it's being set up by Professor Mark Penfield. His office is down that hall on the lower level, you can see if he's in. I don't know when he has office hours, to be honest."

I went in the direction she was pointing and read the black plastic name plates until I found Mark Penfield's office, where conveniently for me the door was ajar and the light was on. Seated man with a full head of salt-and-pepper hair, wire frame glasses, an array of pipes on his desk in front of him, nose buried in a journal. I knocked lightly.

"Yes, come in."

"Hello, I saw the sign out there that said 'Peer Counseling,' and I was told that you were the person coordinating that? Assuming you're Dr. Penfield?"

"Oh, yes. Are you a psychology student, then?" Dr. Penfield clasped his hands and rested them on his knee and leaned back in his chair.

"No, I'm a person who believes in mutual therapy and peer support, though. Depending on when it's in operation, I'd like to participate."

"Oh! Well, the students who will be running the Peer Counseling office will have taken a course so that they're qualified to provide services. Students have to be at least in their junior year, and to have taken my Psychological Counseling intro course as a prerequisite. That's why I asked if you were a psychology student, you see."

I shook my head. "Seems to me like a lot of the problem with conventional non-peer therapy and counseling is the notion that the person on one side of the desk has expert training, and that the person on the other side is the one with the problems. I thought from the name of it that peer counseling would be counseling provided between peers, between equals."

Penfield unlaced his hands and leaned forward, scowling. "Hey, now, you can't just come in off the sidewalk and expect the student body to be like guinea pigs for just any untrained student to practice on! That wouldn't be ethical! If you're interested, you're welcome to sign up for the required classes. But they won't be offered again until next fall."

I rolled my eyes but thanked him for the information and headed off for my next classroom.

My primary attention at school was always on women's studies, but it turned out to be the history class final exam that really brought me to my professors' attention.

We had been assigned Dee Brown's *Bury My Heart at Wounded Knee* as one of our texts for the course, and had heard in detail about how our white European ancestors took the land. Late in the semester we had also been assigned to read a long essay by historian Frederick Turner titled *The Frontier in American History*, which promoted the notion that the land was empty and represented opportunity and potential and so on.

Our final exam was all open-ended written responses to questions, no multiple-choice or simple fill-in-the-blanks. I heard Shantay Solomon from the next row over groan as the tests and blank composition booklets were passed out and recalled our conversation in the hallway. For me, though, the format played to my strengths.

The last part of the final exam allowed us to pick two out of three questions for a long essay, and Question Three said to first pretend to be Frederick Turner and respond to some specific portion of Dee Brown's book; and then write as Dee Brown and respond back to that from Brown's vantage point.

In retrospect, I think that what Professor Rosenstein had anticipated with that question was that students "being Turner" would write something dismissive about Brown and the plight of the Native Americans because the frontier was more important, and probably something overtly racist about the unimportance of the Indians. Then the students could reiterate what Brown had detailed about the broken promises, the essentially genocidal policies, and the fact that it had been their land first. Something along those lines.

But very few students had chosen Question Three, and when Rosenstein asked the class later why people didn't choose it, students said it was too complicated. She acknowledged that and said she wouldn't assign it in that format in the future.

But I had not found it difficult to think in Turner's terms and from his worldview well enough to write from his perspective. I didn't think he *would* be directly racist or would wave away what happened to the Native Americans as unimportant.

I chose the chapter in *Bury My Heart* in which Dee Brown wrote about Donehogawa, aka Eli Samuel Parker, an Iroquois who joined the US government administration as an official within the Bureau of Indian Affairs. Pretending to be Turner, I opined that his initial success showed that if the Indians had made an attempt to be a part of the American nation, this option had been available to them, and that Parker's later disparagement by others was because he had made the mistake of taking an office where his racial identity as an Indian left him vulnerable to being accused of bias. I stated that if he had pursued a course in American government in a different bureau with different responsibilities, that probably wouldn't have happened.

I pushed the notion that America had been a "land of opportunity" for everyone including the Indians but that they had not availed themselves of it, attempting instead to stick to their old ways for the most part, and that the march of progress had left them on the sidelines.

Then, as Dee Brown in response to that, I had written not about racism or genocide, but "culturecide," the methodical destruction of an entire set of cultures, making the argument that the survival of Native Americans as individuals in fake-Turner's imagined alternative outcome didn't make everything okay, that the crimes detailed in *Bury My Heart* were not merely the extinction of the people as individuals but the extinction of their viable culture, that to live as they lived was deemed inferior to how the white European settlers lived.

Rosenstein wrote in the margins of my essay that I had done a better job arguing as Turner than Turner would likely have done himself, and that my Dee Brown response argument had taught her something, and that I had taken the argument in a direction she had not expected.

And, as if that weren't enough to give me a rush of egotistical pride, Dr. Baxwood mentioned it later in the week and asked if she could read it, and said Dr. Rosenstein had been talking about it among the faculty.

So I now had a reputation.

Wrapped in a heavy leather-trimmed jacket I'd rescued from a Salvation Army drop box, I trudged through the early February snowpack, kicked the ice from my boots at the door, and slipped into a desk in Ms. D'Abrigio's Anthro of Women class. She had assigned several autobiographical accounts written by women from different cultures in America. Today we were to discuss Moody's *Coming of Age in Mississippi.*

Tracy Marshall spoke up. "One thing I found a little off-putting was her, I guess you could call it contempt, kind of, for Dr. King at the end. I'm not black and I wasn't alive at the time, and maybe I just don't get it, but I thought his speeches really affected America and woke people up about racism and prejudice, and there were so many people in attendance. I was expecting her to be really energized by that, like things are finally happening, you know?"

Hmm, Tracy Marshall's learning how to be more circumspect in how she says things that might come across the wrong way. She may turn out to be an effective politician yet.

Shantay shrugged. "Maybe she didn't know it was going to have that kind of impact."

Nzuma, in the seat to my right, said, "Maybe she figured the impact it was going to have was going to be mostly on black people, telling them to be cool and wait for God to fix everything and not cause trouble."

I nodded. "I got the sense that she was ready to hear someone say 'this has to change and we're going to change it by any means necessary,' and this wasn't the leadership she was hoping for."

Nzuma held her palm out toward me and after a startled second I high-fived her. She continued, "You got to remember she was wanting to feel she was not the only one all angry and ready to raise hell. All that incremental stuff and 'I have a dream' and all that is good in its own way to reach white people and churches, but you also gotta let your people know that you get it, and she wasn't feeling that. Like maybe he was all set up pretty good and didn't want to rock the boat, we don't have to be in a hurry, and she was being like 'Oh please,' you hear what I'm sayin'?"

"That makes sense," Tracy agreed. "I don't know what the solution is, how to balance between liberal and radical when radical is what you want but liberal and cautious seems to be what gets the job done."

"One thing that struck me," I commented, "was all the time she was so tuned in to racial inequality, but she didn't focus anywhere near as much on women's social position. Things would come up, and strike her as unfair, like the way it mattered more for women to be light-skinned or the way the white woman but not the white man got a lot of flack for interracial relationships, but she definitely tended to see everything from a race-centered analysis first."

Shantay shook her head and sighed, "This book isn't about that. She was writing about race in America. Just because this is women's studies doesn't mean everything we study is all about women's liberation you know!"

Professor D'Abrigio interjected, "As a person occupying both identities, it does make sense to examine her experience from a sex as well as a race perspective. Class, too, her experience of poverty is an important part of what she relates in her story. Do you think, considering the time when this all took place, that she was more likely to consider race the most important issue? Derek, do you think it's wrong to prioritize one issue over another even when they're both valid issues?"

Good question.

One of the significant differences between race inequality and sex inequality was that the races were segregated—not to the point that there was no interaction, but families tended to be of a single race, neighborhoods and communities and even entire towns and villages often were, schools and to some extent places of business often were as well. So black people being mistreated because they were black would often be in situations where everyone in the room with them was also black, and it could be talked about in ways that would probably be a lot less likely if there were always white people present. And also, some people lived their day-to-day lives without encountering people of a race different from themselves, or, if they did, only in passing, not as people you get to know by name and over a longer period of time.

But the sexes were socially interspersed. Yeah, there were sex-segregated facilities and clubs and whatnot, and occupations where one sex or the other was almost exclusively employed, but heterosexuality was the overwhelming norm, and people had siblings and children. Even if your home was headed by two lesbian moms and all their children were girls, chances were high that there would be male people living on your block, that at least one of the women would have a living father or brother, that the children would end up playing in mixed groups.

Anne Moody and the other women in her life might have had

plenty of provocation to get angry about how women were regarded and treated in society, but they were less often in a space where they could discuss it without male people and male people's reactions and feelings to have to consider, and even when they were, they'd be going home to an environment where they had ongoing connections where being categorically enraged at male people would be disruptive. That kind of situation sort of forces one to a more nuanced analysis, one where you see the other sides of the situation because you care about people who are in that other-side context. That's both good and bad. There are important truths best realized when you boil things down to their basic black and white. So to speak.

On a different level of analysis, I was in a different situation within radical feminism than the typical feminists, which is to say feminists who were not male. Real feminists, as Sharon's friend Renna would say. I was fervently against the sexual status quo of our society, but the basic black-and-white kind of analysis where you see society in terms of the men wanting to oppress the women and the women wanting to free themselves from that, the adversarial thing where men are the culprits benefitting at women's expense, pretty immediately clashed with my own experience. I was pushed toward a more nuanced way of understanding patriarchy right from the start. Because my very existence as an affirmatively sissy male threw into question the absolute notion that patriarchy benefits males.

I was in this for personal self-serving politically selfish reasons; whether you called it *oppression* or put some other word on it, I had experienced the sexual status quo as something impinging on me and making my life a truncated and attenuated nonlife. It was specifically its patriarchal elements and structures that made society that way for me, so I was one male who did not benefit from patriarchy.

I might still be better off than I would be in various ways if I had been born female, although even that wasn't a clear straightforward obvious truth. I would also have fit in far better and been far less isolated as a weird misfit, far less identified as a creepy perverted pathetic thing deserving of mockery. All that was true even if it was also true that I could safely walk the sidewalks at night with very little risk, and women mostly could not. The jury was still out on whether I'd be paid a dollar for a comparable woman's sixty cents: I had never managed to become gainfully employed for more than basement-level wages, and had been repeatedly fired for seeming odd, my nonmasculine characteristics being interpreted as an "attitude," or it being deemed a good thing to eliminate employees who didn't blend in as part of a team.

Ultimately, the complexity of feminist analysis of patriarchy was what attracted me to it. Radical feminist theory contained the anger and the righteous clear analysis of the overall situation but it also embraced the complex nuanced rethinkings that I needed. Radical feminism upended the usually unquestioned notion that oppressing someone, having power over them, was something desirable. It said that the very placing of a high value on conquering and wielding power over someone else was, itself, an aspect of the masculine value system, and of patriarchy as a social system.

On my way back to the bus stop, I detoured to see if the Peer Counseling office was open. If it was, I'd drop in for a session. If it were at all what I thought of as legitimate peer-to-peer counseling, I wanted to support what they were doing; if, on the other hand, I found condescension from know-it-alls designated by Professor Penfield as Official Penfield Peers, I wasn't going to let them abrogate the phrase "peer counseling" without a struggle.

But it was once again a deserted office. In fact it looked absolutely identical to when I had seen before, right down to the same stacks of paper on the desk.

"Hey, where are you going?" challenged Tony Blaine. I had my mind focused on a theoretical argument about the way women are portrayed in the media, and the interruption startled me. The security guard was blocking the corridor leading to the front gate exit.

"School, same as usual," I replied.

"Uh huh. Well, everyone's s'posed to go over to day programing and get certified that you're participating in a rehab. I'm telling everybody. So turn your ass back around and talk to your counselor."

"School *is* my program, and if anyone has any questions about it they can take it up with John Fanshaw. Now excuse me, I don't want to be late for my bus."

"If you go out that door, you ain't getting back in. This is mandatory. That means you got to attend or be kicked out of the program."

I stalked past him, speaking over my shoulder as I went. "If you try to interfere with me reentering the building when I get home, I'll see you arrested for an unlawful eviction." I stomped angrily down the steps and across the lawn and headed toward the bus stop.

The "Women and Media" topics that were on my mind revolved around the question of whether women were portrayed differently in films created by male directors than in films done by female directors, and what those differences were.

I had seen *Fatal Attraction* recently, and that was a film I wanted to use as an example. I could say a lot about it in my paper: the lead character, Alix, played by Glenn Close, was a strong woman, and also scary; in a break from the typical movie plot trajectory, it was the lead *male* character, Dan, who we see suffering for his sexual stepping out of line (he was a married man but opted to have a fling with Alix). On the other hand, Alix quickly transforms from human character to horror-movie monster, and the film is replete with the pacing and music of a horror thriller, culminating in the scene where Alix has killed the children's bunny and placed its dead body in a cooking pot in Dan's home. So the strong independent woman becomes a frightening evil horror-movie thing (complete with an apparently immunity to being killed, as we see in the end scenes), and the person finally able to stop her is the conventional good-Mommy figure, Dan's wife Beth.

The other example that I could turn to was feminist filmmaker Lizzie Borden. She had made a radical movie titled *Born in Flames* but it hadn't received much attention. I couldn't find a copy anywhere on VHS, only on a reel in the archives of the New York Public Library, so it had effectively disappeared without a trace. But she'd gone on to make a second movie that was more patterned after successful situation comedies, called *Working Girls*, about middle class prostitutes (the main character Molly being a Yale business school graduate, the others also being decently well-off and not stereotypical impoverished drug addicts). Lizzie Borden used humor and subtlety, humanizing the prostitutes and normalizing their lives while at the same time making the lives of the male clientele appear desperate and truncated. She was able to have an impact with this kind of movie that she hadn't been able to have with a more serious head-on feminist film.

I didn't know what the term paper assignment was going to be, specifically, but I'd become adept at taking an assignment and running with it in my own directions, and using it as an opportunity to dive into subjects I wanted to write about.

That was one of the nicest things about being in school: I could write in fulfillment of coursework responsibilities, and at an absolute minimum, one person—the professor—was going to end up reading it and giving me feedback. It wasn't the full-scale audience that I wanted for my ideas and thoughts, but it was a major improvement over not reaching anyone at all.

"You make it sound like your ideas were so radical that they had to lock you up to keep you from changing the world," Laura Wahlberg proclaimed.

I nodded gleefully. "They weren't like what anyone else was saying, and the people I explained them to at the time were pretty stunned and got all thoughtful. And other people tried to bat them away," I related, making frantic pawing gestures in the air and adopting a panicked expression. "They found them threatening, and for that matter people still do."

Laura sighed in apparent exasperation. "It's a cheap way of saying you've got something out of the ordinary, and it makes you sound like a used car dealer. Or a stereo equipment salesman. 'Come on down to hear Crazy Derek. His ideas are so far out they're innn-SANE'."

I winced at her spot-on mimicry of the Crazy Eddie radio advertisement. "Well, that *is* more or less the pitch. I want people to rethink what they're ready to dismiss as mental illness, and show them that calling me that isn't going to shut me down. I'll claim it as my own and turn it inside out and wear it."

"Very brave and noble of you. But I don't want to convey that weird extraordinary behavior is what gets you locked up. I want to warn them that quite ordinary harmless behavior like what they do every day can also get you locked up, that it can happen to anybody. As long as they think it's limited to people being weird..." Laura trailed off for a moment, then continued, "You told me earlier that you didn't think the people running your campus really understood any of what you'd written."

She hadn't phrased it as a question but she was waiting. I nodded. "Yeah, I don't think they were trying to have me locked up like it was a conspiracy against my beliefs. They got a whiff of what I was trying to say, I think, but it was confusing to them and they decided that if they couldn't make sense out of it, it must be because it didn't *make* any sense. And somehow they thought I might be making a threat against the woman running the Rape Crisis Center. She was a feminist poet and I left my writings behind because I was hoping to get her opinion and feedback."

"So emphasize that. You weren't threatening anyone, you wrote a note to a professional person in a campus office to ask for her thoughts—and that's completely harmless and reasonable behavior for a college student—and their reaction was to have you placed on a locked ward. Could happen to anybody."

I nodded reluctantly.

"And you told me about a woman that got locked up because her husband thought she was having affairs behind his back and he lied about her to the psychiatrist ahead of time. That could happen to anyone. Husbands, wives, parents, children. Family members that convince themselves it's for your own good, but it's really that the family member feels threatened and wants to control their relative's behavior."

Carolyn, yeah. Intense, frustrated sexy Carolyn. Laura reminded me a little bit of her, in fact. Not in appearance—Laura was wiry to the point of being skinny, whereas Carolyn had been curvy and exotic—but they both had that welding-torch intensity about them, in their eyes and voice and gestures.

We were discussing my appearance on Allan Markman's WBAI show, "The Madness Network," as one of the psychiatric ex-patients and liberation movement participants he would interview. How to use that occasion as a public relations opportunity to reach more people and make them aware of our issues.

I could see Laura's point, but from where I was positioned it was annoying that the ideas that had gotten me locked up at UNM never got any attention. I had been shut down from talking about my material by having it dubbed a symptom of my mental illness, and now the psychiatric radicals, although they didn't assume my ideas were the product of an impaired mind, weren't particularly interested in discussing them either.

I was totally on-board with psychiatric patients' rights, but I saw them as integrated into the volatile subjects of gender and sexuality. I'd been treated like something was maladjusted within me for years before I came to terms with my identity, and psychiatric notions of "normal" and "healthy" were very definitely loaded with conventional sex role expectations.

But Laura in particular, and many of the others in Project Release as well, had indicated that they regarded these as distantly peripheral issues. Institutional psychiatry was mostly not about poking a therapeutic nose into people's sexual identities and far more about being an informal police system for getting inconvenient and disruptive people whisked out of sight with minimal concern about due process, and that's what they wanted our outgoing message to focus on.

Some local politician named Frank Padavan had been the subject of a newspaper article, and had been quoted from one of his recent public appearances. He had taken credit for our RCCA and touted it as a wonderful approach to the homeless mentally ill. At the same time, he had promised all of the homeowners and business people in our community that we would be kept off of their sidewalks and out of their stores. Oh yes, the institution's administrative officers and the city funding sources had given him all kinds of promises that we, the residents in the facility, would be kept indoors with an earlier curfew and carefully tracked. He promised that more regulations were being put into place to make sure we stayed where we belonged and didn't constitute a disturbance to the good citizens of this fine community.

We had called another meeting of our residents' rights committee to discuss the article. Fewer people had attended than had come to the original formative meeting, but I pushed for and got their approval to write up and xerox a reply to Mr. Padavan and distribute it all around our neighborhood, explaining that this was our community too. That we had a right to come and go the same as any citizens. That the RCCA was turning out to be just another warehouse just like all the other shelters for homeless people—they weren't doing anything to get us launched as independent people, they were just funneling welfare and social security disability income established in our name into their pockets as rent and salary. And then disregarding our rights and ignoring our needs. I also noted that, as citizens, we were eligible to vote, that those of us not already registered would register, and that our votes would not be going to support the reelection of State Senator Frank Padavan. We urged the rest of the community to vote against him as well.

I had typed it out on my fancy word processor and then had

photocopied it at Kinko's Copies and taped it up all over our district.

I was expecting and hoping to ruffle some feathers, but the feathers that bristled at me most prominently were on Lisette's little felt hat.

"Did you write this?"

I nodded affirmatively.

"Why you go telling everybody this place is just a funny farm where they dump us? I don't want people thinking I live in some horrible ugly place, why you gonna make everybody ashamed to be here? This place works! I never had a place that wasn't as bad as the streets, with everybody got some game going and trying to make me selling drugs or putting out for they friends and shit? You got no right, they should put you out for saying this, after what they do for you!"

I made feeble attempts to explain that I wasn't characterizing us negatively, I was describing the attitudes of the administrative staff toward us, along with some of the people they had chosen to employ, but Lisette wasn't in a mood to hear it and went off to drum up other residents to oppose me.

I watched her storm down the hall with mixed feelings. I didn't think my political sentiments were wrong or my facts incorrect, and I definitely didn't feel like the RCCA deserved kinder treatment from me. But I had written up the flier as if it were the voice of all of the residents, and I hadn't made enough of an effort to make sure the voices of all the residents were being heard. I'd just assumed that my sentiments were widely shared, give or take one Robert Scarborough. Apparently not, though. So I was now guilty of speaking on behalf of someone I hadn't consulted, and effectively stealing her voice and putting my words in her mouth. So much for empowering the people.

I had by now walked past the Peer Counseling center on campus a dozen times or more since talking with Mark Penfield, and the office was never open. I decided to write a letter and see if the student newspaper, *The Catalyst*, would print it. I poked fun at the idea of Penfield and his "certified trained peers" and how dangerous he thought it would be for untrained folks to listen to each other's problems. Then I described my attempts to drop in on the peer counselors only to find the office always closed and deserted.

I dropped the article off at the newspaper's storefront office. A few days later, I moseyed by and inquired, and they perked up and said yes, that letter was definitely going to be published, as is. It was an amusing and yet bitingly critical letter and it expanded my reputation as a hotshot radical who had strong opinions, an easy contempt for established authority, and a way with words.

"Don't hate me," I said.

I had been thinking about it consciously for a week, and probably in the back of my head for a lot longer than that. The discussion in Anthropology of Women about Anne Moody and issues of race and sex and class, and having to pick your battles, select the thing that's going to be your priority. My argumentative discussion with Laura about the impropriety of talking about the ideas and concepts that had provoked my psychiatric incarceration instead of just focusing on involuntary psychiatry as a civil rights violation. The joy I had felt upon meeting the Project Release people and being a part of an actual movement.

Behind the scenes I had been having a discussion with myself about my own priorities. Yes, the concerns and rights of people who had been psychiatrically labeled was a worthy cause and was something I had a personal stake in and cared about. But I hadn't hitched to New York and struggled though all the associated experiences in order to be a psychiatric patients' rights advocate. I had come here to be an out and proud and politicized sissy, and coed feminist. And that was my priority even though I hadn't really found "my people" and connected with a movement of like-minded militant heterosexual sissy males yet.

"I've put in an application to move into the dorms next year, starting this fall," I continued. "I think I really need to be able to spend more time on campus and make connections with other students. I hate to abandon you two, and I'll come back to participate when I can, for residents meetings and stuff."

Mary waved off my apology. "Hey, don't you think I'd love to get out of this place if I could? You'd be shooting yourself in the foot to stay here when you don't have to!"

Cowboy nodded. "You do more for us with the things you write than most of the people here, and you can still do that after you move. And you can come to Jay's events in the city, there'll be people from all the shelters and programs, and people who have gotten out of the system but are still fighting for rights. Jay is living in a place on his own now, in East Harlem." He put his arms out and gave me a hug. "I know you won't abandon us! And we'll come out to your campus and you can show us around."

"Meanwhile," I added, "I won't be disappearing any time soon. Not until next September when the fall semester starts."

I was up late, retyping one of the chapters in my book *The Amazon's Brother*, adding a little section about flirting and courting behavior, describing something I called the "co-reactive dance," where neither of the people involved ever makes an overt pass but they negotiate through subtleties that they are mutually interested.

I had noticed earlier when Suzy came in to keep me company and hopped up into my wardrobe. But I'd since then become immersed in what I was writing.

I don't know how long I'd been hearing the panting sounds from behind me before I consciously registered them. Several minutes, probably; I had the sense that the sounds had been going on as background sounds for a little while now.

I wonder, is it possible that she's giving birth?

Pause.

Of course it's possible. I wonder how likely it is that it's happening...I think it is. Cool! Hmm, I don't want to do anything to startle her, if she is. I'll just keep attending to my manuscript. Unless she sounds like she's in distress or something.

I returned to my typing, staying tuned to the sounds coming from behind my shoulder.

It was the tiny squeaking sounds that finally made taking a peek irresistible. I had to see.

Suzy was licking a ludicrously tiny kitten and biting and chewing at bits of some remaining transparent sac. I counted two other microkittens squirming and emitting high-pitched yeeps, and there was also one still in its enclosing sac. As I watched, Suzy shifted her attention to the final remaining newborn; she poked into it with her nose and I saw it twitch and wriggle, but after a moment she pushed it with her nose to the far corner of my wardrobe and returned to licking the other three.

They were all head and belly, kicking with pathetic little legs they couldn't walk on yet, silly little tails coiled around them, making plaintive squeals with their little eyes closed. One solid black and two darker ones with lighter grey stripes. It was all I could do to keep from picking one of them up. I wanted to kiss those little kitten tummies. But it would have to wait. For now they were squirming across the layer of t-shirts toward Suzy's warmth and finding a place to nurse. Suzy purred.

I slipped down the hallway to the TV room but found that Cowboy and Mary were asleep on the couch. I went back to my room and typed out a note:

The Residential Cat Care Annex is pleased to report the birth to Ms. Suzy of three wigglesome newborn kittens on the surface of my shirt shelf at 1:30 AM this morning. Please consult the facility for visiting hours.

—Derek Turner, Certified Nurse Midwife

I walked back to the TV room and safety-pinned the note to Cowboy's hat brim and went back to my newborn nursery.

Later, I checked the remaining kitten, verified that it was cold and still, and wrapped it in an old plastic sandwich bag and disposed of it outside.

PART TWO: RESIDENT STUDENT

SUMMERTIME

With the end of the spring semester's classes, I spent more of my time travelling to events and meetings.

I attended a community panel discussion in Queens Plaza along with Laura, Cowboy, and Cowboy's friend Jay. The panelists were debating city policies for addressing homelessness.

At one point in the ensuing debate, a homelessness advocate named Tom Duffman criticized the policy-makers who had been instrumental in setting up our RCCA -- but not from an angle I could appreciate: "They wanted to cherry-pick and offer services only for homeless people who could get jobs or function on the same basis as anyone in this room, so they could take credit for their eventual success. We had to sue them in court to force them to open the facility to all of the homeless in the Queens shelter, but I'm happy to report that we were largely successful in that measure."   I was furious, outraged. I slapped my program and handouts on the desk with a bang and stood up. Heads swiveled toward me. "So! You're the idiot responsible for the broken promises. And you're proud of it! I'm Derek Turner and I live in the facility you're discussing. How are you defining success?"

Duffman glared at me, mouth hanging open. Then he straightened and answered. "We made sure that the entire population had a chance to benefit from the RCCA site, including the minorities and mentally ill with impairments who otherwise get ignored and bypassed."

"No, you made sure that *no one* gets any benefit from the RCCA. Does the phrase 'least common denominator' mean anything to you? It was supposed to be services to help us get on our own feet and out of the system. But by making them let in everyone you made it so that the services are a bed to sleep in and food in the cafeteria. If a program can't screen for the people it can help, and it has to be responsible for everyone who gets put there, it's not going to have the resources to help the ones who would benefit from it."

Duffman gave a weary sigh. "I don't see why the most privileged people should benefit by being given more privileges. There's a whole generation of inner city black and brown kids that never got a decent chance in school because the school money stays in the rich white neighborhoods while they get guns and drugs in the hallways and classrooms with old broken blackboards instead of video projectors and science labs. But I guess they don't matter as long as you can get a hand up, huh?"

I regarded him from across the room, shaking my head. "They deserve real help and real programming, but they're not getting it at RCCA. Instead they're getting the same warehousing we were getting before. No one's teaching them the skills they didn't learn or giving them the education they missed out on, they're just...RCCA is like a kennel for stray dogs and cats, no one's getting rehabilitated there. Some of us could be, maybe for unfair and unequal reasons like you said, but now no one's getting any real help."

Duffman shrugged. "I'm okay with kids like you being held hostage until the city decides to do something for the less fortunate. You're white, you're articulate, I bet you haven't missed many meals."

"You think the only people in the RCCA who could have been placed somewhere where they could be independent are white people with advantages?" I retorted. "You got a pretty insulting attitude toward the people you claim to be standing up for."

Jay got to his feet and joined the conversation. "I was in the Queens shelter and I would have been in this RCCA except that I was telling people about their rights as residents and the RCCA staff didn't much appreciate that. You all may notice that I'm Black. I went to school in those schools you were talking about, with the guns and drugs, and the teachers being the ones you buy them from. I have a law degree but when I lost my home I hadn't passed the bar exam. Maybe you want to explain how the RCCA program was going to help me, in between taking away everyone's SSD money and trying to get everyone dosed up on thorazine."

The discussion moderator waved his hands at us in a "sit down" gesture and said into the microphone, "This is disruptive and inappropriate. There will be a Q and A after the discussion, but I'm going to have to ask that you hold your comments until then."

Jay made as if to argue, but the moderator cut him off. "If you don't sit down we can arrange to have you removed from the premises."

Jay and Cowboy whispered to each other and then Cowboy indicated with a hand-gesture that they had decided to leave, and I followed them out.

I also took a day trip to Long Island University in Brooklyn. I had continued searching for something akin to an organization or coalition of men who agreed with feminists and wanted to bring an end to patriarchy, which was something I hadn't found through spontaneous interaction since hitching to the city. In a library book, I found mention of a group called the Society for Men Against Sexism and Heterocentricity (SMASH), and I made an appointment to see Dr. Brimmel, who was one of the co-founders.

I waited perched on an orange-cushioned metal chair in his receptionist's office until he came out and ushered me in. I seated myself across from his desk; he made an urbane "over to you" gesture and asked, "So, how can I help you?"

"I came to New York looking for other males who are really at odds with sexist expectations and want to join with the feminists in opposing all that," I stated. "I've found plenty of gay rights and places for gay guys to come together socially, but I identify as a sissy, not as a gay male. And there's no social awareness of feminine males who aren't gay, or places for us to congregate or discuss our issues and stuff."

Brimmel nodded, smiling. "At the risk of repeating myself, how can I help you?"

Flustered, I sort of gawped at him for a moment or two. "Umm, I, well, you organized this SMASH group, and I wanted to, well...connect with some allies...?"

He kept looking at me as if I were not entirely making much sense. "So you would like to join SMASH? Here is a form you can fill out and send in," he said, passing me a brochure.

"Well, I want to do more, really build a movement. I see a magazine article now and then about men who think feminism is good for us, but they don't seem to be making it a priority the way the women are."

Brimmel shrugged, continuing to smile at me. "I know, but what can you do? You're right, it doesn't seem to be a male priority."

"Well, do you...you know, have meetings?"

"Yes, we have an annual conference. There's information about it in the brochure."

Dr. Brimmel did not seem to be reacting to me like someone who had just found another ally for his central cause. He didn't quite ask me if there was anything else he could help me with, but I was starting to feel a bit unwelcome in his office, so I thanked him for his time, asked him if he wanted my contact information—he belatedly got out a sheet of paper for me to write down my name, address, and telephone number—and then I shook his hand and departed.

A more recurrent travel destination for me during the summer was Identity House, down on Sixth Avenue. I had come across it during my wanderings when I'd first hitched into the city, and had gone in to see what it was about. The place had been festooned with posters on the wall about gay and lesbian life, the self-affirming act of coming out, and warnings about the HIV or HTLV virus and AIDS, and the importance of raising social awareness. I hadn't really made any significant contact at the time. There had been some shy young guys and a few ostentatiously seductive ones, and a lot of unspoken inquiries, body language and eye contact and all that. It didn't seem like a useful resource for me.

But during my freshman year I had often been drawn back to my thoughts from back when I had first come out on campus at University of New Mexico in 1980, when things had sort of clicked into place within my head. I had thought of myself as specifically *different* from typical guys, different in a way quite similar to how gay and lesbian folks were different. Also, it's what so many people had thought or assumed about me. So although I didn't have same-sex erotic attractions, I had a lot of the same characteristics as a sissy that society associates with being gay.

There was also the sense that transsexual people were being thought of as part of the gay and lesbian community now, or at least as activists working toward a common goal, and I definitely had lots of things in common with the transsexuals even though I didn't want to transition my body.

So I was going back to see if I could make some kind of useful contact and maybe even meet other people like me.

I walked up the concrete steps self-consciously, pushed open the glass door and slipped inside.

"Hey there, welcome," said a thirty-esque guy with wire-frame glasses.

"Hi," I nodded back at him. I broke eye contact and glanced around. A woman with spiky styled blue-tipped hair and wearing snug dark blue jeans was sitting on the arm of a couch, watching a red-haired girl stapling paper to a large green sheet of construction paper. A black guy with large oval earrings was singing softly along with his radio over in the other direction.

I felt awkward, as I often did in gay and lesbian environments. Didn't want to display overt interest in the attractive gal; lesbians presumably don't come to gay and lesbian centers to be stared at by guys. Didn't want to focus attention on any of the guys, lest they get the wrong idea. *Stupid social clumsiness. Like they're going to think anything faintly approaching friendliness from me is an act of sexual aggression. Yeesh.*

I took a couple deep breaths and let my body relax, and hovered on the verge of the various clusters of people, listening. After a moment I realized that's actually pretty much how I behave in pretty much *all* social environments, not just among gays and lesbians. *I go through life walking on eggshells terrified that someone's going to think I'm sexually interested in them. That's part of my experience as a sissy male, that so many people react to the idea of me being interested in them with disgust and irritation.*

Another pair of guys came down a flight of steps, in mid-conversation. "...another month of apartment-hunting and still haven't found one, you know?" the blond one in the black tee shirt was saying as he descended.

"I hope so too," the Hispanic guy in a mesh shirt following behind him said. "They got the subway diverted up eighth and I didn't know, so of course I had to walk with it down the block. The only nice thing about it was the delicious pizza delivery boy on his bike at midblock. Bike shorts. Bow wow wow puppy chow!"

"Faggot!" taunted the blond one, giving him an open-handed push-away gesture.

"Uh huh. Good one, too!" replied the Hispanic, with a mocking grin.

I felt comfortable with them. Something about their very overt and open comfort level was contagious. When they both went behind the desk and began putting out things on clipboards and straightening piles of fliers, I felt pretty sure they were staff or were a part of the operations of the place at any rate, and stepped forward.

"Hi, I'm Derek. I've come here before a couple times, but I'm looking for...I'm basically like a girl, a femme I guess you'd say. My attraction is toward female people, so I'm not gay, but the femme thing makes me different, and I'm looking for a place where I'd fit in."

"I'm Hector. This glossy glamorous thing is Mishi. Hmm, well, we have a bisexuals support and socialization group that meets the fourth Thursday of every month. That might be a good scene for you to check out."

Hmm. Maybe...probably any group that tends to pull in the exceptions. I pondered, then asked, "Is there anything like that for people who are transsexual?"

Hector looked at Mishi, who raised his eyebrows and said, "You know, we should. We really should. Get an Identity House transsexual group together."

Hector laughed and said, "Yeah, they could meet on the *fifth* Thursday of the month."

"Hi, everyone! My name's Beatrice," she said, pronouncing it *bee-truss*. "I'm the facilitator. I'm bisexual, although all my sexual relationships have been with women since I was in high school. If you would put your name on the sign-in sheet when it comes around, you can leave off your last name if you're not comfortable, we just need it for a head count."

Then we went around the room introducing ourselves.

"Hi, I'm Irwin. I'm twenty-three, and I'm still sorting things out. I find some girls cute and I find some boys cute. I live on the lower east side."

"I'm Teodor and this is Hector. We've been together a couple months now. Both of us have had girlfriends in the past but we wanted to try this."

"Hey everybody! I'm Suzanne..." Suzanne flipped her hair off her shoulder, smiled broadly, and twisted her body to look at all of us around the table. "It is so nice to be here with so many nice looking people!"

"Oh, so, my name's Hanna? I live in Brooklyn. Sheepshead Bay? I came a couple times before so this is, I guess, my third meeting? And I'm twenty-five in September."

My turn. "My name's Derek, hi everyone. I'm twenty-seven. Everyone thought I was gay, growing up, because I wasn't very masculine. I'm actually not. I'm not really bisexual either, I'm a sissy femme who is only attracted to women. I don't really fit in anywhere."

"I'm James. I'm bi, I'm twenty-five, I like to draw comics."

"Yo, I'm Gina. My partner broke up with me last year when she heard I sometimes date guys. Like I guess that gave me boy cooties or something..."

After introductions, the meeting proceeded with a minimum of formality. Boys flirted, girls flirted. Suzanne, in particular, was the very sparkly center of both male and female attention and a lot of the conversation revolved around her animated presence.

The person I was most interested in on a pure chemistry level was Gina, who seemed deliciously smouldery and insouciantly cynical at the same time, but pretty early in the evening she answered someone else's question to say that she wasn't interested in male dating prospects at the moment. I would still have wanted to interact with her more, but she was in quiet conversation with Beatrice, while two other people, Hanna from Sheepshead Bay and the comic artist guy James, were the ones most often directing their conversation to me.

"I like the waterfront, you know? The birds and seeing the shells. But it's so far to ride into the city, so I should probably move?" Hanna seemed to be as socially inept as me, a bit dorky and self-immersed. I tended to like that; I often found people who didn't blend well socially to be the most fun to talk to when they weren't trying to make a social impression.

James, meanwhile, was more interested in discussing issues I cared about. "So, what you were saying about 'how' and 'what,' that's interesting, dividing it up like that. So, like, if I'm feminine but I'm still a man, *how* I am is feminine but *what* I am is a man. Why does the world have such a problem with that?"

The meeting was coming to an end, and James was keeping the conversational volley going. My intermittent dialog with Hanna was more mundane and, to be honest, more inane. Hanna was headed back to the far end of Brooklyn while James said he lived in Forest Hills, which was midway back to the environs of Creedmoor Hospital, so I left with him.

We caught the F train, getting into our seats to the tune of "Stand clear of the closing doors."

"So you said you create comic books, is that correct?" I asked.

"Yeah, I started drawing characters in the corners of my notebooks in grade school. I'd get in trouble for drawing instead of paying attention in class, you know?"

"Do you do the stories to make a specific point or show what things are like, or more just for entertainment?"

"Well, my heroes are gay or bisexual and have lots of sex with the other characters."

It was late enough at night for the train to be making only local stops, so it puddle-stopped its way through western Queens. By the time we got past Roosevelt Avenue and Jackson, there were only a couple other people in the subway car with us. James was holding a bunch of Identity House handouts and he lifted them to show me that he had unzipped his pants and was fondling himself surreptitiously.

I had come to the meeting hoping to connect with people around social issues and concepts of being different, although admittedly attaining a personal connection hadn't been far from my mind. I really should have anticipated that most people would come to the meeting hoping to get it on. This was awkward. I really didn't want to be sitting next to some male while he entertained his own nerve endings. I felt violated, intruded upon. But from his viewpoint maybe he'd feel that I'd led him on by leaving the meeting in his company, and he probably expected more.

"I need to be by myself right now, sorry, nothing personal," I told him. "Have a safe trip home." The train happened to be right at the Woodhaven Boulevard stop and I got up just as the F train doors were about to close and dashed between them to the platform.

I stood there waiting for the next train, thinking about my behavior, and his. *Well, that sure was elegant and dignified. Yeesh. Way to handle things and keep your poise. So, okay, not only am I terrified of accidentally making the wrong person think I'm expressing sexual interest in them, if anyone does it to me I run screaming for the hills. But I'm not sexually uptight, naah...*

My next visit to Identity House was all business and the politics of details. The Gay Pride March was imminent and I joined others at the table, cutting and pasting and stapling. Organizers were making arrangements by telephone and people came in with boxes of silk-screened tee shirts to sell.

One person in a cast of thousands, I marched with my sort-of colleagues down the avenue. I was wearing my denim jacket despite the heat, because of the embroidered patches. I wished I had my skirt: back when I'd first come out on campus at University of New Mexico in the eighties, I had briefly owned and occasionally worn a denim skirt that I'd found at the Salvation Army thrift store. I had lost track of it over the years. I now wished that I'd gone in search of another one for this occasion, something to signify why I was marching.

"Hey, would you mind carrying a sign?" Beatrice asked me. She held several that had been made from construction paper and thin wooden paint sticks, and offered me one that said "HE SHE." It wasn't exactly my sentiment or how I would represent myself, but I hadn't thought to make my own sign any more than I'd planned the ideal thing to wear for the occasion, so I shrugged and took it from her.

We marched for hours. Down in the village, at the end of the parade route, Beatrice asked for the sign back. She handed it to another marcher and assembled a group that marched with a banner that said: THINGS PEOPLE HAVE CALLED US. The other signs in the cluster had things on them like "LESBO," "FRUIT," "SEXUAL INVERT," "HOMOPHILIAC," "PERVERT," and so forth. *I kind of like the term "invert,"* I thought. I marched along behind and to the side of the cluster, disincluded.

I suspected that Beatrice, and perhaps the other Identity House people, viewed me as a supporter and not as a part of the identities that they were housing.

Later that summer, I flew to New Mexico at my parent's expense. They asked me to come visit and mailed me the round-trip plane tickets. I came off the jetaway and they were waiting for me at the terminal and we embraced.

Once back at the ranch house down in White Rock, my Dad gave me another hug and said, "I'm so proud of you. You said you were going to go off to school in New York and you went and did it. Then you made straight As and the Dean's list. I admire that you made a plan and stuck to it."   I proposed to my parents that I cook dinner. "I haven't had a chance to cook in ages. We don't have a kitchen in that facility I'm living in, and I miss it."

"Well, I was just going to throw something together from what's in the freezer and larder," my Mom said. "I originally thought we'd have leftovers from Tuesday but we finished most of that off, and I didn't really have a plan for tonight."

I nodded. "I can cook from what I find. Do you mind? I'll clean up after myself."

"Oh, I'd love to have someone else cook. I didn't expect you to feel so ambitious right after a long plane ride, but if you do, I'm happy to sit on the sofa until you call us!"

I made foods that I'd grown up with, family recipes and preparation methods I'd learned at this very stove. Macaroni and cheddar in the oven with a pone of cornbread, and a batch of fresh peas from their garden. Foods of our family. Foods I'd been missing.

My mom came downstairs while I was poking around in my closet looking for things I might want to take back with me. She hovered at the doorway for a moment, then said, "I'm proud of your success in school, too. I realize this is what you said you wanted, and I didn't support you on it when you told us you wanted to go there. I always knew you had it in you to do anything you wanted in school, but I wasn't sure you'd apply that and stay focused. I'm glad I was wrong. It's so good to see you doing well."

INTO THE DORMS

Fall semester, 1986. The day came for me to move into my dorm room on the first floor of Building Five. I packed most of my clothes and a handful of books, manila clasp folders from the college, my booklet of contacts and calendar, and other first-tier essentials into a soft-sided suitcase I had purchased used from David Gaffney, another RCCA resident. The loop bus picked me up where the county transit bus let me off, and I lugged my possessions through the corridors of Academic Village and out one of the spokelike radiating corridors to the residential buildings that surround it.

"Turner...yeah, okay. Lemme see your bursar slip. Uh huh. Your room is Thirteen-A, right down there on the ground floor. I'm Leroy Allison, and I'm your RA, you got anything you need to talk to someone about, like you got a complaint or you having trouble getting settled in, you come to me." Leroy Allison gave me a bored level stare and held out my keys. "I put you on the ground floor because there are ladies who they aren't comfortable where someone on the outside is where they can maybe get in at their window." I nodded; that made sense. I had not been developing a very charitable attitude toward this man, who struck me as arrogant and pompous in a petty-official kind of way, but his last remark made me try to suspend my reaction.

I unpacked, made my bed, and made notes about additional things it looked like I'd need there. I wouldn't be going to classes until day after tomorrow, and didn't plan on returning to RCCA until tomorrow morning, when I'd bring a second set of Derek-possessions from the facility at Creedmoor. For now, I rummaged through my cassette tapes, selecting Bloodrock, a dystopian rock band from the 70s, and stuck it into my portable boom box. The tones of "Hangman's Dance" washed over me, and I stretched and pivoted and looked around my dorm room.

No more halfway-house bullshit to deal with! This was going to be nice!

It was somewhat hot and stuffy; it was an early September day, and students had been coming and going all day long, installing themselves in their dorm rooms and letting the air conditioning out. I glanced out the window and saw that, even though I was on the ground floor, the back of the building was on a downhill slope, so my window opened onto the concrete ceiling of a storage area.

After a couple minute's consideration of the matter, I opened my window and crawled out onto the flat building ledge immediately outside, taking my cassette boom box with me, and stripped to my underwear and sunbathed while rock music played.

After about ten minutes an adjoining window slid open. Leroy Allison poked his head out. "Yo, you can't be doing that. We got to keep standards. If everybody was doing that the campus would look sloppy, so I need you to get back inside."

I shrugged and pulled everything back into my room. Yeah, so I live on SUNY campus now. Another institution, what can you do?

Through the open window, I heard something happening outside in the pedestrian walkway that went between residential buildings. Curious, I stepped out and found a cluster of people centered around a dark-haired guy with a cane who held a softball-sized rock in his hand.

"Oh, hey there, I was telling these ladies, and this gentleman over here—what was your name? Marco, right? And here we have Shauna and Patrice, and I'm Mike—I was telling these folks that just outside of my dorm room I discovered this rock, and it is quite a special rock, is it not? See, it has a patch of green over here on this side, and some sparkles over here. I think a rock this special deserves a name, so we are holding a contest to see who can come up with the perfect name for this fine stone." Mike nodded toward the girl to his right. "Shauna, who lives in Building Six, has suggested 'Rocky,' and Marco, from Building Five, says we should call it 'Peter'. I began this quest over at Building Seven, which is my own fair abode, and that's where I met Cindy, and Patrice, who is majoring in business administration..."

I was totally blown away. This guy had picked up a rock and started walking around and now knew several dozen people and was entertaining everyone with his silliness. In due course he turned to me, got my name and which dorm I was from and that this was my first semester as a resident student, and my nomination for the rock's name: Paul Simon.

I followed the cluster of people as he went on to Building 4 and drew in a few more people, and then he turned around and asked if anyone had any smoking material that wasn't exactly tobacco insofar as he was momentarily out of his own supply. As was his roommate, who was, like himself, named Mike, and who had, like himself, a cane, but was black, thus making the pair of them White Mike with a cane and Black Mike with a cane, two Mikes in the same dorm room.

I nodded and did a mimic of toking on a joint and pointed to my pocket and he waved me closer while continuing to banter with other people. He learned a few more peoples' names and then said the rock was going to be known as Peter because it came from petro and it was a good tradition to name your rocks Peter.

Folks thinned out and thanked him for the entertainment and said they were glad to have met him, and then he confirmed that I had some weed on me (I did) and we headed to his room. He was Michael Aleissa and this was his first year at Old Brookville and he was majoring in biological sciences.

"I went to high school a few miles from here," he told me. "Didn't want to go to college after I graduated, I wanted to do something else for a while, you know? Got a job in a research lab. After a few years I started wishing I had the biology and chemistry education so I could move up. I'm twenty-four, I guess that makes me an older returning student or something."

"I am, too," I responded. "I got you beat, I'm twenty-seven, and this is my third poke at being a college student."

"I think we're gonna have to teach these younger kids how to have fun. I was expecting more of a college night life here on campus."

"Well, people are still moving in, I think, but I have to say, you've done a damn good job of stirring up some night life. You had a pretty good party crowd there, with that thing you were doing about giving a name to the rock."

Michael opened the door and waved to his roommate. "Hey, Other Mike."

"Hey man. Say, did you have any luck finding any cheeber? I need some chronic."

I took out my bag and Michael Aleissa pulled out a one-hitter pipe and the three of us proceeded to get good and stoned.

The Women's Studies course catalog listed several courses that I was particularly interested in—"Feminist Theory," "Sex, Gender & Sexuality," "The Family: Institution in Crisis"—but none of those were being taught this fall. In lieu of any of those, I had signed up for Psychology of Women and a crosslisted Health Services course titled Sex in Humans. The Psych of Women course would be taught by Baxwood's colleague Rachel Rosencranz.

I plopped down in an empty seat. Dr. Rosencranz handed out a syllabus and began outlining the course. "Throughout history, the nature of women has been a topic of recurrent debate, and has been defined and redefined. Usually by men. We're going to look at some of those definitions and discuss them from a critical vantage point. I want you all to keep a journal and as you read, I want you to write down your thoughts and your questions, and you'll be turning those in every two weeks. For Thursday's class, I'd like you to read the excerpts from Aristotle, St. Augustine, and St. Thomas Aquinas."

I scowled. I knew I had leftover frustration due to not being able to take the classes I wanted to be taking, but I wasn't looking forward to reading the horrible things these ancient moldy men had written about women and women's place in the world.

There was a letter taped up all over the campus from Stephen Balcombe, Acting Vice President for Student Development. Apparently there had been a dance last spring at which there had been an incident of violence, and because of that he was calling a moratorium on any and all dances on campus.

I was annoyed. Mostly with the tone of the letter. We are college students and I felt it was inappropriate to issue this parental-sounding insulting missive and have it occupying all the public spaces as part of our welcome-to-campus experience. There might be occasions or situations where school administrators needed to intervene in our social activities but this letter reeked of "You misbehaving unruly students have been very bad and so I'm taking away your dances to teach you a lesson." Someone should remind him (and the campus as a whole) that we students weren't going to stand by while someone purported to make decisions that affect us without including us in the process, and informing us of their imperial decision in such an insulting manner.

And, with my history of having rubbed professor Penfield's nose in it about the "peer counseling" office last semester, I thought that somebody ought to be me.

This was a college campus with a rich history of student power; it had been created with the intention of letting students shape their own curriculum, and then later had been charged with providing an education for people who usually haven't gotten a fair opportunity to attend college. It had a faculty devoted to empowerment of the underclasses and criticizing inequalities and structural oppressions and whatnot. So Balcombe's letter was a gauntlet thrown down, whether he intended it that way or was just clueless and oblivious.

I sat at my typewriter and wrote a scathing reply to be printed in the *Catalyst* in their next issue, and then dashed off to the newspaper office, only to find that it wasn't open and didn't appear to be staffed.

I recognized Omar Mason sitting at a long table in the Student Government office, going though a stack of mail. "Hey, how's the campaign?" I hailed.

He gave me a friendly wave. "We're making progress. I hope you're going to vote in the student government elections. Of course I hope you vote for me, let's be real, but the important thing is to be a participant and use your political voice."

"Right on. Absence of voice is actually what I'm here about. I wanted to put in a letter to the editor over at the newspaper, but it seems like the *Catalyst* is shut down. What's up with that?"

Omar smiled a wry smile. "Starting last fall, there was a little clique of journalism hotshots that decided the paper belonged to them. We got a lot of complaints from the student body that they only published what they agreed with, and in the spring they started tearing down student government. Saying we'd been spending student fees on ourselves, accusing us of not doing anything but partying. Jim Dortman told them it was libel and they couldn't print that shit, I mean excuse me, but I've been in this organization for two years and our meetings are open, we are totally transparent, you hear what I'm saying? So they wrote more about how we were trying to censor them, and Dortman cancelled their budget line and they couldn't pay the printers for any more issues. They tried to hold a rally, you know, freedom of the press, in the Academic Village main corridor, but the students all laughed at them, 'cause they'd dug themselves into this hole. Anyway, they're not doing the paper this fall and no one else has stepped up to take over. So for the time being..." He shrugged.

"I see. Well I might want to get involved somehow. We need a paper."

But I didn't feel like waiting for that to happen. The time for this letter was now, not next month or whenever a new editing staff was able to resurrect the newspaper. I rode the bus in to Kinko's copies and paid for them to photocopy a thousand copies, then went back and taped my reply to Balcombe in all the places where his letter had been posted.

> Woman was merely man's helpmate, a function which pertains to her alone.
>
> Woman does not possess the image of God in herself but only when taken together with the male who is her head, so that the whole substance is one image. But when she is assigned the role as helpmate, a function that pertains to her alone, then she is not the image of God. But as far as the man is concerned, he is by himself alone the image of God just as fully and completely as when he and the woman are joined together into one.
>
> —*Saint Augustine, Bishop of Hippo Regius (354–430)*

These readings were every bit as awful as I'd anticipated. I was not enjoying my sojourn into the pathetically sexist mind of this decrepitated church fossil.

That was Augustine; the other two we had to read materials from were no better:

> As regards the individual nature, woman is defective and misbegotten, for the active force in the male seed tends to the production of a perfect likeness in the masculine sex; while the production of woman comes from defect in the active force or from some material indisposition, or even from some external influence; such as that of a south wind, which is moist, as the Philosopher observes. (St. Thomas Aquinas)

> The male, unless constituted in some respect contrary to nature, is by nature more expert at leading than the female, and the elder and complete than the younger and incomplete...

The relation of male to female is by nature a relation of superior to inferior and ruler to ruled. (Aristotle)

Why was Dr. Rosencranz making us wade through this? It's not like anyone in the classroom would be likely to be unexposed to this kind of thinking. The Moral Majority and the elders of the Mormon Church were still saying plenty of things like that. And the mere fact that we were Old Brookville students taking a Women's Studies class was a pretty good hint that we didn't agree with this.

I could see how leading off with these readings might make sense in a course about women's role or how women were perceived, but it seemed like an odd (and unpleasant) start for a course about women's psychology. I was skeptical but curious to see where she was going with this.

Meanwhile, since keeping a journal and making comments in it was part of the course assignment, I wrote down my contempt for these people's notions about women and my misgivings about using them as a starting point.

I plopped down into a seat in Rosencranz's class the next morning, feeling cranky and argumentative. But I resolved to sit on my attitude as much as possible and let her teach.

"What did you think of the readings?" she asked us. "These famous men don't think much of us, do they?"

She called on Shantay, who proclaimed, "I don't think Aristotle has got any business talking about women not being as good at leading, because he lived in ancient Greece and women in his time didn't get a chance to lead, they had to stay in their home, so he never saw women act as leaders."

There were other comments in a similar mode, expressing disagreement or posing questions about the authors' position to write what they'd written. They said it a lot more politely than I would have.

Dr. Rosencranz offered a summary about an hour into the class. "The one theme that has echoed down through the ages, from the Greek philosophers on through the medieval theologians and on into the political and social leaders of modern times, is that women are evil and men are good. Women are sinful and morally depraved. So the authority to lead, to be in charge, has to go to the good people, who of course are always men."

I couldn't sit on my hands any longer, and signaled that I had something to say. "I think it's a bit more complicated than that," I said, "at least the way it ended up in modern western culture. 'Good' and 'bad' are words that have different meanings depending on the sex of the person. For boys, 'bad' is affirmative, being a bad boy is all about getting away with something, being a rebel, not letting anyone discipline you. 'Good' is passive, being...you know, put in your place, silenced into obedience. For girls, 'bad' isn't affirmative in the same way. Bad boys may be strong but bad girls are weak, pulled down into misbehaviors, misled into their own peril and all that. And good girls are the strong ones. I think maybe it has a lot to do with how human sexuality, sexual behavior, is tied into how we think of behavior in general."

Dr. Rosencranz shook her head. "I think we're in danger of drifting off topic and into the weeds. If boys can get away with being bad it's because they aren't already thought of as bad to begin with."

She shifted gears. "I want to read to you a study performed at Harvard. The sex of the subject was hidden from the interpreter and the interpreter was asked to assess whether the subject was behaving rationally or reacting emotionally. And they concluded that the female subjects were no more likely to be regarded as driven by their emotions or less rational than the male subjects."

Later, I wrote in my journal that so far the whole discussion of women's psychology reminded me of a joke about a politician being betrayed by their former ally. The betrayal took the form of a grossly inadequate and diluted denial after a listing of horrible charges: "I have been hearing for years that my esteemed colleague Senator Smith is a lying reprobate, a swindler, a corrupt and unethical slimeball who sells his vote to anyone who will make a little contribution, and an immoral alcoholic who fornicates with depraved prostitutes. Well I am here to tell you that Senator Smith lies no more frequently than other Senators, the court cases in which he was accused of embezzlement did not result in any convictions, and furthermore the women with whom he has associated were never proven to be engaged in actual prostitution. Senator Smith is *not* utterly unqualified for his position, I don't care what else you may have heard!"

"Hey you troublemaker!" Michael Aleissa greeted me, waving from down the corridor. "Man, you really roasted that guy Stephen Balcombe. What is it that he does here?"

"Well," I said, striding up to where he stood, "he identifies himself as 'Acting Vice President for Student Development'. Whatever that may mean. I don't know his actual job description. But the way I look at it, from a students' rights perspective..."

"He's full of shit," Michael summarized, cutting to the chase. "Yeah, I got that. If that's the way he's acting, he can go develop himself into a less harmful job, couldn't agree with you more."

I nodded.

"How're things going with your professors and stuff?" he asked.

"Getting settled in." I sighed. "I don't seem to be as much in tune with my coursework as I was last year. How about you?"

"I showed Professor McMillan this trick for titrating an organic soluble with a variable-speed centrifuge, and it's so much faster than the textbook process, you don't learn these things without some real-world lab experience. He's thinking of putting me in charge of the chem lab!"

"Quite cool!"

"Hey, I need to run something past you. I met this fantastic woman during the summer, a real renaissance woman, you know?"

"Lots of diverse talents and interests, huh?"

He paused, then continued. "Like a Renoir. Her name's Jenna. Well, she has a best friend Marcie, and I got to know Marcie too, from the three of us hanging out. And, I couldn't believe this at first but I swear, Marcie was flirting with me and Jenna was right there and joking about me and Marcie getting it on. So I'm like, 'Can this be happening, they want me for a threesome?', and I'm pinching myself."

I grinned and nodded. "That sounds quite cozy."

"So I won't give you all the bedroom details but it was really a taste of heaven, or a lot of tasting of heaven. But so now I want to continue to see Jenna, but I really like Marcie, too, and I can't figure out what to do about it!"

"What do you mean?" I replied, puzzled. "They know about each other, obviously, and you like them both. What is there that needs to have something done about it?"

"Well, doing a threesome is really special but I want to have some one-on-one time with Jenna. And yet Marcie is cute and I'm thinking I want to spend some time one-on-one with her."

I nodded along slowly and waited, still not getting it.

"Well, when I'm with Jenna I think 'Oh, this is the girl for me' and I'm ready to focus all on her, but then with Marcie I start thinking 'I don't want to give this up,' you see what I mean?"

"Not yet. Go out with Jenna and be with her and be in love with her. Then have a date with Marcie and be fully with her. Sounds to me that's what they want, to share you."

"D'you wanna come over later and meet them? Maybe once you see how it is you'll understand my problem."

CONFLICT AND PLEASURE

"Hey, it's Derek! Have a beer, dude. Hey, everybody, this is Derek, who I met my very first day on campus!" Michael waved me into his dorm room. "This is Jenna, the Renaissance woman I spoke to you about earlier..." Michael slipped behind Jenna and ran his fingers through her reddish blonde hair, leaning in to plant a delicate kiss behind one earlobe. Then he pivoted on his boot heel and leaned his face into that of the other girl, bumping noses with her. "...and this cutie is Jenna's good friend Marcie."

"Oh, hello!" Jenna said cheerfully, giving me a wave. Marcie wiggled fingers at me and nodded.

"Derek just wrote this absolutely cool memo about this jerk Stephen Balcombe, who is our -- what is he again, student life coordinator? -- who told us we weren't allowed to dance. Derek really let him have it and it's posted all over campus."

"Vice President for Student Development," I specified. "He put up notices saying there had been some kind of violent incident last spring at a dance so we weren't going to be allowed to have any dances on campus from now on. I kind of thought it's his job to consult with us, not just tell us what we can and can't do. I mean, by his logic, if there had been a violent incident in the parking lot I guess we'd be prohibited from parking, you know?"

Jenna rolled her eyes and Marcie, watching her, giggled. Jenna said, "I hate dealing with little officials who enjoy making rules and saying no to people. I had to go to DMV to get a replacement driver's license and the form said to use black ink. The only pen I had was blue ink so I asked to borrow one. 'We aren't in the business of lending out pens.'" Michael shook his head. "I could never be in the business of saying no to delectable women. I would get fired after the first week."

Marcie said, "I would have leaned over her desk and asked what business she *was* in, because it sure isn't customer service!"

The diminutive Marcie, with her bright cheerful mannerisms, didn't seem like an imposing figure, but I could see that she had an edge.

Jenna nodded thoughtfully. "I thought of asking if her daddy knew what she does for a living, but it was easier to just grab a pen from the empty desk next to her. So I told her 'In that case, I won't bother returning it'." She smiled sweetly. Different edge.

Michael was playing deejay, picking out an album and positioning the needle to drop on a specific track. "Hey, down in the bio sciences lab we've got some insect habitats. I could turn some ants and roaches loose under Balcombe's office door, that would teach him to mess with us!"

I stared at him, not being clear on whether he was serious or not. It didn't hit me as funny. Jenna's eyes had tracked over to him, too, and there was something quizzical and reserved in a disapproving mode on her face. She caught my glance and gave a microshrug and a brief glance upward.

Michael then shook his head and made a dismissing hand-motion. "Naah, he's not worth it. You already nailed him."

"If you ask me," Michael stated, "there's nothing that tastes as good as a woman right out of the shower, wouldn't you agree?" He dropped the needle on a U2 track and took a hit off the joint.

I wasn't particularly experienced or adept at oral sex and wasn't sure how to reply, so I just smiled.

Michael circled to come up behind Jenna, while ostensibly continuing to aim his conversation at me. "You're a women's studies student, so I'm sure you would agree that so much of the problem in this world is male selfishness. I always say 'she comes first, and that means she *comes first*'."

Marcie, in the other chair, winced like she had a headache. She shifted and chirped, "Some of the world's problems come from guys acting like every time a girl comes he gets to carve a notch."

Jenna was doing it again, eyeball-conferencing with Marcie and raising an eyebrow just a fraction. It wasn't that she was one of those people whose thoughts and feelings are out in front for anyone to see whether they'd rather hide them or not; it was more like she had a broadcast mode turned on, and was tuned into Marcie and communicating with her below the audible threshold. And because I was reading along, she was acknowledging and including me in the conversation. It had the effect of making Michael odd man out; he alone didn't seem to be participating.

He spread his hands wide as he faced Marcie. "There's that, too, no doubt about it. Always trying to prove you're a man. Treating it like it's a performance. I try to get away from that and just be in the moment and appreciate it for the beautiful experience that it can be."

There was a lull in the conversation, during which Michael put on another record and Jenna got up to use the bathroom. When she returned, Marcie tapped her forearm and said, "Remember when Michael and my Dad first met?" Marcie turned to me and explained, "My parents are from France and live in a pretty ritzy neighborhood near Locust Valley. They manage a rich family's estate grounds and live on the property, so they're like butlers or gardeners, they're not billionaires or anything. But they're kind of stuffy and old-fashioned..."

"Old-fashioned? Them?" said Jenna, mocking disbelief.

".. and they think everyone ought to dress up nice and be respectful to their elders and all that. And so Michael is picking me up but he doesn't come to the door because of his leg, he just honks. And my dad goes out with me to see who this American is who drives up and honks for his daughter, right? Michael's wearing a t shirt with holes in it and my dad is like this...," she frowns sourly, "and asks where we're going, and Michael says we're off to taste wines on the east end."

Jenna laughed. "Yeah, and your dad said something about how only French wines were worth drinking and Michael starts lecturing your dad about the superiority of Long Island wines."

Michael interposed, "I never said French wines weren't any good, but here your dad is, living in an area that makes excellent wine, and he dismisses it without ever having tasted it."

I chimed in, "Yeah, I agree with Michael. I don't mean Long Island wines are better than the best French wines but there are some really nice ones out there. I like Hargrave's merlot from last year, for instance."

"Oh, I know," Marcie nodded. "But to *mon pere*, you don't correct an older French man and tell him his country's wine is no better than what he can get by the side of the road locally, so now whenever he sees Michael he sighs and scowls at him."

Michael said, "Yeah, it's like 'Marcie, that uncouth gutter snipe is here again, do you want me to tell him to leave?'"

Jenna laughed. "Well, Marcie's dad doesn't really approve of anybody very much so don't take it personally. I think he thinks I'm a bad influence."

Marcie began, "If they only knew half..."

Michael cut her off, speaking to Jenna, "Does he glare at you and speak about you as if you weren't standing right there?"

"Not quite like that"

"Maybe you should try sitting down in the living room and talking."

I noticed that Marcie's face had lost some of its buoyant cheer. And I watched Jenna as she answered Michael, and saw her monitoring Marcie. It seemed to me like Michael was far more focused on Jenna and that Marcie was perhaps feeling very fifth-wheelish, only getting his attention incidentally.

After a little while, Jenna asked, "Hey, Marcie? Do you think we need to be heading back?"

Marcie looked back gratefully and nodded. "It was nice meeting you, Derek. Bye, Michael, don't get into any trouble until we see you again. Save the trouble for next time we're around!"

Michael turned to me. "Derek, would you mind escorting the ladies to their car in the parking lot? I would, but with this leg...I know it's probably safe but everything on this campus is black this, black that, everybody's black here. Even my roommate is black, we got Black Mike and White Mike, and we both got our canes, and I guess everything's equal and fair, although maybe he's safer when he's walking around."

Jenna turned toward me and asked, "Do you feel unsafe on this campus? Are the black students here hostile to white students?"

I shook my head. "No, not at all. I'm not even sure we're really a minority, we might just be less in the majority than a lot of white people are used to being. Anyway, no, I've never felt either unsafe or unwelcome here."

"Yeah, it doesn't feel that way to me either."

"I'd feel better if you'd go with them to their car," Michael persisted.

I looked to Jenna. "I'll do that if you two don't mind, although I suspect you know how to take care of yourself."

We stepped out onto the concrete walkway, Michael calling out his good-nights from the door, and down into the asphalt parking area.

I asked Marcie, "You okay?"

She smiled wryly. "I'm fine. I'm used to it."

Jenna glanced my direction, then asked Marcie herself: "Really? You're sure?"

But Marcie was insistent that all was well with the world and that we needn't be concerned about her.

Jenna shrugged. "He can be a really nice guy, really thoughtful." She seemed to be talking to both me and Marcie. "I'm kind of worried about him a little, he seems really uptight about the black and white thing."

"Yeah," I agreed, "he keeps bringing it up and saying the same things over and over, especially the stuff about him and his roommate, like he's disturbed by how much they have in common or something."

"Well," Jenna said, opening the driver's side door, "I hope we get to talk some more. Really. This was nice."

I thought so too.

Sex in Humans, a Health Services course cross-listed with Women's Studies, was being taught by Professor Amy Teller. "Okay," she asked the class, "is anybody in here familiar with the structuralist functionalist branch of theorists?"

I raised my hand. She nodded and continued. "Then you know they're basically the conservatives, the apologists for the social order."

"Well, not necessarily," I dissented. "I just got finished rereading Elizabeth Janeway, and she uses a lot of Talcott Parson's theories to take apart lots of commonly held beliefs about the sexes, to show how the beliefs have a function to preserve and maintain the way the sexes are set up as opposites."

"Well, see, that's sort of my point. She uses structural functionalism to justify the sexist status quo and the structure of the family."

I shook my head. "No she doesn't! I'm talking about *Man's World, Woman's Place: A Study in Social Mythology*, it's a feminist classic, and it's a takedown of those beliefs!"

Dr. Teller looked annoyed. "Well, I think she's probably what we would call a 'liberal feminist'. Anyway, the type of theory known as *conflict* theory is the sociological perspective that progressive social researchers and activists tend to use, and structural functionalism is the kind that, generally speaking, is used by conservatives, that's what I'm trying to say."

She went to the blackboard and wrote "STRUCTURAL FUNCTIONALISTS—CONSERVATIVE" and circled it, then "CONFLICT—PROGRESSIVE" and drew a second circle around that.

She faced us and continued, "Beginning in the sixties, feminism has been a part of what socialist activists started. As they began examining the oppressions in our society, such as racism and social class, they realized the importance of examining gender. The family as we know it didn't get here to create a safe nurturing space for children, that's not the main purpose of the family as an institution. The family was formed as a way to transfer property down the male line. Property is capital, it's the most basic capital, it's how capitalism got started. And men were the owners of capital, the owners of property and they owned their wives and their children, they were capital too, they were also property. Attributes that were useful for the male ruling class to have in their women, like obedience and being gentle and supportive, that was defined as 'femininity'. As girls and women, we are praised for characteristics that make us useful domestic slaves."

Hands shot up. Omar Mason and Carl Jenkins and Shantay Solomon. Dr. Teller looked from face to face and grinned. "That hit a nerve, did it? I've got an article I'm going to pass around, 'I Want a Wife' by Judy Syfers. We ladies are taught to take pride in our femininity, and to be admired and recognized for what we bring into our relationships. But instead of thinking of these things as female characteristics, what if we think of them as *useful* characteristics, useful to have in your partner. Or your servant. Why don't we demand the same useful traits in our male partners? Because men just aren't like that? Because we're lucky to get a partner who wants to stay with us?"

I was familiar with the article being passed out to us; it was in one of the compendiums I had on my bookshelf, *Woman in Sexist Society* or maybe *Sisterhood is Powerful*. I grudgingly admired the professor for how she had provoked the class; they were ready to be argumentative but she had us all engaged. I wasn't sure, though, whether she intended to start a discussion or just wanted us to learn passively in her class. She'd ignored the waving hands and people had put them down and were taking the Syfers piece as it was being distributed.

Teller made her points about how the characteristics that are designated as feminine are things that one would seek in a subservient person that one would wish to control or exploit, using the article about the attributes of a wife as a jumping-off point.

Carl Jenkins finally got called on. "A lot of these same ways of being you say are thrust onto women were expected of the black man too. I think you've got to look at that as well. And I mean, sure, we want our women to have gentle, well, feminine characteristics, but we don't demand her to take a lesser role because we know what that's like, from our own experience."

Dr. Teller nodded. "All these different oppressions tend to function the same way. But it's important to realize that although you may experience racism, you as a male are not a victim of sexism. Socialist feminists began with an examination of class struggle and then saw how that same inequality plays out as racial oppression and when they took a look at the relationship between the sexes, hey, they found it there too."

I held up my own hand and eventually she called on me. I said, "I've read a lot of things written by Robin Morgan and other women who were a part of the left, what they called the *male* left, in the sixties, and they say that the political left was very sexist. They came to participate as radicals but were expected to make coffee while the guys were the leaders and it was from breaking away from them and going off on their own as radical feminists, not so much just extending the Marxist analysis of class and all that, that got them started as radical feminists."

"There was a lot of splintering," Dr. Teller said, sort of interrupting, since I hadn't finishing formulating my question. "Especially for lots of white middle class women, they didn't have a lot of solidarity with working class people and minorities and once they thought they could have a movement all about their own oppression, some of them went off by themselves and retreated from a more universal concern about human rights and human suffering. But I think you'll find that the most useful, the most progressive analysis of sexist oppression, is to be found in the socialist conflict theory tradition."

Omar called me aside as I was leaving the cafeteria. "Hey, Derek. So, here's the situation, man. The student gov advisors want the *Catalyst* to be taken over by a journalism student, or a bunch of them, that's how it's always been in the past. But there's no one left who was part of it last year, and we asked around in Karl Gilman's Media and Reporting class but nobody was hot to take it over. There's people who don't want you having anything to do with the newspaper, they think you'll be a hothead worse than who we had in the spring. I'm tellin' you man, that thing you posted about Balcombe, you have riled some people up. Not sayin' that's a bad thing, you catch my drift, but just so you know. But I told them you were interested and we got to have a student paper. You want to take a look at the *Catalyst* office and see if you think you can figure out how to put out an issue? Maybe get a group of friends together and make a go of it?"

Omar dangled a key and I took it. "I'll see if I can find some instructions or a guidebook or something," I said. "I've never done this kind of thing, but I definitely want to see the newspaper come back to life."

The newspaper office was abandoned as if for a fire drill; piles of mail, stacks of typed and handwritten material, random photographs and fast food styrofoam containers were interspersed with scissors and push pins and X-acto razor knives and scotch tape. I turned on the overhead fluorescents and sat at the most prominent of the desks.

The mail included bills from a place called Senator Printing, a couple of ads apparently intended to be included in the next issue, and a series of acrimonious missives from the student government about overdue requisition forms, denied budget items, and accusations of libel.

Under a stack of ledger-sized paper, I found a portion of a newspaper page where the columns had been cut out from the paper they were printed on and pasted onto a template. "Aha," I realized, "that's how it's done. Somehow they get printed out in these narrow strips, and then you cut them out and paste them down to make the newspaper pages."

Off to my right stood a tall blue metal machine with a typewriter keyboard and a zillion other buttons. The brand name was Linotype.

The bills from Senator Printing appeared to be for running off three thousand copies of an issue back in April.

I was going to need help with this, that much was obvious.

Dr. Baxwood looked up to see me hovering at her door. She gestured. Come on in. I slid into the seat across from her.

"So how's the semester going so far?" she asked.

"Umm...," I said. Really erudite. Feeling awkward. "Umm, listen, can I ask you...am I a disruptive male in my women's studies classes?"

She smiled and nodded sagely. "Sometimes. You *do* like to hear yourself talk. What you have to say is never an attack on feminism and it's obvious you have sincere good political intentions. Sometimes you go off-topic. A disruption isn't always a bad thing in a classroom, although it can be frustrating to the person trying to teach the class. Did you have something specific in mind?"

"Well...I have Rachel Rosencranz for Psychology of Women, and I've got Amy Teller for Sex in Humans. And it seems like I've made both of them mad at me in their courses, or at least they don't like what I had to say and cut me off. And I don't mean to be that guy, you know, creating problems for the women's studies teacher, but it's frustrating."

"Well, I've had to cut you off myself sometimes. I wouldn't take it personally. Sometimes a student brings up something that's relevant or interesting, but maybe not relevant or interesting to everyone in the classroom, and there's only so much time in the class period."

I sighed. "I came here to be an activist. To join up with other people who had the same kind of politics, the same sort of concerns. But sometimes the way things are presented in class, I feel like I'm being erased. I'm a sissy libber, I guess you could say. I got socially oppressed, or at least ostracized and badly treated, the same way gay males get treated, but it's not because of sexual orientation, patriarchy is intolerant of people who break sex role behavior standards and stuff. And in Rosencranz's class I was trying to say it isn't as simple as 'girls are bad and boys are good in this society'. And with Teller, she's saying sex inequality is all from class and that feminists who look at it differently are elitist white women or something."

Baxwood pushed her brown plastic-rimmed spectacles farther up her nose; she looked off somewhere above my head for a moment, then raised a finger. "I think if you're trying to make a big deal about being a different kind of person than other men, you're going at this wrong. I do think patriarchy is bad for men, in fact I think it's bad for all living things on this planet. It confines all women, and it confines all men too, if we're going to go there and talk about that. Not just special types. You don't want to have it look like you're saying you should get a free pass because you're different but other men are the culprits and we can all blame them because it's their fault."

She began pulling stapled articles from manila folders on her desk, flipping through them, as she continued talking. "In my intro course, I have my students talk about who was expected to do the dishes in their family when they were growing up. Dr. Teller...well, I have heard Amy Teller say that war and poverty are important, and the fact that forty percent of black males are in prison, and America's role in global colonialism, and that that's what we should be focused on, not who does the dishes. Aah, here it is..."

Dr. Baxwood now had an article between thumb and forefinger, but for now just used it to point at me. "Dr. Rosencranz isn't quite that extreme, but she's got some similar beliefs. I was a Redstockings, and I was in some of the first consciousness-raising groups with Kathie Sarachild and Carol Hanisch, and I think the socialist left misses some things. They have more of a top down way of thinking about social problems and we learned there are advantages to looking from the bottom up. But to tell you the truth, I'm not too concerned with a lot of the arguments about different kinds of feminist theory. That's more of a male thing, to get all invested in arguing about how many angels fit on the head of a pin, that sort of thing. But I know you want to talk ideas, I see how excited you get in the classes when we talk about the readings.

"You need to go to grad school. That's where you'll find these discussions, and you'll thrive there."

She held out the article toward me. "The Unhappy Marriage of Marxism and Feminism," it was titled. Heidi Hartmann. Oh yes. I want to read that. Baxwood smiled and let me take it.

"Will you walk us back to the car again?" Jenna asked me.

Jenna and Marcie had been over to visit Michael again, and he had once again suggested I hang out with them. We'd had a good pleasant evening of it.

Marcie had brought a board game, with a combination of tokens and cards and dice and questions the players were supposed to ask each other, but it proved complicated and apparently there were pieces missing. She had given up in frustration and asked if either of us had any games, and I'd said that I knew card games from playing with my family, and taught them all how to play cutthroat hearts.

Over giggles and triumphant dumping of the queen of spades, Jenna talked about her coursework at SUNY Farmingdale and Michael described the use of colored stains for making microscope slides and the off-label use of the centrifuge for hyperchilling a bottle of vodka. Throughout the evening, I again had that exciting intimate feeling, the awareness game, of being in on an unspoken secret with Jenna in particular and sometimes with Marcie as well.

Once we had departed Michael's dorm room, Marcie asked if she could make a pit stop at my dorm room because she had forgotten to go at Michael's before leaving. And she and Jenna agreed that they wanted to see my room anyway.

"So," Marcie began as I opened the door and turned on the light. She smiled a perky smile.

"Yes. So," Jenna agreed. "You're probably wondering why I called this meeting..." Marcie giggled, as Jenna adopted a mischievous expression for a moment.

But then she turned serious and sincere. "We don't know all of what Michael told you but we thought it made sense to explain a few things. I met Michael last year and we spent some time together. He's a good guy, you know that, and kinda cute too. Well, so he met Marcie from spending time with me, and, you've seen what he's like, he's a flirt, and Marcie is a flirt, so things happened, just playing around at first, but ..."

Marcie took over. "I asked Jenna what I should do, and she said if it wasn't bothering me and I liked it, I should have fun. And I was like, 'So you don't mind?', and she says, 'I don't have a branding iron and I don't have a stockyard,'" Marcie explained, nudging Jenna.

Jenna smiled a wry amused smile. It was a smile I was seeing a lot of. It was a smile that I liked seeing. "Well, that's how things got started. I'd have dates with Michael, and Marcie would have dates with Michael. And sometimes we'd hang out all three of us together. It's not like Marcie and me were itching for a threesome, it just kind of developed, and it seemed nice at first. But after a couple months, it was like whenever it was all three of us, Michael feels this need to show me he'll give up Marcie any time I ask, and that kind of sucks for Marcie, and it's like he doesn't see that."

I nodded. "I've seen that. It's like he wants you both to know that he cares but he also wants everyone to know who he wants if he can only have one...," I said, turning more directly toward Marcie, "... and it must make you feel like you've been thrown into the dumpster along with the MacDonald's wrappers when he's cleaning up for Jenna to come over."

Marcie laughed. "Yes! Exactly! I didn't ask to be his one true love or anything, but he wanted this, I didn't tie him to the bedpost and ravish him, and it does suck!"

I looked at Jenna. "And you don't like seeing her treated that way."

They both nodded. "And you noticed."

Marcie did that eye-conferencing thing with Jenna. "Jenna watches out for me. When we met..." More eye signalling. "...we were on a mental hospital ward, self-harm and anorexia and stuff. There were three of us then, Eisie was the third."

"I've been on a locked ward myself," I acknowledged. "It brings patients together sometimes. Being in a situation where you only have each other against the staff can really make a special connection."

"I'm not surprised," Jenna said. Then, "Oops, that could be taken the wrong way, I guess."

I grinned. She knew I wasn't going to take it the wrong way.

"Well, I really do need to use your bathroom," Marcie said, and I slipped past me to the toilets in the dorm suite area.

Jenna turned her hands palm upwards and spread her arms. "Marcie and I fooled around a little. She liked it and wanted more. My attitude was...this is nice? but after a bit I wished she had the equipment to finish the job, you know? I like her a lot though, she's special to me. And I think sharing Michael is a way for her to keep on being with me if you know what I mean."

For all that I appreciated Dr. Baxwood's thoughtful feedback and advice, I hadn't much cared for being told that it was a silly *male* thing to be all concerned with differences in theory—would she have said the same thing to a female student who had come to her with the same exasperations?—and I didn't agree with her dismissal of such things as not significant to feminism.

Words and concepts are important. As an isolated individual who isn't part of an identifiable movement of feminist heterosexual sissy males, nearly all of my social power comes from communication, from being able to put these complex thoughts down in such a way that other people can understand what I'm saying. The feminists who'd had the strongest impact on me so far had been authors whose writings had made things clear to me or provoked me to think in new and different terms.

On the other hand, to be fair, Dr. Baxwood had given me a bit of a mixed message, hadn't she? She'd handed me an article about a dispute within feminism between different theory types and their believers, and she'd also told me I should go on to grad school where I could discuss that kind of thing in more detail. I quite liked the idea of grad school. I knew that a lot of people in my classes were mostly here at college so they could get good jobs when they got out. I figured it would feel different to be in a place where everyone attending was there to take the subject matter seriously, to theorize and analyze things in our own right.

I read the Heidi Hartmann article through a couple of times, flipping back to reread certain sections. One thing I found interesting was that the author was pushing the notion of socialist feminism as the solution to what she called Marxist feminism—the "unhappy marriage" of Marxism and feminism. She started off by saying it was like a classic English common law marriage, where the two become one and the one is the husband. In this case feminism and Marxism were treated as one, and that one was Marxism.

But although Hartmann was praising socialist feminism as the solution to that, I was encountering the exact same problem with socialist feminism. I had read a lot of articles, some assigned in classrooms and some that I'd come across on my own, where the author identified herself as a socialist feminist, but only used feminist concepts to study sexual inequality.

For class differences and race conflict and colonialism and poverty and war and everything else, they would write about the working class and the means of production and the role of capitalism. Then, when they'd write about women's oppression and sexual inequality, they would discuss patriarchy as a system, but they'd still throw in some lines about how it was that way in the first place because of men controlling the means of production and wanting to pass down property and all that.

More to the point, maybe, it was only the feminists who called themselves "radical feminists" who started off from looking at how people interact and the politics of personality and behavior at that level, and how certain personal priorities and values lead to the big structural institutions behaving the same way. To me, this was the bottom-upward approach that Baxwood valued, and the other stuff was all top-down. And the top-down socialist feminist stuff all seemed to start with the notion that the evil culprits—men, capitalists, white Europeans, the nobility, whatever—oppressed other people because they could. The bottom-upward radical feminist theories were more inclined to look at the behavioral pattern of behaving like an oppressor, and valuing having power over others, as pathological. Masculinity, basically, as the root of political problems.

For me, that was important. I wanted to talk and write about the institution of heterosexuality, how it was set up, all the personality and behavioral pieces that it is made up of. It was mostly the radical feminists who were writing about porn and sexual objectification and the subject-object way that sex is set up in patriarchy, and that clicked with the kinds of things I wanted to talk about.

According to Omar Mason, Dr. Gilman hadn't had any success trying to get a cabal of journalism majors to take over the newspaper, but apparently Gilman had been telling everyone that there was some guy, Derek Turner, who was going to get the *Catalyst* up and running, because several people walked up to me in the hallways over the next few days to say they'd be interested.

After the third or fourth such encounter, I began telling everyone there would be a meeting in the *Catalyst* office on Wednesday after 4:20 classes let out.

I walked down the corridor leading to Building 7, key in hand, and found a cluster of people already waiting. "Hi, are you Derek?" asked a black man in his forties. When I nodded, he continued, "George Morehouse. Do you know Max Coyle? He said there was going to be a newspaper staff meeting and I should drop in. I'm a Business and Marketing major and it would be good experience to see if I can sell some ads."

A sandy-haired guy and the girl standing with him wearing a red vest turned out to be Joanne and Roderick, exchange students from Northumberland. "It sounded like it might be fun to work on a newspaper," Joanne said.

I opened the door and turned on the lights. "I don't know what you were told, but I'm not...I haven't ever been involved in putting out a newspaper," I told them. "As best as I can figure out, we have to typeset the stories and articles and print them out, then the columns can be sliced out and pasted down on these things," I said, indicating the ledger sheets with the pale blue column guides. "It looks like this machine over here has something to do with the typesetting, but I haven't figured it out yet."

George Morehouse looked thoughtful for a moment, stroking his chin. "There might be an easier way," he said slowly. "I type my papers for my courses on the little Macintosh computers up in the info technology center. One thing I noticed is that you can set the margins to any width you want, so it ought to be possible to make it as skinny as a newspaper column. And then to print it, they have laser writers, and they look really sharp, like the print in a book. So we may not need that typesetting machine."

A couple more people entered the office. Max Coyle I recognized, as one of the students who had spoken to me earlier in the week. "You said you wanted to write movie reviews, right?"

"Yeah," he said. "If you'd print them. The last folks, from last year I mean, they wouldn't print anything that I wrote."

Tracy Marshall wanted to be sure the newspaper wasn't going to be the publicity organ of her opponent Omar Mason. "It's the duty of the school newspaper to be fair. I don't know what Omar told you, but if he's going to try to control what goes into the paper..."

I shook my head. "Honestly, no one has tried to tell me anything about what can and can't go into the paper. You should know me, I want the paper to be a place where any student can get their material printed. As long as it isn't printing actual lies, I mean. I don't know much about running a newspaper, but I want a place where I can post my opinion column, shoot my mouth off and all that. And I want everyone to have that ability, it's supposed to be our newspaper."

"Well, I hope you'll make some effort to report on actual news, events on campus, cover what's happening...hey, you'd print a regular bulletin from the student government, right?"

"Of course. If y'all can put something together for the student body and get it to us, that would be great as a regular feature in each issue."

Joanne and Roderick said they'd try to write some actual news coverage pieces.

This was looking quite promising.

It was true, what I'd told Tracy Marshall. I really just wanted the newspaper to exist in order for me to be able to publish my snotty little column. Be a radical on campus, advertise to the college community the contents of my head and, in particular, position my sissy lib form of feminism within the general context of radical campus activism.

"You're okay with talking about this?" Jenna confirmed again.

I nodded. "I'm pretty 'out' in public about it. I once had a tee shirt made to order which said 'The world is held together by nuts under tension' and it had a picture of a hex nut. And underneath that, it said 'Mental Patients Liberation Front'."

Jenna laughed. "I would love to see people's reactions to that!"

I grinned back. "Most people didn't want to engage with that, although I *did* have a few people come up to me and say 'Hey, I really like your shirt'."

"So...you said you had been on a locked ward, like me. I'm not ashamed of it either, but I've had as much as I can take of people being all tragic and understanding about me having a broken head. And I'm not used to talking about it because it's really not anyone's business, you know? But there's a lot that I don't talk about with most people." She looked at me head-on at this point and smiled a small smile and added, "But you're kind of easy to talk to."

Good! I want it to be that way!

Jenna paused for a moment. Collecting her thoughts. "My Mom thought it was good for me and my sister for the family to stay together. That was her excuse at any rate. Maybe she was just scared to leave him. He would hit her and yell when he came home drunk. When I got big enough, I told him if he ever tried that shit on me he'd better be prepared to kill me, because I'd come after him with a baseball bat if he left me alive."

She sighed. "So I was going to be free from that, right? Well, the first guy I was seriously involved with, he didn't seem to be anything like my old man, but he started to get jealous, and accusing me or...he started off asking me to reassure him, like tell him what he wanted to hear so he'd quit imagining things, but then he started getting to the point of saying he didn't believe me. The first time he hit me, I said 'That's it, you don't get to do that,' and I broke up with him, but he came around and said he was sorry and...well you know how it is. I thought I chose to give him a second chance. He's a lot smoother than my old man was. 'I need you,' and 'I'm so sorry'. And it got harder to make myself believe I meant it when I said 'That does it, you're history'. And he didn't believe it. Why should he? He always got me back."

Jenna couldn't fight him physically and she couldn't break free. "Every time he hit me, a little piece of me died," she said bleakly. "I was so angry and I hated myself for becoming my Mom all over again. So I started cutting. And that's how I ended up at St. Agnes."

I told Jenna about my own experiences. Making good on my reassurance that I was okay talking about this. "I wasn't a cutter, but I once swallowed nearly a whole bottle of Seconals. Reds. I didn't think I was trying to kill myself, I thought to myself at the time that I was trying to get stoned. Oblivious. But when I looked back on it, I think it was actually a suicide attempt, and I was just lying to myself about it, pretending I was doing something a lot more...a lot less severe, you know? But I had to have known that would be a lethal dose."

Jenna nodded solemnly; I continued. "I had been hitchhiking and these truck drivers who picked me up...kept brushing me with their hands. Not groping. Nothing where I could be sure it wasn't just my imagination, but every couple minutes I'm getting a hand up against me somewhere."

Jenna's face twisted in revulsion. "Yecch! I hate that creepy shit!"

"When I asked...I had suitcases with me, and the driver had stowed them when they picked me up. So later at this truck stop, I asked for them back, I didn't want to ride any further with them. And he pretended he didn't know what happened to the smaller suitcase and invited me to look inside the truck if I thought there'd been anything else. Any other piece. So I was about to get into the truck and he was on the ground, waving me up, you know, 'Climb up there and look around if you want, don't accuse me and my partner of stealing your shit'. And all of a sudden I got this image in my head, like a movie trailer for *Deliverance*, of me climbing up those stairs with him behind me, and his partner turns out to be waiting up there in the truck cab..."

I sighed and rubbed my eyes for a moment. "Nothing happened, I mean, I didn't do it, I didn't go up the steps, I just left him there, and left the suitcase, you know, wherever they had hidden it, but I started thinking I had done something that made all this happen. Like the way I had acted or how I was dressed. Years later, I told somebody about it and she referred to this as the time I got raped. I think she meant that it affected me in a lot of the same way as if it had actually happened. The way it made me feel about myself, like there was something wrong with me, and stuff like this was my lot in life and I brought it on myself because of how I was."

I looked at Jenna for a couple beats and decided to go ahead with it. "I'm more like one of the girls than one of the boys. Always have been. Later on I came out, described myself as a militant heterosexual sissy."

Jenna had a look on her face like the things I'd just said had had impact, but she wasn't pulling back from me; her face wasn't closing off. After a couple moments, she asked, "So, is that how you got hospitalized, from taking the pills?"

"No, actually. That didn't happen until a couple years later. I wasn't upset and stressed out then, I'd just come out on campus and I was feeling pretty good. But I freaked a lot of people out. I guess they'd heard of gay rights and some of them had heard about transsexual people, but they didn't know what to make of me. And I was writing about this stuff and handing out the things I'd written, and one of the people on campus thought I was threatening her and reported me to the campus police."

"But you hadn't actually threatened anybody. I can't imagine you threatening anyone, you're the most mellow peaceful person I know! They wouldn't listen to your side of the story?"

"They decided I wasn't making any sense so I must be crazy, and if I was crazy she must be right to feel threatened. They got me to sign a paper, I thought it was a consent to speak to the doctor there in the emergency room, but it was apparently a voluntary commitment. It didn't say I agreed to be locked up or anything but that's what they did to me."

Excerpt from *The Amazon's Brother* –

She won't risk rejection either? Unfair of me to expect her to do what I hate doing?

Okay...the co-reactive dance: micro-advance and micro-retreat, never an overt invasion of the other's space, no objectionable moves. Come out to meet me halfway. Every little step of the way. Oscillations. Flirtations. Waves. Tentative, intense, all the way in. Lots of suspense. Very hesitant. Nothing taken for granted, not sex, not love, not continuation. Keep raising the emotional ante. Tension. I like it that way.

Oh, you don't? Fine...say what you want, then. End the suspense.

Scared I'll say no or misunderstand? You don't say! Ahh, being human is so...

Jenna had called earlier to ask if I felt like hanging out. She had arrived alone, saying that Marcie was busy at home and hadn't come this time. Shortly after her arrival, she had indicated that my remark from the last time we'd been together, about having also been on a locked ward, had been on her mind. Hence her next question, about whether or not I was okay talking about it.

I didn't know the scope of Jenna's interest in me. It certainly seemed that she liked talking with me, that she liked my company and wanted to be friends. I myself didn't always define the type of interest that I had in an interesting woman, and part of my peculiar sense of sexual identity—and my brand of feminist personal politics—had to do with my right to be ambivalent and undefined in that sense, to just take things as they go and see where they would lead. After all, it wasn't *my* responsibility to make romantic or sexual things happen. In the current situation, though, I had a pretty good handle on where I'd like this to go with Jenna. I wanted it all.

But I liked how things were now, and didn't want to ruin our rapport if she wanted a confidante and didn't regard that as compatible with boyfriend.

In 1980, when I came out, I had declared a moratorium on ever feeling like I had to do the Boy Role thing of being the sexual gas pedal to the girl's brake pedal; I had said I'd be damned if I'd ever do more than 49% of the sexual advancing to make things happen, because I needed to feel desirable too, I needed to feel like sexual interaction was a mutual thing and not some kind of favor I was seeking. I didn't want to be the appetite symbol. I wanted to share that, and to share being the sex object.

Well, one alternative to *either* person being the overt sexual instigator that had occurred to me was the co-reactive dance thing. I had an option besides being sexually aggressive or being sexually passive.

I could find out if Jenna was inclined to dance.

CATALYSTS

I hopped off the bus at the corner of Hillside and Winchester and walked up the ramp to Creedmoor's old Building 4—the RCCA site. Tony Blaine was ensconced at the security desk in the foyer. "Yes, can I help you?" he asked me, behaving as if he didn't recognize me.

I resisted the urge to reply "Probably not" or some such thing. "I'm here to see Cowboy and Mary," I stated.

"I don't see nothing here about you being an expected visitor. I'll have to call the office," he said, reaching for the desk phone.

"Hey. Front desk. Yeah, I got Derek Turner here to see Allan Hauser and Mary Margiotta. There's nothing on the log...yeah...no...oh, right....okay." He crossed his arms behind his head and leaned back in his seat, appraising me. "You can go in this time, but you have to call ahead from now on. You got to get your friends to put you on the list. Next time I ain't gonna let you in."

I didn't dignify this with a response, and walked on into the hall and down to the TV room that my friends had commandeered as their lounge.

"Hey, welcome back!" they greeted me.

"Hi, Mary, Hi, Cowboy. Hey, what's with the security desk saying visitors've got to be on kind of list now?"

"Oh yeah," Mary snorted, "they just started with that shit. They say it's for our protection! But it means no one can come by to see someone here and check in to make sure everything's okay. Like Jay has several residents here he checks up on, make sure RCCA hasn't kicked them out or had them locked up in Building 40. So now he won't be allowed in unless they knew he was coming that day and put him on the list."

I plopped down on an unoccupied ottoman. "Sounds like their usual bullshit."

Cowboy nodded. "You don't know the half of it. They're pushing all the residents to open a bank account at Chase and sign papers here that give RCCA access to their banking records. And they've changed the receipts, because Jay was going to take them to housing court. They want to say the people staying here aren't paying rent and aren't tenants. Now we're clients and paying for a treatment program, and they say that means they can still kick people out any time they want."

Mary said, "We're going to try to get a Section Eight and move out into an apartment. RCCA can kiss my ass. Treatment! I wouldn't treat a dog that bit me like how they treat us here!"

They asked about my experiences at school and I told them about the student newspaper. I asked about some of the other residents and they filled me in on how they were doing.

"Oh, say, can you keep a kitten in your dorm room?" Mary asked.

"No, pets are against the rules. I could probably get away with it, but I don't think it's a good safe space and I'd be away too much."

"Well, come on down. You can say hi to Suzy and the babies at any rate."

Joanne and Roderick, the two Geordie exchange students, not only brought in actual news articles but went down on elbows and knees with scissors and glue and did most of the pasteup for the first issue of the *Catalyst*. We received a movie review column from Max Coyle and several pieces from student government—some welcoming the student body and giving general advice, some providing direct news of what the student government had been doing—from both Tracy Marshall and Omar Mason, who also posted campaign speeches and ads with logos urging people to vote for them. George Morehouse also brought in a couple news articles, one about a theatrical performance and one about a sporting event.

For my part, the "Contemptuous Cat"—that was what I decided to call my opinion column—made its debut with a diatribe about the male role as appetite symbol and how it perverts sexuality to invest all the appetite in one sex and the desirability in the other. I described what would have been called "subject-object dynamics" in a feminist theory article but in plain language and with as much attitude as I could convey.

I took potshots at beauty pageants and some lyrics from top forty songs I had heard playing on the radio.

We hauled the master copy of the newspaper over to the printing company in Westbury and I introduced myself to the folks at Senator Printing and ordered up the same number of copies as the previous issue from the spring semester under the prior newspaper leadership.

By the following Tuesday, the student newspaper had made its triumphant return to campus.

Nzuma approached me in the corridor near the vending machines. "I have been reading what you wrote in the paper," she began. "You make a lot of good points, but I just got to ask...you're not being one of those people who come out against porn, are you? Tell me you don't get on board with that shit!"

I had mentioned pornography in passing as an example. I raised my index finger. "I think a lot of what gets portrayed as sexual is very objectifying. It's very polarized."

"Aww, you are! I can't believe it! Look, there's a lot of difference between rape and abuse and stuff, and just settlin' down for some good fun. These feminists who want to ban porn are taking away from trying to stop real violence against women, because we got to make a distinction between sex and violence. We say we are for stopping violence but we don't have no problem with sex, you hear what I'm sayin'?"

"I didn't say anything about a ban," I replied.

"But you saying it's bad," she said, shaking her head disapprovingly. "Hey, Marshall girl, get over here and help me talk some sense into this boy!" Nzuma gestured with curved hand to Tracy Marshall, who veered in our direction.

"He's all in on that McKinnon Dworkin stuff and saying porn oppresses women," Nzuma shorthanded.

"You're not serious!" Tracy said, staring at me. "C'mon, you need to read some other feminist opinions. Haven't you ever heard of Susie Bright?"

"Yes, I know about so-called 'sex positive' feminism. I am not a prude or anything, and that includes liking sexy pictures or movies or whatever, I wish there was more of that kind of stuff that I did like. What I'm saying is that a whole lot of what's out there in that, that zone, that category, that it's really sexist in how it shows the sexes. It's not just violence, I mean there is a lot of violence, but even putting that aside, there's a lot of the man doing things to her, that it's about his sexual hunger and that sex is him being the one who does it and she's the one it gets done to. That's pretty basic male dominance, wouldn't you say?"

"Dominance can be pretty hot, when it's consensual," Tracy retorted, smiling. "I don't have a problem with that, or with rape fantasies, as long as it's not against anyone's will. You can't strip all the power out of sex and have this totally...like diplomacy, you know, very polite, I'm sorry but sex isn't like that."

"I don't have anything against any of that as long as it isn't set up so that it's always the male person who is doing the power thing. There can be very non-diplomatic and impolite power where some of the time she's the one doing the active power role. And that's what I'm saying, that's what I'm complaining about, it's not shown equal. It's always her as the sex object and him as the appetite, and that's not good for society."

"Oh, come on, what about the dominant women with the whips, doesn't that count?"

"I think it probably does but most of what's portrayed is the other way. Also, even the women with the whips, they're like a commodity, like it isn't for them, for their appetite, it's because the guys want that."

"Well what's wrong with that? Women want a dominant man sometimes, and that's us wanting, that's our appetite, why doesn't *that* count?"

"Fine, but show that. The way it's shown, it doesn't..."

"I think you want to put too many rules on things. And you're trying too hard to be a good feminist but you've been reading..."

"Hey, wait, hey, I do my own thinking. I read, but these are my own ideas from my own experience!"

"The thing that gets me," Nzuma interjected, "it's always the women who are doing the sex work or acting in the porn who get put down whenever somebody starts going on about how it's all bad and stuff. They don't say 'Ooh, you are bad if you go watching that,' they go 'Hey you dirty tramp whore you shouldn't be strippin,' or grindin' that thing, you got bad morals'. Same when it comes from feminism. 'Oh sister you are betraying us, take off that makeup and quit that shit, come march at Take Back the Night instead'."

I nodded. "But I'm not trying to blame anybody. This isn't about having culprits. What I'm talking about is the eroticizing of power, of this particular power difference. We can change what we program to be sexy, by what we show and what we watch. If it was more balanced it wouldn't have the same effect."

I had spent another evening hanging out in Michael's dorm room with the other Mike, Jenna, and Marcie. The two Mikes had taken turns cueing up their favorite songs from a wide assortment of tapes. Black Mike liked a mixture of dance house music and international acoustic folk, and White Mike's tastes were classic rock and jazz. The girls had brought a couple six-packs of beer and we sipped and talked.

I was finding that I really liked this non-monogamous dynamic. Jenna was with Michael, but Michael was also with Marcie, which set the stage for it being okay if Jenna should end up also being with me. And while it was true that there was some unresolved uncertainty about whether she was interested in me in a boyfriend-girlfriend way or just as a friend, there was no accompanying pressure there to resolve that—it wasn't like I had to grab her before someone else did and put her off limits to me. She was *already* with someone else and yet *not* off limits. So I didn't have to know where things were headed, and I liked that.

I discovered that one of my favorite authors had put out a new book last year, although this was the first I'd heard about it.

Marilyn French had written *The Women's Room* back in 1977, my high school senior year. When I came out as a militant sissy a couple years later, it was recommended to me by one of the feminists at the Siren Coffeehouse in Albuquerque. French had used the fictional story of Myra and her friends in the late 1950 suburbs to show the reason women needed feminism; her characters were vividly portrayed and their situations and concerns undeniably real and palpable. A lot of people were upset by the book, saying it wasn't fair to men and so forth, but it wasn't at all a polemic. And a lot of other people said the book spoke for them and that they identified with the characters.

This new book, *Beyond Power*, apparently wasn't fiction. Marilyn French was writing feminist theory this time, a full-on theory of what patriarchy was and what the feminist issues were.

I located a copy in the library and was pleased to find she'd cranked out a 533 page volume.

I soon found myself nodding and occasionally scribbling down page numbers to xerox. This was radical feminism. It directly targeted the notion that power over other people was intrinsically desirable, and theorized about the origins of that belief, the psychology behind it, and the social structures that were founded upon it. This was the kind of feminist theory I liked, that I agreed with. The socialist feminist theories didn't make this kind of analysis.

On Thursdays, Jenna had her Farmingdale coursework and then a part-time job to attend to before she had free time, but had shown up around 8:30 with a six-pack, tapping on my door.

"Hi!" she greeted perkily. "I decided to interrupt you from your drudgery. Or nondrudgery. Are you drudging?"

"Mostly just vegging. I was working on an Contemptuous Cat column earlier but I've pretty much finished it."

"How's the newspaper business going?"

"It's kind of fun, although I have no sense of knowing what I'm doing. They keep calling me the editor. I don't know how *I* ended up in charge!"

Jenna took a seat and unzipped her coat and unwrapped her scarf. She had on a linen top with textured strings that had little beads sewn in. "Ooh, I like that. That's so pretty. You leave this with me, I wear it," I suggested, smiling sweetly.

"And go home with nothing but what's underneath? I can't go home with a behavior like that!"

"These are matters of apparel, not of behavior."

"Oh, believe me. If my mom sees me show up without a shirt, it's a behavior." Jenna smiled wryly. She popped open a can and handed one to me.

"So how's retail? You get slammed with customers?"

"Pretty quiet. We got one lady who came in and insisted she'd been promised a large dog bed tax free, because it's a rescue dog. I said 'You must be mistaken' but she was one of those who wasn't going to take no for an answer. So I told her she had to list her dog as an exemption on her taxes, that's how it works." Jenna drank from her can.

"Things at home?"

"Oh, same old same old." She drained the can and opened a new one.

I sat facing her for a few seconds. I wasn't sure but something didn't seem quite right. "I'm glad you came by. It's unusual to see you on a Thursday."

Jenna returned my gaze. After another couple beats, she sighed. "I had an argument with my mom last night. She said something about the sacrifices she'd made for me and Lori, my sister. I asked if she meant staying with my Dad. We yelled at each other some. It brought up all the old stuff."

"Yeah, I can see how it would. And her saying it like she was doing you a favor staying with him."

"You got that right."

"Do you...does it freak you out sometimes when you end up feeling angrier than what seems to fit the situation?"

"Yeah, like a volcano. I hate that. And I hate the way it seems like I'm never going to get it behind me."

"Well, there's a sense in which you probably won't. I mean, our past is a part of us. I think it gets easier though."

"I don't *want* this part of me! Oh, I know what you mean, I don't want to forget. I learned some hard things. But do I have to feel like this every time something bumps into the wrong places?"

"Like being a marionette, you mean? Tired of your strings being pulled?"

Jenna shook her head. "I don't know if it's that. More...umm, I think it brings up too many memories of when I felt all that rage before and it was a time when things didn't go well. So I have this dread, you know, as if feeling like that now means things are about to not go well again." She shifted. Her stare was off in the distance for a moment. Then she looked back at me and continued. "I couldn't protect her. And she didn't protect me. It makes us both mad and I guess we're both ashamed."

She glanced around. "What time is it?"

I leaned over and looked at my alarm clock. "About nine fifteen."

Jenna looked pensive. Bit her lower lip. "She'll be wondering where I've gone but she won't have eaten without me yet. Walk me back to my car?"

In the parking lot, she said, "She's not a bad mommy, really. I just didn't want to grow up to be her."

She located her keys and unlocked her car. Gestured for to me to get in on the passenger's side. She slid in and closed her own door. Facing me, she said, "How do you do that? I didn't want to be part of the world tonight. And I was doing a fairly good job of succeeding in my mission. What's your magic? How do you so easily make me feel good enough and strong enough to participate? I've always been stubborn enough that if I decide something, that's what I'm gonna do, and no one can change my mind. How come I let you?"

She took my hands in hers. *Yes please*, I thought. *Can I have this? I like what we have but I want so much more.*

Jenna leaned toward me. I leaned toward her. When we met in the middle, we kissed.

I lay sprawled on my bed, reading the latest *Catalyst*, proud of our little student newspaper. I'd already read the opinion pieces and news articles but had only skimmed the rest. Max Coyle's movie reviews sprawled out over most of a full page, starting at the top of page six and continuing on below the fold. Each of four movies had multiple columns devoted to it, describing the director's background, prior films of the primary actors and actresses, and interesting elements of the plot. One of the movies was a film that Coyle had obtained an advance publicity viewing of, a Japanese movie called *Tampopo* which wasn't in the theatres yet. From the description it sounded quirky and interesting. Coyle said he had expected to find it silly and contrived but ended up giving it three and a half stars.

Jenna came by; I'd been expecting her, anticipating and impatient enough to be deliberately distracting myself. I tossed the paper onto my desk and opened the door and greeted her. "Hi!!"

"Hi yourself!!"

We didn't hug or touch. Just looking at each other, smiling, savoring.

"You had some kind of finals today, yes?"

"Yeah, math. It's over with now. I may be over with, too. I don't know what my professor's going to think of my brain when he gets to my test. One of the questions was 'What are the characteristics of x in the equation $3x^2 + 2x + 6$' and I put 'It's one of the letters near the end of the alphabet and it's made with two perpendicular lines'."

I shook my head in mock disapproval. Jenna smiled archly and brought her head closer to mine. We bumped our noses, glancing into each others' eyes from close range.

Jenna started playing with my hair. "You looking forward to seeing your folks for Christmas?"

I nodded. "But I'd rather spend Christmas with you. I do want to see them, but it would be so nice to just hang out with you. Not have to work on papers or be anywhere. Couldn't you tell your mom your bed is too cold and you've found a bed warmer for the holidays?"

Jenna smiled but shook her head. "I can't go home with a behavior like that."

We took turns removing some outer layers, returning to snuggling and exploring shapes and skins in between, until we were perched on the bed in our underwear, limbs intertwined, petting and nuzzling. Enjoying the process, not hurrying.

"I actually do have to write papers," Jenna amended. "I took an incomplete in anthropology. You know how things are at the house. I couldn't work there. I went over to Marcie's but...well, that didn't lead to doing schoolwork either?"

"You wanna borrow my word processor for the holidays? You could take it to a coffee shop or a library, anywhere they'll let you plug it in." Jenna had admired how I could compose a paper and print it out later after proofreading it and making corrections.

"That's awful nice of you, but I'm sure it's expensive and I'd hate for anything to happen to it."

"Well, the alternative is to leave it here in the dorm and hope no one breaks in while all the students are gone. It would be safer with you, and someone should be getting some use out of it while I'm gone."

"Well, okay, it does seem like I might get that paper finished if I didn't have to work on it at home."

"You have to promise to write to me though."

"I hate writing letters!" Jenna pouted.

"But I like getting them," I counterargued.

I brought the word processor out to her car, and, along with it, a pair of self-addressed envelopes with my parents' Los Alamos address on them, stamps already attached. I handed the latter to her with the sweetest, most innocent smile I could put on. Jenna took them from me with an imposed-upon scowl.

"My mother was the first person in her family to stay in school past fifth grade. I think she knew what she wanted and she didn't care if no one supported her in it. She was so proud of her graduation from Oconee Women's College and the doctors and patients she worked with said she was one of the best nurses around."

My mom paused to stir the potatoes and turn down the burner, then continued. "I think for her it was a calling, something she knew she needed to do. I felt that way about getting involved with Head Start, when you were about in third grade back in Valdosta. And then teaching elementary school at West Gordon.

"When I switched careers to work at the lab and do spectroscopic analysis, that was a different kind of thing. It wasn't something I needed to do, but I needed to have something and it was an opportunity and sort of a challenge I guess you could say.

"This social science that you're doing...nobody in our family ever had any interest in that direction, so maybe you feel like your grandmother, taking up nursing. From some of what you have been saying, I guess you see it as your calling. Do you think you know what you want to do with it, after you graduate with your degree?"

This was a far more thoughtful and diplomatic approach to asking how I was going to support myself with a women's studies degree than I had anticipated, and it was the first time she had really acknowledged what I was doing other than voicing her approval for me going back to college and doing well there.

"Well...I didn't set out to go into women's studies with a career in mind. I have a mission. I want to explain to people what it is like to be a male feminine person who is heterosexual, and to push for some social change that comes from making room for people like me to exist. But one of my teachers said I should think about graduate school, and that got me to thinking maybe I'd like to be a professor, and teach courses about this. It would be a way of bringing my ideas out and passing them on. And I'd write books and papers and get them published."

Mama nodded. "I think you would be a good teacher. If it's what you want to do. I always pictured you as a professor, teaching astronomy and physics or maybe chemistry and biology, you were always good at that. I never thought about social science. I guess we don't take it as seriously. But your father is right. We always said we would support you and Jan in whatever you decided to do with your lives, and you seem pretty serious about this. And I can't deny you're doing well in school. I'm happy to be proven wrong."

The first envelope I'd self-addressed for Jenna arrived the first week I was back in Los Alamos. But there was no letter inside. When I opened it, there was only a smilie face and her signature inside the envelope itself.

Five days later, though, I received a real letter.

I had to send you that first one because I was thinking, I'll be damned if I let him tell me I have to write him a letter, you know? I hate writing letters!

But I wish you were here.

I got into a massive fight with the old man last night, and after it was all over I told him I was tired of being in the midst of such a fucked up situation. He missed my point entirely and told me basically it was all my fault, i.e. for loving my mother and for not sticking by him in a time of need! Then he cried and told me he was all alone in the world with no one to share with.

That ripped my heart out, but I couldn't tell him that. I split, and headed for the campus. When it dawned on me that I would have to drive infinitely further than that to see you I went to the beach. At first, I felt real lonely and empty, but after a while a real neat warmth started to fill me because I know all my strength was coming from me. Nothing personal, but I'm glad I didn't have enough gas to get to New Mexico! Today, I'm a little harder, a little colder, and a little angrier, but all these things will help me in the future because I am willing to let them. Please do me a favor, hmm, throw a big cold snowball at yourself, compliments of me!

The *Catalyst* office phone rang. Classes weren't in session yet but I was back early and hanging out there, since I wasn't officially supposed to be in the residential dorms just yet. "Hello, *Catalyst* office, Derek Turner here."

"Hey Derek. This is Tracy Marshall. I hope you had a good Christmas vacation. Did you go see your folks?"

"I did! I had a very nice time! How about you, did you spend time with your own family?"

"I live with them, so yes, we had a nice Christmas together. Listen, this isn't official yet but it will be later this afternoon or soon after, depending on when we can get a quorum. But I wanted to go ahead and let the paper in on it. May as well. Omar Mason won the election for Student Government President."

"Oh. Umm, my condolences. You ran a very intense and well-organized race. Honestly, I was impressed with all of you who were doing this, we should all be proud that it's taken seriously here."

"Yeah, thanks. I think I did too. Omar won fair and square and I'm going to concede and tell him you said that, he worked hard on this and you're right, he does take it seriously.

"You know, one thing that really came out as a theme...don't print this, okay? Can we be off the record? This is just me talking and I'd prefer not to read this quoted in the newspaper or anything? Thanks, you're a good media person, I know you wouldn't say that and then break your word. One thing that sort of became a theme in this election was how things like 'commuter student versus resident student' are sometimes a stand-in for race and racism. I didn't start off using it that way, but Omar made me look at how it can be coded and people can hear it to mean that. Do you think reverse racism can exist? Sometimes I feel like there are black students who were all set to vote only for a black candidate. Maybe I played into his hands with the commuter student positions that I took. Anyway, it's been a learning experience for me. What are your thoughts on the matter?"

"Well, one thing that's interesting is that you didn't ask about sexism. A lot of people here seem to think that race is more polarizing than sex, and maybe you do, too. Did you feel like there were students who took an attitude because you were a woman candidate, apart from the issues or the race thing?"

"I do, but it gets wound up with race. Sometimes I think the black students...black culture as a whole, even...have more of a problem with white women than they do with white men. Like they think we're more likely to be prejudiced. If we're scared of...if there's a bunch...let's say there's a parking lot and a cluster of...people, and they're mostly guys and they're mostly black. And you're a white woman going home. If they sense that you are worried about them, it becomes a race thing.

Often times it's a sex thing. It's a sexual thing anyway but they can...I think they believe we'd be different, they'd say 'She wouldn't act that way if it was a bunch of white guys,' and I think that's not necessarily so. And it colors...bad choice of words, huh? It permeates everything."

"I've been pondering that kind of question a lot. Being here at Old Brookville makes you think, doesn't it? I think race hits harder. The oppression is more severe, even if the sex oppression is older and more fundamental. With males and females, you've got people living together at home. Guys have moms, sisters, daughters, wives. And vice versa for feminist women, they can't see us as the enemy completely because they live with male people that they know and love, so it's more nuanced. With race, it can get to be a lot more like hey, those people are Other, and I wish they would all go away. It's easier to not have any sentiment and just see them as bad. As oppressive. Or whatever."

INTO THE DARKNESS

I had, of course, come back early in hopes of hanging out with Jenna before classes resumed. So far it wasn't working out as I'd hoped for.

After three or four phone calls to chat and try to set up some time together, Jenna had made some space in her busy life and brought me over to the house. I'd met her mom and sister. On the one hand, it had felt like an important event to be introduced to her family, and to meet people who were a central part of her everyday life, and I'd be able to listen and discuss her home life from a more informed perspective. But she herself had been very shut down, remote and superficial to her family and also to me during that visit. This was Jenna the busy person, walled off and with lots of demands on her time and only superficially available to others.

Her mom had asked me friendly questions. Where I was from, what it had been like to be home for Christmas and see my family, how I liked Old Brookville campus, and oh, she had heard that I was the student newspaper editor, what was that like, did I enjoy it? Jenna's sister had been more joking, popping a clever one-liner first at me then at Jenna or her mom. She also seemed to me to be a walled-off person, at least on this occasion. Using clever snark and perky snips to insulate herself.

It was all quite interesting but I wanted a chance to sit with Jenna and *talk* about it and how she felt about the family dynamic and so on. I wanted to get back under the hard shell and be with her. And instead she drove me back, quiet and distracted during the drive, and let me off in the parking lot. I wasn't able to lure her in to hang out, and in subsequent phone calls in days to follow, she was the same way. Sorry don't have much time to talk, I'm very busy.

The *Catalyst* continued to lure interesting and talented students in to participate. I came in to the newspaper office for our weekly meeting and a middle-aged woman with ash-grey hair shook my hand. "Hey, so we finally meet! I love the Contemptuous Cat! You should totally do a column about the Financial Aid department here. Oh, I'm Carrie Warrens. I'm in Karl Gilman's journalism class. So, listen, how'd you feel about another columnist? I've been wanting to do a spoof of Miss Manners. I could write a pretend advice column about etiquette and stuff."

Carrie showed me a couple of printed articles she'd written on spec. One was about a jazz historian who was scheduled to come to campus to talk about the ethnic and cultural origins of jazz; the other was a contest announcement, "Draw the College President," which pretended to be offering a prize for the best likeness, the hidden implication being that no one knew what the reclusive official actually looked like. The drawing was really nicely done, a caricature of a bug-eyed college student wielding a paint-dripping brush. "Great illustration," I noted.

"Oh, you haven't seen them yet," exclaimed Carrie and she and George pulled out a whole sheaf of cartoons this same guy had submitted. Apparently his name was Sheldon Isaacs and he was an art student. The faces he drew were grotesque, freaky, distorted, with maniacal grins; the shading and detailing, like tiny little hairs sprouting from someone's nose or little bloodshot veins in the eyeballs, were meticulously drawn in. Fantastic...if he'd keep giving us these and let us publish them we had our own in-house artist!

Dr. Baxwood had asked me to come to her office. She made us each a cup of coffee, then began talking. It felt less like she had something official to tell me and more like she just wanted to chat, although it was sort of a continuation of our previous conversation.

"They aren't all apolitical and unconcerned, but most of our students don't engage with course content as political. When we were students ourselves, we took over administration buildings and the police were sent in, and we printed our own manifestos and taught our own alternative classes in the hallways. Teaching the truth about the Vietnam war and race and how the people who write the textbooks take money from the corporate conglomerates that benefit from the war. But this is a different era."

I nodded. "I've read some things that Robin Morgan wrote about coming of age during that era and I've always felt I sort of missed out on the excitement. Being a radical when it felt like we were making actual changes."

"We like having you in our classes. You have very interesting things to say in the classroom and in your papers, but sometimes the questions that you ask or the comments that you make are just going to go right past the other students, who haven't read as extensively as you have and they won't be able to follow the conversation. You've asked about your role as a male in women's studies classes and whether your presence is an issue...it's only an issue when you want to have a conversation in class that no one but you and the professor can participate in. And to be fair I don't think that's because you're male, but your willingness or inclination to try to have those conversations in class, perhaps, is. A well-read woman student who was in your situation would most likely be less inclined to become the center focus if no one else were asking similar questions. I'm not sure that's better, a better behavior, we as girls get a lot of training in being selfless and not standing out in public spaces such as classrooms."

I nodded; that made sense. I asked her, "What made it so students in your era wanted to make society accountable to them? Everyone else, before or since, seems to see society as something we have to adjust to, that it's not going to change. But your generation saw that society is something that's in our heads and if you change people's minds you change everything. How do we get back to that?"

"I wish I knew. A confluence of things. A large postwar generation, the Vietnam war, the racial tensions coming to a head in the sixties, American prosperity and parents promising children they should have the best life possible...you're right, we felt like society was being changed and we were the main ones changing it. Critical mass. A lot of people thought society was in the process of being changed, and that meant they were listening and thinking about how to change it and acting like we could. It's harder when you interact with people who don't think they can change anything."

The classes I was most interested in were once again not being offered this semester, so I signed up for Women and the Health System and Intro to Social Work. Then, because I wanted to get better at speaking in front of an audience, I signed up for Public Speaking and Voice & Diction classes. I'd always had one of those soft quiet voices that don't project very far. I could put things into words pretty efficiently, but it would derail my concentration every time someone would interrupt to say that they couldn't hear me, and could I please speak up.

I counted the rings, hoping Jenna would pick up. She eventually did, after the fifth. "Hello?"

"Hi, you! Are you free to talk?"

"Somewhat. What's up?"

"Just thinking warm fuzzy thoughts about you and wishing you were here."

"Hmm, I see. That's very sweet. I mean it. Unfortunately I have to be here, not there."

"Waaah. Sorry you're tied up. How are things?"

"Oh...mostly okay, actually. Hanging in there. Thanks for asking. Listen, I hate to cut this short but I can't really stay on the phone. Maybe after this weekend."

"Okay. I'll be thinking of you."

I took the train into the city and joined Laura Walhberg and the others from Project Release on the sidewalk. The American Psychiatric Association was having a conference here in Manhattan, discussing the likely expansion of the criteria for imposing involuntary psychiatric incarceration. The traditional rationale was "danger to one's self or others." It was a standard that was abused and stretched, as it was—anyone could be perceived as "dangerous" if the psychiatrists didn't need to convince anyone other than themselves that a danger existed. But now there was a move in several communities to include "gravely disabled," which would mean being able to cast a net over anyone they deemed messed up enough to "need it."

We were handing out fliers and, to attract attention, doing street theatre. Laura had shown up with a butterfly net. "Nancy is going to be here in a few minutes with a set of white medical scrubs, she'll look like a doctor or an orderly. I think we could take turns being the patient and trying to get away from her and her butterfly net."

"Sounds cool. If we can engage with people on the sidewalk and they seem amused, she could turn on them and go after them with the net."

"Oh, I like that! Meanwhile, whoever isn't being the victim can hand out fliers and answer questions."

Some of the people who stopped to talk with us were psychiatrists who were attending the event. A woman in ash-grey office wear and very professional looking hair asked us, "So what's your alternative? You have to do something when people are at risk."

Laura retorted, "Why do we need to provide an alternative? When something is wrong, the alternative is to not do it!"

"But if it's reasonable to intervene when someone is dangerous, why isn't it reasonable to intervene when they're incapacitated?"

"Our society has a lot of people who are known to be dangerous. Racists, neonazis. They don't get locked up for being dangerous, they only get arrested once they actually *do* something. Why should it be different for us?"

"Oh, so you don't even accept the existing rules." She shook her head, but accepted an informational flyer and a position paper from me when I handed them to her.

Later, a pair of shrinks came out of the conference building and mocked us as they came past us on the sidewalk: "Oh, look, I guess they think we're out to get them."

"If the proverbial shoe fits," I replied. "I wasn't seeking psychiatric help, but people of your profession stuck me in a place with locks on the doors and bars in the windows and wouldn't let me leave when I wanted to. I'd say that qualifies as being 'out to get me'."

"Did it ever occur to you that people were trying to help you cope with your condition?"

"I was coping fine with my condition. It wasn't causing me any distress whatsoever at the time. My difference is not a disease, and if I'm not seeking a cure, I sure don't want to be 'cured' against my will. Involuntary treatment is immoral and wrong."

Mark held out his hand and Nancy passed him the long-handled butterfly net, and began removing her lab coat costume. Louise gripped her shoulders in a quick hug and grinned. "Oh, that was great! You were perfect! Did you see those creepy doctors, the ones who asked if your therapist knew you were out here?"

"Because of course we all have a therapist," Mark interjected.

"They can't imagine that we're off our leashes without a keeper somewhere to track us."

"Oh, here," Louise said, offering an aluminum pan, "have some pita with baba ganoush, you must be starving. Anyway, some people on the sidewalk started asking them questions and they ran into the building! They're so unused to being challenged!"

"I wish we could do something to show the mental patient being pinned after the bug collector catches you in the net. That's how it feels when they've got you under their control, like you're a butterfly and they want to pin you so you'll quit flapping around."

Laura said, "Well that might be too complicated, but we could get some large piece of styrofoam. Think about how we'd act that out though. Anything that looks like a pin big enough to stick in my head could get the police saying we've got a weapon and we're dangerous."

Rosary Mariana was passing out a stapled photocopied collection of things she'd hand-written. "This is about psychiatry as a patriarchal tool of oppression," she announced.

I reached for a copy. "That's an important connection that doesn't get stressed enough in women's studies or here in the movement," I commented.

"Well, Freud. They'll talk about what a sexist pig Freud was. But they use medical model psychiatry as a way to discredit Freud and it's just as bad."

"I know, it's all about the worship of normality. Conformity. Any deviance from what everyone else is doing is a disease of the mind and we have to fix it. You don't act like all the other boys, you must be crazy."

"Or the girls. Tell me about it. Oh, you don't want to be a doormat, you're so *angry*, well here, the stuff in this needle will fix that. Have you ever read Adrienne Rich?"

I nodded. "Compulsory Heterosexuality and Lesbian Experience."

"Yeah, that's her," Rosary nodded back. I was internally gratified that she looked a little surprised. She continued, "Well, she wrote this thing about brutalized society and how if you're going to rebuild it you have to start with the most oppressed people."

"Well, that can be a good way to look at it, but it can also feed into that whole thing of 'well *my* oppression is worse than *your* oppression so I'm more legitimate when I speak about it,' which isn't very productive."

"I don't know, I think that's real. If a Black or Latina lesbian with a disability goes to the microphone, I think the white straight women need to listen and not assume they know all the shit they need to know because they're oppressed as women."

"Yeah, but..."

"You probably find that threatening because you're a white man, but it's true, you need to listen the most."

"Well, I was listening to a couple students in the *Catalyst* office the other day, one was a black guy and one Jewish, and they were saying they're never allowed to complain about anything at home. Their moms and dad would be all 'Oh you think you got it bad, your grandfather was killed in the gas chambers at Treblinka,' or 'You have it easy, your mom's people were slaves in the Carolinas,' you know? And so these guys were comparing notes and laughing about it, but it's true, there's always someone who's had it worse than you, been more oppressed, but that's not really a legitimate reason to say 'shut up, you've got no grounds to complain about your lot in life'."

I kept calling Jenna and asking her to hang out and she kept making excuses. Finally she became annoyed and said I was pressuring her. "My life is very complicated right now. I feel like you understand that, and that you understand me when I talk to you about it. That means a lot to me. But when you pester me about when I can come over, well, I found myself thinking, 'Oh, now Derek is doing it too, just like everyone else, why won't people leave me alone?' And I feel bad, I don't want to think of you like everyone else, you're different, you're the one person in my life who doesn't make me feel like that."

One of my favorite mystery-series authors, John D. MacDonald, had occasionally described his main character, a guy named Travis McGee, as a fellow with an affinity for rescuing women in distress. Birds with broken wings. I was starting to wonder if I had that kind of tendency. I liked the unshielded intimacy and the specialness of being trusted, and of being let in behind someone's everyday defenses.

But feminist theory was making me question whether it was healthy to have my sexuality tied up with another person's vulnerability. Wasn't that a certain type of power trip, an inequality? Well, perhaps not necessarily, not if I was bringing a reciprocal vulnerability to the table. But was I? Or was I seeking people who were more deeply hurt or troubled than I was, so I could be the one taking care of my partner? I did seem to experience caring-feelings and sexual feelings as things that went together, that belonged together. Maybe it wasn't particularly advisable, that combination? I'd have to give it more thought.

But any way I examined it, it was starting to look like maybe Jenna was not in a place where she could be fully involved with a partner, at least for now.

This was going to be really hard. I wanted this. I wanted what I had with her, and the potential for a whole lot more. Walk away from it?

It's not fair!! I finally find someone I click with and really like. I want to be in love. I'm always on the outside and lonely. Can't something nice work out for me, please, just this once?

Vince Ashton
10:50—12:30 Room 139
Public Speaking EL2 261

The short stocky balding man put down the chalk and indicated the blackboard with his thumb. "If you're here for public speaking, you're in the right place. If you're not, you're in the wrong one. I know some of you young people take a misbegotten delight at being in the wrong place. You know, the way that people who don't have a job somehow find themselves in the welfare office waiting for a handout instead of walking up and down main street with their resume in hand.

"Speaking to an audience is a tool for helping people to realize the difference between wrong places and right places. Sometimes we deploy that tool as a way to convey *information*, what we like to call a *speech to inform*. Sometimes we use that tool in order to transmit a *viewpoint*, which we refer to as a *speech to convince*..."

"Yeesh," I thought, "does he actually believe what he just said, or is he fishing to see if any of us will try to use our speaking skills to contradict him?" My hand shot up in the air.

Ashton came to the end of a sentence and nodded in my direction. "We've got one over here, don't we? You look just like the people I used to see back in the misguided sixties. And we know what happened to them! Well, I can see you're itching to jump in, what do you have to say?"

I took a deep breath. Fortunately, the classroom wasn't a very big space and I was used to speaking up in college classrooms at least. "I've been among the unemployed a few times in my life," I stated. "And I've done that walk up and down main street, asking every single business in town if they could use a worker. Then at the end of the week, I'd go to the unemployment office and they asked me to fill out exactly three places I'd tried to get work, and they were just as condescending about how I should seek employment and not just show up for a handout. I know some people want to believe that anyone who wants a job can get one, but that hasn't been my experience."

"Well, did you consider cutting your hair?" he replied, making a sweeping palms-up gesture with both hands.

"One person, a deli owner, said he'd hire me if I got a haircut. I got my hair cut and came back and he still wouldn't hire me, and now I didn't have my hair. I shouldn't have to do that to get a job, but having short hair didn't help me, I kept looking for jobs with my hair short and still no one had a job for me."

"Well, see, that's commendable. A lot of people aren't willing to do that. Of course you probably still had an attitude, like the one you brought in here with you, and that's why no one would hire you, but at least you recognized that you had to make some changes. Now let's move on. The packet that's being passed around is your schedule. You'll see on page two that we have three class sessions devoted to *speeches to inform*, and I'll need you each to sign up for one of those blocks on the separate signup sheet that's making its way..."

I gave myself a score of 70 for that exchange. A little bit meandering but I thought I'd made my point. Then I'd let him cut me off when he didn't like the way it was going.

Meanwhile, yeah, apparently he really did think this way. Great. This is going to be fun.

I couldn't seem to focus. I was trying to reread a photocopied article about midwifery in the 1700s, trying to engage, but when I turned the page and folded it back at the staple, the remainder of the sentence on the following page didn't make sense to me. After a moment I realized I was reading words but not paying attention to what they meant.

I'd been to a *Catalyst* meeting earlier the same afternoon. Carrie and Sheldon and Max and the others had been enthusiastically tossing out ideas and joking around but I, the editor, hadn't really been paying any attention, my mind wandering to other things.

My thoughts kept cycling back to Jenna. I had a constant debate rehashing itself inside my head—*I miss her, she's what's important to me right now, I need to do something to fix this. No, I need to give her space and wait and let her decide she wants to reconnect, or I really will lose her.* And a darker thread mixed in—*I've already lost her, it's over and nothing else seems to matter to me any more.*

I picked up a flier that the college administration wanted printed in the newspaper. It described the "Accreditation Program for Experiential Learning." APEL for short. It was designed for older returning students like George and Carrie, apparently; if a student had worked or otherwise participated in endeavors that were equivalent to college classes, they could write up a description of what they had learned and obtain college credits for it.

Something clicked into place. *I could do that. I pretty much educated myself in feminist theory before I came here. And if they aren't going to offer a feminist theory class so I can discuss the things I really want to talk about in a classroom, I should hurry up and get out of here and move on to graduate school. Baxwood says that's where I belong.*

I shoved back the covers and extracted myself from my dorm room bed. To my right was the mass-produced particle-board contraption that passed as a desk, and on it were textbooks and lists of assignments and my halfhearted essays and homework efforts. I stared at them, flipped through the pile of written materials. Somehow they seemed to belong to some other person, some other time; I didn't feel connected to them. I wasn't due in Women and the Health System until 2:30.

My mood darkened and crumpled and crumbled and blackened. It was over. It was over. As horrible as it was to contemplate, I did not have Jenna in my life. I could not sustain any kind of ...anything. Something was dying, bleeding, inside me, ripped out and dying right now. My skin hurt, my bones hurt, my face felt hot like I'd been weeping for hours and hours and hours; my eyes felt raw and burned. I shuffled around the cage of my dormroom, and eventually collapsed at my desk and just sat there for a long time, unable to move, then finally, just to have something to do, I lifted a cleaning rag and began dusting off my word processor.

A wave of despair crashed over me, and I felt so over, so useless to myself. I couldn't imagine anything mattering to me more than the dust I was removing from the screen. Jenna. Jenna. Why? *Why?* I reached out with my dustcloth and just pressed it against the screen and then closed my eyes and sobbed quietly, shaking, supporting myself by pushing against the glass.

I stopped it and rubbed my dull eyes. I needed a place to be, something to focus on. How much longer before I could reasonably go to class? I looked at the clock. Incredibly, only a couple minutes had gone by since I'd last checked. It felt like I'd been mired in this, stunned and overwhelmed and miserable, for hours and hours.

I looked around me. *This is your life now. You get to do things you don't care about and feel horrible and alone and lonely and miss Jenna and everything lasts forever and when it's over you get to do some other thing you don't care about while you feel horrible and alone and lonely and miss Jenna. This is all that's left. Oh Jenna, oh Jenna. Why? What did I do? I'm so sorry. I hoped I would make you happy. Why wouldn't you want to be with me? There's something wrong with me. I'm broken. I thought maybe I could have love but I never will.*

I felt an infinite ocean of uncried tears and I knew once I got started I'd be crying for a long long long time. Then afterwards I'd wake up and it would still be true and I'd still be facing the same thing. I glanced at the clock again. Maybe four minutes had passed since I'd first checked. Conceivably, just possibly, five. My day stretched out in front of me, a long string of remaining hours, and beyond that a horrible terrifyingly bleak life sentence. *I have to stay alive until I die and it's all going to be like this.*

"I was wondering what had happened to you," Sharon Solerno declared, giving me an appraising stare. "So you just don't care about anything any more, is that it? Romance gone sour and now nothing matters?"

Sharon had an unsurpassed talent for making me feel like a whiny spoiled manchild with nothing legitimate to complain about. I glared at her for a moment, then said, with a sigh, "It matters, dammit. Being in love isn't like a dessert bonbon or something, it's right at the heart of my politics. That someone like me could have a decent shot at actually having someone. I'm politically active because being kept out of all that pisses me off, okay? But I thought I had something nice taking place, and...and I put a lot of myself into that, believing in it, letting myself think it was really happening."

She nodded slowly. "But even though this is ripping you up, from what you said you already knew all that romantic love stuff was fucked up in our society. So getting back to you losing interest in your classes and the newspaper and all, what do you think is going on? I mean, are you going to change your major to business and go work on Wall Street?"

"No! God no!" I closed my eyes for a moment, even put my hands over my eyes. Staring into my personal darkness. Sighed again and looked back at Sharon. "I've been thinking about this thing called an APEL portfolio, where you get credit for things you learned before you came to college. I think if I could get at least eight credits from that, I could finish up here at Old Brookville and go on to grad school a year early. I'm impatient to dig into the real stuff that I came here for. Not the watered-down stuff. You know they haven't taught an actual course in feminist theory in over three years? I'm tired of my teachers saying 'Oh don't bring that up, you'll confuse the other students'. And I feel like too many of my classmates didn't come here to discuss complex ideas in their women's studies classroom, they're here to get a bachelor's degree so they can get a job, and they took women's studies just because it was four credit hours in a convenient part of their schedule."

I cut Sharon off before she could retort to that, reading the smirk on her face without needing a translator. "Oh, of course I'm privileged, and yes I know how that sounded, I can hear myself talking. Look, I'm not saying there's anything at all wrong with coming here to get the system's little legitimacy letters so people will hire you. Hire *us*, I should say. I've never been particularly employable *myself* and if being a college graduate fixes that, it's a nice side effect. I don't blame anyone for jumping through the hoops they set up for us to jump through, I get it. I just mean I really want to talk about the ideas and theories, it's what I came here for, and Professor Baxwood and other folks say I'll find all that in grad school and be patient. Well I'm not patient. I've never been very good at patient and I'm going to be twenty-nine next January because this is my third time doing college. I've been wanting to be a part of a movement and connect with other radicals and raise hell since 1980, and it keeps on not happening."

She was now giving me this look, like *oh my, look what we have here*. Not quite *oh look what the cat dragged in*, but still with some critical attitude. "Well now, it sounds like you do care about something after all. I don't know if you'll find what you're looking for but you know what you want and it seems to matter to you. So you know what to do." Sharon shook her head, smiling a little bit. "You really *don't* get it, even though you think you do, and you have so much to learn. But you sure are interesting. It's good to see you."

I stood outside the large glass window of the *Catalyst* office for a while, watching George and Carrie and Max gesturing and talking. After a few moments, I sighed and opened the door.

"Hey, Derek!" they greeted me.

"I still can't get over how my movie reviews are actually being printed," Max said. "I used to bring things in to last year's *Catalyst* staff and they really looked down their nose at me. Like, 'You ignorant peon! You think anyone would want to read what you wrote? Begone, and don't darken our doorstep, you uncouth gutter snipe!'"

Carrie laughed at his over-the-top caricature and they began embellishing the portrayal of elitist snobby journalists.

I sat.

I didn't have a column written. I pushed around some pieces of paper, advertisement circulars and stuff that had come in the mail and whatnot.

After a while George got up and said he was off to a business management seminar. I rose and followed him, far enough behind him that it wouldn't be awkward not to engage in conversation, and made my way back to my dorm room.

POTENTIALS

"Hello class. I apologize for being late; the shuttle bus at the Hicksville station departed without me and I was forced to wait for the next. My name is Mrs. George Louise Frieze, and, if you are here to study Voice and Diction, I will be your instructor. I hope you are having a good day so far." The short, deliberately precise middle-aged woman deposited a massive pocketbook on the desk and unbuttoned a thick grey-black outer garment and arrayed it on the back of the chair there. "Mine has been lacking in certain aspects, but none for which any of you here are responsible," she added.

From my vantage point, I saw a couple students in the rows in front of me glancing at each other. Illustration one, under dictionary definition for "nonplussed." For my own part, I couldn't help grinning.

"I do not know what lessons you were taught back in your formative years about the process of pronouncing the English language," Mrs. Frieze continued. "Back in my own days as a schoolgirl, we had something that was referred to as 'phonics'. This was supposed to simplify the gap between the word *as written* and the word *as spoken*. We were expected to learn an assortment of diacritical marks and concepts such as the *short a*, as in 'hat,' and the *long a*, as in '*bake.*'"
As she spoke, Mrs. Frieze sketched a pair of letter a's, one with a curved line over the top and the other with a flat bar in the same place.

To my surprise, she turned in my direction. "Your expression indicates to me that this isn't entirely unfamiliar. Do we have a fellow victim of phonics in our midst? What's your name, may I ask?"

"Derek Turner. Yeah, we had those and other marks we were supposed to learn, like a hat over the vowel or a pair of dots. I didn't think it was so bad actually. The dictionaries would use those to explain how to pronounce words and I learned a lot of words from reading and didn't know how to say them."

Mrs. Frieze nodded. "That was the intent, to be sure. As you say, it wasn't all bad. But what it *was* was inconsistent. The phonetic rendering of the word 'bother' would be like this..."—she wrote bô-⟨th⟩ ə r on the blackboard—"...and for 'father' it would look like this—" here she sketched out fä-⟨th⟩ə r. "Look at the vowel sound in the first syllable. It's written two different ways, but it's the same sound. That's inconsistent. So is English spelling of course, but there's no reason to study phonetics if it's merely going to supplant one inconsistent way of rendering sounds on paper with another."

Mrs. Frieze singled out a girl in the second row. "You look as if you're somewhat unclear. Please ask questions. If I can't make myself understood, I will accept the blame for that, but you don't give me a fair chance if you don't tell me when I haven't succeeded. Your name, if you don't mind?"

"Sheila. Sheila Henry."

Mrs. Frieze waited.

"Well, I never thought about *bother* and *father* being the same. I guess maybe they are, but it feels different because one is done with an 'a' and the other is with an 'o'."

"Perhaps for some people they *are* different. In this class we are going to study how sounds are classified. We're going to learn about *fricatives*, and *plosives* and you will learn what *alveolar* and *palatal* sounds are and how they are made. And we are going to learn a new nomenclature, in which every sound has one and only one symbol, and every symbol stands for one and only one sound, regardless of what language is being used. The IPA. International Phonetic Alphabet."

I was discovering that although nothing tended to sound interesting or appealing, if I could ignore that (or if there was sufficient external pressure on me to go there or to participate or whatever), once I was immersed in something, it felt very good to have my attention focused on something that wasn't Jenna.

I began pushing myself to read the APEL program descriptive materials. I came to this college with an education in feminist thinking that was already in progress. It did make sense that I should receive formal credit for that. And if doing so meant I could move on to graduate school ahead of schedule, so much the better. I wanted to have theory discussions with other people who thought in theoretical terms. This was how my head worked. I could make the points that I wanted to make, jumping off from any one of a number of different starting concepts. It was like climbing a mountain: you could start from this side or from that side, but the paths would converge and you'd gain elevation and soon you'd be where you wanted to be.

The central proof for what I'd experienced and what I'd learned, I quickly realized, was *The Amazon's Brother*. It was a combination of personal testimonial about what I'd gone through as a sissy femme male person and demonstration of my ability to theorize, to knit my personal experience in with the existing body of feminist theory and make a contribution, to theorize from my own authority as a differently positioned male person within a patriarchal context.

So that would be the core of what I submitted. All I really had to do was a writeup, explaining how the book had come about and analyzing it and explaining what it represented from an educational viewpoint.

For the second speech we were to do a "speech to inform." Professor Ashton had suggested doing a "how to" instructional speech as one acceptable approach to this.

He had continued to sprinkle socially conservative zingers, opinions that he presented as established fact, into every class session. Then he didn't allow rebuttals or contrasting opinions, quickly pulling the conversation back to the course topic of how to speak in public any time that anyone tried to argue.

So I came up with the idea of instructing the class in how to make and utilize a water pipe. I knew I'd hold their attention and it would be a good departure from the overly cerebral kinds of topics I usually gravitated toward whenever I spoke in class.

I got a mason jar, a length of chemistry lab tubing, and some caulking sealant, so far so good, now what to bring in for the bowl? Aha...the hollow shaft of a metal ball point pen barrel. Perfect. I went in with my paraphernalia in a paper shopping bag, including a Bic lighter and I picked up some dried autumn leaves on the way over to the classroom. I brought water with me in an empty plastic two-liter soda bottle.

I described the process for the class as I assembled the pipe in front of them. Punched a hole in the mason jar lid for the pen shaft, another for the tube, caulked them up, added the water, screwed the lid down, then pulled out a paper bag full of dried leaves. "This is *potential oxidation tissue*, conventionally abbreviated P.O.T.; although we don't normally use oak and maple leaves from last fall, they will do on this occasion..."

I crumbled them into the bowl I'd created from the pen shaft, lit the Bic lighter, put the hose in my mouth, and inhaled; the water bubbled, the flame was sucked down into the leaves and they caught and incinerated nicely, the air chamber filled with leaf smoke, as did my mouth, and then I stopped, released the hose, bowed, and exhaled a spume of smoke and got a round of applause.

"That was totally inappropriate," yelled Ashton. "I can't believe you thought this was okay to do in a classroom! You're promoting drug use! You have no business behaving this way on college property!"

"You're supposed to be critiquing my speech to inform, not making editorial comments on the political correctness of my content."

"How would you feel if President Pettifleur were to walk in this very moment?"

"Well, perhaps now you know how I feel when you're always introducing ideological content that's irrelevant to the subject you're here to teach."

He gave me a C for the speech but I gave myself a considerably higher grade in the place where it counted.

Omar Mason waved to me from down the hall. He waited until the current of students carried me there. "Hey. Hey, listen. Umm, tell me something, do you think Tracy Marshall was serious for real about that commuter lounge thing, or just using that as a way to...let's say a way to give folks, commuter students, a reason to vote for her?"

"You mean like a dog whistle kind of thing?"

He smiled wryly and gave me a nod. "You think it was?"

"Actually I don't, really. She seemed pretty bent, upset when she saw how it could look that way."

"Well, I think we have enough money from student fees, we could do that. Maybe. If we cut some corners. It's not like we couldn't use it for something else, you see what I'm saying though. Maybe the *Catalyst* could do a poll and we see how many people say they'd use it."

"Yeah, we could do that."

Someone else called out to him and Omar and I did our "catch you laters." I started thinking about the things Tracy had said, and that got me thinking about Mike and some of the things *he'd* said about being white on campus. I started to get an inkling of an idea for what to write my column about.

THE CONTEMPTUOUS CAT
White Cat in a Black Neighborhood
by Derek Turner

I went to my first Black Student Union meeting the other night.

You see, I've been hearing things from some of my white resident friends—and it seems to me that I hear this more often than I used to—about how unfair it is that this campus is "black this, black that, everything is geared toward Them." You know. The music at the dances is "all" black. The fraternities and sororities are "all" black. Eat in the cafeteria and the college radio station is playing black music. And, of course, "My God, everywhere I look, after the commuter students leave all you see are these black faces staring at you like Hey White Stuff, you in the wrong place, maybe?"

Uh huh. Yeah. Look, I knew when I came here that as far as the resident student population went, I was going to be part of a white minority. If I had wanted to go to a school where the average complexion was considerably lighter, they aren't all that hard to find, you know. It's not why I came here, but it didn't bother me.

I don't want to give you the wrong idea. I do not quickly and snugly fit in to the black community here, and I'm not an insider glancing out in smug disgust at some prejudiced white people who won't or can't do likewise. No, I don't exactly fit in, either. I'm from a different subculture, remember? Oh, as it happens, I'm pretty unorthodox for a white person, but I do sort of match a certain part of a white subculture in my values, tastes, ways and manners, and experiences. It would be insulting and pretentious to go around acting as if by being friendly I (or my beforementioned white friends) could change that and "join" the black students as part of their culture. So do my white friends have a point?

I think they're missing the point. Being a minority does not usually translate as "don't be prejudiced against the majority or

They won't let you fit in." It usually does translate into being left out, rendered invisible, being overlooked, glancing around and feeling like the whole damn world was designed by and for someone else. And here we are in this little inverted microcosm within a white culture, and the white students have this opportunity to experience what it is like being a minority—and never mind discrimination or prejudice, I mean just for once not being the Holy Norm—and they don't get it!

Okay, I'm cheating. I really am a misfit in white culture. I already knew what it is like to be a nonmember. Once again, don't get me wrong: with a haircut and some external pretending, I could and can pass for orthodox white if I choose to do so, even if inside I'd resent it like hell; and that's an important difference. But I'm not a total novice to the business of being outnumbered and overlooked and feeling like I don't belong.

And I think we've got a problem. It isn't really race hatred, but it could become that in the presence of a hot campus issue or two polarizing blacks and whites. No, the problem is that for the most part we aren't bridging this race gap. We seldom talk about race and when we do, we too often repeat simple liberal statements about how things ought to be between different races instead of sharing what it is like being on our respective sides of the situation. That's what happened when I attended Black Student Union: I got a brief education about what it might be like to be a black person in this society.

We need more of that, and I think we need to get more personal about it when we do. White students (and teachers, too, I expect) probably have a decent idea of what certain prominent black leaders think or thought of white people & culture in general, but I'll bet I'm not alone among white people here who don't know what black people here in our college community think of us. And wonder about us. And wonder what we think of them. And so on.

We need more of that, and in both directions. Black people are not immune to the tendency to bond with the familiar or to fear the different. It is an unfortunate truth that just because someone has been the outsider in one situation doesn't keep them from practicing conformity and being uncomfortable with the unusual in another context.

Many blacks may feel that, while white people remain ignorant about black life, blacks are, if anything, overexposed to the dominant white culture and its norms. But it needs to be kept in mind that the voice of "dominant white culture" is not a composite of all white people but only the mainstream of prescribed "normal" white experience against which all of us are judged; and blacks often participate in applying those same standards in collusion with that voice in viewing and judging those who do not conform.

There should be room on campus for all of us to be our individual selves and to learn appreciation for our diversities [personal insert: if I want to wear my white man's hair long and stringy I ought to be able to do so without being jeered at and called "Jesus"; you know who you are].

We all need to take the risk of opening ourselves to these different values, tastes, and customs and admit our sometimes embarrassing ignorance of the things that others here may have grown up with and take for granted.

At the same time, we need to reevaluate those things which we do take for granted. Taking something for granted is the core of prejudice, which means to judge before taking a look at. For whites, I'm afraid, that tends to mean we need to develop a sense of ourselves as a race instead of behaving as if "race" meant everyone else and we are "normal." In today's world, too many of us white people have sort of grown up thinking that not being prejudiced against other races means believing that They can be normal just like us, too. That, of course, confuses being equal with being the same, and it begins with an incredible arrogance, a sort of cultural chauvinism that has come to replace blatant racism as the primary white attitude toward race: race means them.

But all of us have heard about the need to build a sense of community here; and all of us, in order to participate in creating that with one another, need to open ourselves to each other's curiosity and explore our differences in an atmosphere of respect. If everyone who has been rolling eyes and whispering about what They do had the courage to admit to Them, "Hey, it's different to me, and I'm curious; it's weird to me, explain," the Us necessary for Our Special Place might emerge. We could be one enough to say "we" and still assert that We are not all alike. I'm convinced of it.

And it would be our personal triumph.

Where did my stapler go? I just had it a moment ago!? Yeesh...how did my dorm room become such a pigsty? Aah there, right in front of me.

I stapled the top sheet to the form and then ran both of them through the three-hole punch and then into the binder. My APEL portfolio was complete.

I was seeking four credits for feminist theory and four credits for autobiography. If the committee granted me what I was seeking, that plus the one semester's worth of transfer credits from my brief stint at the University of New Mexico would give me fifteen above what I'd earned here in regular coursework at SUNY Old Brookville. I would be able to graduate a year early. I wouldn't have a junior year. I'd go straight from this year, my sophomore year, to a senior year.

It made sense to pack up and move on. The courses I was taking now weren't really propelling me forward. The public speaking and voice and diction courses in particular hadn't turned out to be particularly relevant to my reasons for signing up for them. Neither one was going to improve my skills at speaking to an audience with a more listenable voice.

I picked up the three-ring notebook and took it to the library to xerox everything before turning it in.

I exited the classroom, spiral composition book and pen in hand, and strode out into the hall. There was the usual chatter from clusters of students milling around or walking together. As I emerged, some of the conversation stopped. A couple of white fellows sitting on the radiator did the opposite: *"Whooo!"* "Hey, Mr. *Catalyst*! You're asking for it, man."

They seemed amused, not hostile. *Do they think that article is going to fire up a local Klan chapter and cause them to come after me or something?* One of the guys was shaking his head at me, grinning. I was curious but decided against trying to interrogate them to obtain a better sense of their thinking. I waved and nodded and continued on my way.

Outside, in the lane between the Academic Village core and the dorms, Omar called out to me, angled himself to walk in my direction. Once at close range he pronounced "You rock, man" and high-fived me.

Scarcely thirty yards later, Nzuma accosted me. "What did you write?! Derek, I can't believe you'd go all paranoid on us. I been hearing about it all day. You can't be tellin' me you're all scared of black folks on campus, tell me you ain't!"

"No, of course not. Did you read it?"

"Well, not yet. I gotta tell you though, everybody talking about it!"

"Well, you should read it and see for yourself what it says, don't you think?"

She scowled at me dubiously, shaking her head, but said no more.

"Hey, yo, man, if you think this campus is 'black this, black that,' why don't you just leave? We don't need your shit." The person speaking was a fraternity brother. Rho something-or-other. Or something-rho. They referred to themselves as the Rho-men. I'd written a previous "Contemptuous Cat" column ragging on fraternities and sororities for hazing and for the whole demeaning practice of making their pledges humiliate themselves to prove how badly they wanted in, and the column had drawn his ire; he'd confronted me about it and since then had yelled out challenges and attacks when he saw me.

But my current column was being misconstrued. Maybe he was particularly biased against me because of the column about the Greek organizations but it seemed like a fair number of people were somehow thinking I'd written something in my current column other than what I'd actually said.

I decided to look for the Black Student Union coordinators and ask if I could address the group and answer any questions before this got any further out of hand.

"Okay, everybody, if you'll take a seat we can call this meeting to order and get started," Shantay Solomon said. The Black Student Union meeting was having a large turnout. The storefront-window office space—identical in layout to the *Catalyst* office—could comfortably hold 35 or 40 people, but tonight's meeting had nearly twice that many crammed in.

"We got some good feedback about the Black History Month speakers we had, and Keith is going to talk to us about doing a program called 'From Jazz to Rap' which is gonna be pretty cool," she continued. "But we got a guest speaker here, Derek Turner who you all know from the *Catalyst*, has come here to be with us and answer questions and concerns about his latest column. Derek, how do you want to do this?"

"I was thinking, maybe I should start off by just reading the column out loud," I answered. "Does that make sense to everyone? Then we can discuss whatever concerns or issues need to be addressed." There were a lot of nods.

So I began reading, just doing the column verbatim, adding a little bit of acting for the parts where the sentences were supposed to be somebody else speaking, to distinguish that from my own voice as the column's author. Everyone listened attentively, and when I finished, someone started applauding and all the others joined in. I felt a burst of relief. I hadn't thought I'd given anyone here reason to resent anything I'd written, but then I hadn't anticipated people reacting as if I'd written a hostile column, and yet apparently some had taken it that way, so it was gratifying to have the BSU people clapping and not glaring at me with their arms crossed or something worse.

"Thank you, Derek," Shantay said. "We appreciate you coming here tonight."

"Thank you for letting me address the group," I replied, then, to the room at large, "Does anyone have any questions or things they want to disagree about that I wrote?"

Keith Johnston stood up. "I think what you wrote says everything you need to say, and I thank you for it," he said.

Nzuma came over and shook my hand. "I should've *known* you couldn't have written something racially prejudiced, I didn't want to believe that about you, and I'm so glad it wasn't true."

Omar said "I told you so" to someone and I also overheard someone else say "That took guts," which provided an extra boost to my feeling of triumph.

Later, I walked back to my room, shaking my head. I was startled by how many people had apparently been inclined to believe I'd written something horrible when all they would have needed to do was pick up a copy of the newspaper and read it for themselves. But I realized I'd seen it happen many times, that people's situation, the context in which they encounter something that's been said or written down in words, can make them react to it in ways that don't have much to do with what was actually in those words.

It had happened to me rather dramatically back at the University of New Mexico when I first came out. I'd written a little piece about how the ways that sexual orientation and gender identities are set up in a society are central to how the society is overall, whether it's militaristic and coercive or cooperative and free. But it had been perceived as a threat when I left a copy of it in the mailbox for the Director of the Rape Crisis Center, and the university had been so concerned that I might be making threats that I'd been incarcerated for a month in a psychiatric hospital over it.

People are often so churned up about volatile social issues that they hear or read what they think a person *might* have said or written and often can't set that aside long enough to find out what they actually *did* say.

In the speech class, Dr. Ashton had handed out a photocopied article explaining different types of informal fallacies. He warned us that we needed to avoid using those types of constructions in our speeches, because he would be pointing them out; that they were illegitimate types of argument that only ignorant people would fall for. Consistent with his behavior all semester, he then went on to give several examples of bad logic, all of them using socially progressive factions or people as his negative examples.

While I continued to dislike Ashton and his class, I was enjoying the exploration of fallacies. I wished he was correct when he told us that arguments of this sort would be rejected by most people, but unfortunately I saw people utilizing this kind of argument all the time, and seldom being called on it. Ashton himself was doing so, in fact, with fallacies embedded in his own presentation of the fallacies. "These bleeding heart liberals are *bad*, because, see, they used an informal fallacy here, therefore we can dismiss *all* of their positions and arguments." *Unwarranted generalization. Fallacy of composition. Argument ad hominem.*

The sign posted outside the cafeteria stated that cafeteria services, library, administrative offices, Academic Village core, bookstore, gym, and campus bus services would be closed down for spring break starting at 10:30 PM next Friday and not starting back up until Monday of the following week at 6:30 AM.

Well that's just wonderful. I guess all the students who underline *matter* ununderline *are going home or going on vacation. What the hell am I supposed to do for food, stand outdoors and photosynthesize??*

I'd been hearing lots of other students chattering about going to Florida or New Orleans or some other destination. The way that spring break was described and depicted in advertisements and in the media didn't make it sound like my kind of thing. Lots of loud drunken kids, casual sex, least common denominator blend-in crowd activities. It hadn't bothered me to not be going anywhere and I hadn't been feeling left out. But I'd failed to realize the campus was going to close down like that.

We had a handful of kitchenettes interspersed among the dorm suites, but I'd never seen them open. The administration had had them locked up the year before I started, apparently because the resident students had failed to keep them clean or had vandalized the equipment or something.

I hadn't made any arrangements to fly back to New Mexico to be with my parents and it was kind of late to try to plan anything like that. I'd have to think about what I was going to do.

I stepped off the N22 in front of the old Creedmoor gate on Hillside and walked toward the RCCA facility. Queenie saw me and sauntered in my direction. "Well, look who's here. Is this old home week? Now don't you look all spiffy!"

"Hey Queenie! Listen, can I con you into doing me a favor? I don't feel up to dealing with Tony Blaine or Jerry Durst today. Go down to the TV lounge and poke your head in and tell Cowboy to come out?"

"Oh, that Tony, something awful he is, for sure. Well, I suppose I could. Cowboy owes me bus tokens from yesterday. Say, you don't happen to have a cigarette, hon, do you?"

"I don't smoke, remember?"

Queenie looked at me dubiously. Being a smoker was sort of the default here at the RCCA. Most people did. After a moment Queenie went inside.

"They can't do that," Cowboy proclaimed. "It's a public institution, right? State University of New York. And they've got a policy against making people homeless."

"You should contact Jay," Mary added, "and have him come out and give a talk on campus."

"That's not a bad idea," I replied. "Especially if I can get some club or classroom to invite him to make a presentation. Meanwhile, I'm a newspaper columnist, and I intend to write about this. But technically they're not putting us out of the dorms, they're just not making it possible to feed ourselves. I can buy food in town, but they're cancelling the circle bus too, so I'd have to walk all the way from the front gate to the dorms with bags of groceries."

"Well, we've got something we wanted to show you anyway," Cowboy told me. "And it might solve your situation. Wait here. Mary, let's go get some chips and fill up your thermos with hot water for tea, from the lunchroom. We'll meet you back here in about ten minutes."

I sat on one of the park benches out front of the entrance ramp. Birds clamped their feet on twigs above me and cheeped songs at me. It was a nice day and I lay back against the bench and basked in the sunshine.

Cowboy and Mary returned with bags and baskets and beckoned me to follow them. Together we walked around the deserted east side of Building 4, the part that had been the old Queens Men's Shelter that preceded the RCCA's opening.

Cowboy glanced around; I gathered that he was checking to see if anyone was observing us. Then he and Mary led me across the deserted parking lots in back to the hidden inside wing of the next building over. "This is Building Twenty-five," Mary told me. "It's all boarded up but we found a way in." They approached a window and showed me that the boards weren't attached. Cowboy raised the wooden-framed panel of glass windows which slid up with a skreek. Then he helped Mary over the side into the building and indicated for me to follow her.

Inside the building, tattered shreds of paint hung down from the ceiling, reminiscent of cobwebs and evocative of decay and abandonment. Clearly it had been a long time since Creedmoor had made use of this space. Cowboy switched on a lantern flashlight and gave me a tour: "This looks like a nurse's station. Over here, this is the kitchen. Look at all the metal bowls and trays and stuff. There are big stoves over in that corner, and through those doors is the cafeteria, looks like they stacked all the broken furniture in there..."

After showing me the sights, they arrived at a closed door on the second floor which swung open when Mary turned the doorknob. "This is where we've been staying. RCCA won't let girls in the guys' rooms or vice versa. It's not fair, Moby and Leese can be together because they're both women, but they won't let us share a room."

"Yeah," I nodded. "It's weird because they're Catholic Charities and officially don't approve of homosexuality, but that means they don't recognize it exists either. It's like with the priesthood or the nuns. It's sometimes been a safe place for gay and lesbian people."

"Well, we go back over to RCCA during the day and get counted as present for activities but they don't do bed checks. Not yet anyway. So we go out the window just like you used to. We used your trick of cutting the security chain and putting on our own combination lock. Then we go over here. It's warm enough. There's no plumbing or electricity but we bought a box of trash bags and line one of the toilets in case we need to use them during the night, then the next morning tie them off and get rid of it."

I nodded. Yeah, this would work. There were grocery stores and convenience stores a lot closer to this building than to my dorm room at SUNY, and I could kill time reading at the library or going for walks during the day, or just hang out with Cowboy and Mary when they weren't required to be at RCCA events and activities.

With help from Cowboy and Mary, I picked out a room—relatively empty, small, with room for a bed and a bedside table—and brought in a bed with metal bedsprings, a bedside table, and a couple of chairs in decent condition. Then I followed them to where they'd found a fallout shelter. Among all kinds of other interesting artifacts, like silver iodide for mouth sores and water decontamination pills and glass syringes and kits of dried powered food, there was a stack of plastic-wrapped comforter-like padded blankets with pillows. I ripped one open. It smelled weirdly chemically but had obviously been isolated from the air for all these years. We dragged these upstairs, picked out a reasonably okay mattress without holes in it, then wrapped it in one of the garbage bags and put the comfortor-thingie on top along with the pillow. Mary gave me sheets and a bedspread they'd brought over from RCCA.

"You feel like going exploring?" Cowboy asked me. "You're not going to believe this. Mary and me, we've been checking this place out with flashlights and there's some seriously weird shit you haven't seen yet." Sure, I said. What the hell.

They took me back the way we'd just come, down into the fallout shelter. Cowboy pointed to a door at the far end of the room and pulled on it. After a moment it shuddered and scraped open far enough for him to squeeze by, and I went in after him, Mary behind me.

In front of us, a hallway stretched out to the limits of the lantern flashlight's glow. I followed Cowboy and after about a hundred yards or so (it was hard to measure distance under these circumstances but that's what it felt like), the hallway abruptly bent to the left by about 45 degrees and also began heading downhill.

Down we went. The walls gradually lost their sharp right-angle edges and the smoothness of institutionally painted solid wall gave way to lumpy brickwork. I started to see puddles on the concrete floor and took care to step over them. Our footsteps and intermittent conversation echoed.

We came to a metal gate, standing open. Steel supports ran across the floor of the tunnel, then up the sides, with hinges. A heavy chain with a massive lock dangled from the crossbars of the gate. We stepped through the opening and continued. A little farther on, we came to an intersection. The tunnels to our left and to our right had gates on them like the one we'd stepped through a moment before, but they were closed and locked.

"I don't think we're in Building Twenty-five any more," Cowboy pronounced. "I think all these old Creedmoor buildings were connected underground and if we could keep on going we'd come up inside one of the other buildings."

After another ten minutes or so, we came to another junction. This time the way in front of us was blocked; the gate was closed and chained. Just on the other side of the locked gate was a four-way intersection. The path to the right and the path continuing ahead in front of us were on the same level we were currently on. But to our left, the connecting tunnel descended at a sharp angle.

"I've been thinking of getting some bolt cutters," Cowboy said. "I really want to know where that goes. We might be the first people to go down this way in forty years. I bet the folks who administer Creedmoor have no idea this even exists. It was probably built during the cold war. There might even be a whole emergency retreat center down here, like a town just waiting in case it was needed, with provisions and houses and rooms."

We stared for a while down the mysterious dimly-lit passages for a while, then made our way back to our illicit domiciles.

PARTICIPATIONS

My spring break experience woke me up about what the summer was likely to bring. I made a few inquiries and quickly confirmed: I was not going to be allowed to stay on campus during the summer break. It was much too long to spend in the abandoned hallways of Building 25, too. I needed a place to be. I had a few months of spring semester remaining to me, and it made sense to speak with my advisors and mentors and see if I could set up with something like an internship or job for the summer.

Dr. Baxwood pursed her lips and gazed into the distance for a moment. "I think you should definitely do a women's studies internship, we recommend that for all the students who are concentrating in women's studies. But I don't think summer is a good time for that. You need to be writing up your experience as you go, and meeting with your professor to discuss what you're doing. It just doesn't work as well if you do the internship all by yourself in isolation and then discuss it afterwards."

"Hmm, I guess that makes sense. Well, actually the reason I was asking about the summer was that I live in the dorms, but the college seems to assume everyone goes back to their families when school isn't in session. I don't really have a home around here. I could go stay with my parents in New Mexico but I don't really want to do that. There's nothing to do there unless I had a summer job, and I'm afraid I'd go stir crazy after a month of living with my folks. Also, financial aid is based on me not receiving support from my family and me staying there would kind of muddy the waters."

"No," Baxwood agreed, "I wouldn't have wanted a summer's stay with my parents either. Well, let me think a moment." She walked over to her bookcase where the coffeemaker stood and poured herself a cup of coffee. "Want a cup?" I nodded; she handed me a spare cup and I poured one for myself. Baxwood sat back down and sipped for a minute. "You don't have any place to go because you were in some kind of homeless institution, is that correct? Do you know who Mitch Snyder is?"

I nodded to the first question but shook my head to the second.

"He's an activist down in Washington who's done hunger strikes and marches to make the city do something about homelessness. He lived for a while on a cardboard box over a subway vent and he's been arrested several times, and there were several news articles about how the homeless are treated a stone's throw from the White House. He finally embarrassed them enough to get them to fund a shelter, and now his organization runs it. Anyway, he's from around here, and they might could use a volunteer who is also a homeless, you know, has a history of being homeless and you speak out about it and write about it."

"Yeah, that sounds great."

"Meanwhile, you should still be thinking about doing an internship this year for credit. I've got a list of possibilities here, hold on a sec. Yeah, here it is."

Some of the sites and organizations on the list operated as spaces that weren't set up to have any male people present, and she made a pencil mark by those. Of those remaining, one looked particularly interesting to me, the Coalition Against Domestic Violence. Dr. Baxwood said she'd write a cover letter to introduce me, and I could call them and set things up some time between now and the fall semester.

Meanwhile, she would contact the Community for Creative Nonviolence, the organization that Mitch Snyder was with, and see if they'd like to have me come down for the summer.

I had to register for fall classes. I didn't know yet whether I'd get any credits for my APEL portfolio. If I didn't, and I had counted on those credits, then I might end up short of enough credits to graduate after this year.

I thought about it. I looked at the course schedule. "Well... if I registered for the Internship in Women's Studies like Baxwood recommended...hmm, I could take three regular classes...and if I could do a research project, which would make me look good to graduate schools...I could do interviews with other people who were either masculine females who weren't lesbians or feminine males who weren't gay, and look for common threads and stuff...that's, like, twenty credits. And I could do the remaining fifteen credits in the spring if I don't get an APEL credits, so I could graduate this spring no matter what."

I was belatedly enjoying my Women and the Health System course now that I had at least partially extracted myself from the dreariness of my mope. In the assigned text by Barbara Ehrenreich, and in the lectures, we'd covered nurses and midwives in the era before the male medical establishment took over. I found it interesting that the treatments and interventions the midwives and folk healers used were often more fully grounded in legitimate effective practices than what the doctors were doing—like using the tree bark that aspirin was later distilled from, in the same era that the male doctors were still using fleams and practicing bloodletting.

Meanwhile, although neither my Public Speaking nor my Voice & Diction class had turned out to be particularly relevant to my concerns about speaking effectively to an audience, I'd become entranced with the International Phonetic Alphabet that Mrs. Frieze had introduced us to, and had even spent a weekend in the Macintosh labs with an application called FONTastic, designing an IPA font so that I could type from the computer keyboard and generate the characters for phonetic transcription.

I decided to wait until the Fall semester to pen my Contemptuous Cat article about the school closing down the dorms and not making any concessions to students who had no simple easy home to return to between sessions. I definitely saw it as a social justice issue, one that the campus ought to be concerned about, but I figured if the article were to stir up some concern that could lead to taking action and making changes, starting that just as the spring semester was coming to a close wasn't good planning.

Dr. Janet Dixon in the Old Brookville Psychology Department was interested in helping me with my proposed research project. I wanted to ask some open-ended questions to be answered by women who felt like they were more like men than they were like other women, and men like me who felt they were more like women than other men. I specifically wanted to focus on those whose sexual attraction was to the opposite sex because the stereotypes of butch women were that they were automatically lesbians, and of lesbians that they were manly and butch; and even more so for sissy femme males that we were by definition gay guys, and of gay males that they were all effeminate. So the experiences of those for whom the stereotypes were true—while still of interest—were likely to be something of an embrace or acceptance of notions that were already known, and what I wanted to do was to use this research to introduce identities that were not acknowledged in our society.

We talked briefly in the hall between classes. "You would sign up for a Psychology independent study. I'd assign you some material to read, and you would use their theories to put your own concepts and your research into a context. We'd work together to get your research, your method, the questions and all that, worked out."

I nodded. "So I'll go ahead and register for that. When do you want me to come in? After the fall semester starts, or do you want me go ahead and get started on some stuff?"

"Fall will be soon enough. You know where to find me!," she added, pointing back over her shoulder at her office door.

"Hello. May I speak with Derek Turner?"

"This is Derek," I informed the phone.

"My name's Reggie Thompson and I'm calling from the Community for Creative Nonviolence. I just wanted to confirm that you'll be coming down here to work at our office on Second Street. According to my notes here, you'll be starting this Monday?"

"Yeah, tomorrow's the last day of tests and classes."

"It will be great having you here. I look forward to meeting you. So you've made travel arrangements?"

"Yeah, I have a ticket for Amtrak and I'll ride down Sunday afternoon."

"Oh, you're coming by train? How are you going to get from the rail station to the office?"

"It doesn't look far to walk. I looked it up on a map at the library. And I'll have plenty of time to kill."

"Okay, then, I guess we're all set. See you in a few days!"

The railroad car was mostly empty seats, one of the distinct advantages of boarding the train at its point of origin. I picked one on the left hand side and slid over against the window. After the conductor came by to verify my ticket, I cushioned my head with a folded sweater and dozed off.

We pulled into Washington DC in the dim early morning hours and I got off, slinging on my backpack and reading from my scribbled instructions for how to get to the center. I had wanted to be at the office when they opened, not wandering in near closing time in the afternoon (or after closing, if the train was running late), so I'd selected the crack-of-dawn train.

The city streets were mostly deserted and business storefronts were dark and shuttered with security gates down. After a little while the route I had mapped took me out into the suburbs, with simple houses on grassy lawns and sidewalks running next to the street. My plans, to the extent that I'd formulated them, were to hole up in a diner or deli where I could sit somewhere and nurse a few cups of coffee while waiting for Creative Nonviolence to open up, but I came to my destination without once having encountered any open place of business where I could kill time. I shrugged off my pack and dug out a science fiction book and put on my sweater and leaned back against the pack to read and let time go by.

I checked my watch every now and then, doing so a bit more often after 8:30 AM arrived, and kept an eye out for any personnel arriving.

It was 9:45 AM when a police cruiser pulled up next to the curb. Two officers stepped out and approached. I waved.

"Good morning. Are you lost? Do you know where you are? How did you get here? Can I see some ID?"

"Hi, my name's Derek Turner. I'm a college student and I made arrangements to work as a volunteer here for the summer. Here's my driver's license. I came down my Amtrak, here's my ticket stub."

"Why did you come to this location and decide to loiter here? Don't you realize how shocking and intimidating it would be for you to be lurking unannounced like this? Have you had anything to drink? Doing any drugs? Why are you here?"

I kept explaining that this was my first day, that the office was to have opened at nine, that I'd gotten here early because of the train schedule and that, no, it hadn't occurred to me that being here waiting when the office folks came to work would be a problem, and that, yes, I had done similar things in the past and that no, I didn't see anything wrong with it, and why should I?

Finally one of the two officers stated, "Well, we were contacted by the people who work in this office. They saw you on the lawn and were afraid to go into the building because they didn't know who you were. No one told them to expect you. It sounds like some kind of communications screwup, to be honest. Your story checks out. But they don't want you here. I've explained to them that you came down to do some kind of internship but they say they don't want to work with you."

After a breakfast and several cups of coffee and some chapters in my book—giving myself additional time to cool off first—I got up from my seat and went back to the pay phones in the back of the diner. I dialed Reggie Thompson's number.

He'd already heard about the morning's incident from the office staff. "Yeah, not exactly off to a good start, I'm afraid."

I took a deep breath. "Look," I said, "here we have an organization for promoting the concerns of homeless people. And the people who work in its office are *scared* of someone who was sitting on their front lawn because he had no place else to go? Seriously? Have any of them ever actually *met* a homeless person? I'm sorry but that's utterly fucked up. I came down here to work with this organization. I got myself down here. I got myself to the office where I was supposed to report to work. I made arrangements to be volunteering here because I've got nowhere else to be when school's not in session, so I'm kind of the population this organization's supposed to be helping out, which is why I thought it would be a good fit. Meanwhile, I'm decently well dressed and groomed, I wasn't crouching in the shadows next to the doorway, I was out in plain sight on the front lawn *sitting down and reading a book*! How the hell does that become 'threatening behavior'?"

"Listen, I hear you. You got a perfectly valid point, my man. I already tried talking with them, but they're not being flexible, they really don't want you working with them. But be that as it may, we got some other options if you still want to be involved down here. You can work with my partner, Carol, doing mailings and filing and stuff like that, she's the outreach coordinator and she does most of her CCNV stuff from out of her home. How's that sound?"

"Well...yeah, if I can still do something useful down here, sure. It doesn't sound like I would have been very comfortable with the office folks anyhow. They might have come in from lunch break and seen me sitting in an office chair and started to worry that I was about to mug them or something."

"Mmm hmm. All right then, let me make a few phone calls and... can you call me again in about an hour? I'll let you know what the situation is."

I grabbed another stack of letters and bulletins from Carol's wicker basket. I skimmed the top page, with particular attention to the top salutation area and the bottom beneath the signature, and circled the telephone number when I found it. It was my job to assemble a calling list of prospective donors from this pile of correspondence and merge it with what she already had, avoiding any duplicates.

We all agreed that this was a good use of my time and skills. I had good attention to detail and worked well on my own, and Carol and Reggie thought that after the fiasco with the front office people, it made sense to minimize my exposure to any additional people who might be hostile and judgmental about someone who didn't exude upper middle class respectability.

I was still disconcerted about that. In most of my life I had *been* regarded and treated as a middle class respectable sort, at least when I sought to be. I had the nuances and the vocabulary and the comportment of a person with educated parents and professional stature. In fact, back in Los Alamos, in my school days, the other kids had regarded me as stuffy and hoity-toity, and I had had to learn how to speak more informally and casually among the stoners and counterculturally-influenced people I'd ended up hanging out with in later years.

I could speak like an educated professional. I'd used it often in the homeless shelter system, and even when the social workers or administrative officials had known full well that I was one of their clients, it had served me well. It was the privilege of class in America, the *lingua franca* of the homeowning and economically secure people who are accustomed to being participants in the running of things, and I could pull it out like an identification badge produced from my back pocket.

But in this case I'd been prejudged on the basis of visual appearance (and, apparently, the inappropriate behavior of sitting down on the grass lawn of a social services' office space) and had been given no opportunity to whip out those credentials. Maybe it was good to be reminded of how unfairly people in our society are assessed. How most homeless people would not have that additional resource and would constantly be viewed as misbehaving ignorant people even if they were hard-working and responsible and quite capable folks.

"So how are you making out?" Carol asked me.

"I'm making good progress," I replied, indicating the two piles of paper. "I'm over halfway through these, and most of them do have at least one phone number."

"But some of those are going to be duplicates of what we already have, don't forget that. Donors can get annoyed if they get called again right after they've made a contribution. So I need you not to rush, and check each one against the master list."

"I know, I didn't forget. What I've done, I copied your master list into this other module, this thing over here that says 'Spreadsheet,' and look, it lets me sort them by name or by phone number. That makes it easy to check whether the person or their phone number is already on the list."

She looked at me dubiously. "This list was set up by my associate, and he said to only use the word processor. I don't want anything to be confused or messed up by going against his instructions. We depend on this list!"

"I'm not using the spreadsheet to replace what you're using, I'm only using it as a tool to make it easier to check for duplication. But if you're more comfortable, the word processor part has a search command, and I could use that to look for duplicates. It's just slower to do it that way."

"Well...I guess if it isn't going to affect the list that we use, you may as well keep using your technique." She picked a purse from a hook and adjusted the strap. "I'm picking up the boys from the academy and we'll need this table for supper. You might want to go out and get yourself something to eat. I don't know if you want to spend some time in your room or if you'd like to, maybe, go see a movie or something, but I like the evening to be family time. If you do go out, I'd appreciate it if you were indoors by nine, so I can lock the door."

Although the main tourist attractions of Washington were the monuments and the main political buildings, the place that lured me was the Library of Congress. They had every book that had ever been published right there on their shelves, and although you couldn't just check them out and take them home, you could request them to be brought to you to read there at their desks, or at least you could for the ones not considered fragile rarities.

I had them bring me a copy of Valerie Solanas' pamphlet, *The Society for Cutting Up Men (S.C.U.M.) Manifesto*, an infamously man-hating piece to which my attention had been drawn by a feminist at Albuquerque's Siren Coffeehouse in the spring when I came out.

The *SCUM Manifesto* had been treated by feminists as a work of humor, a sharp skewering of a lot of male pretensions that made a lot of valid points even as it used them to support the premise that men should be completely eliminated. At the same time, it had been reacted to with predictable horror and pointed to as "Exhibit A" by people who claimed feminists were extremists who hated men. That, too, was mostly regarded with amusement by many feminists, who, instead of working hard to distance themselves, shrugged and said "Well, they're going to call us man-hating extremists no matter what we say, and if they're going to take a piece like this seriously as a genuine reflection of the women's movement's agenda, they're going to have to stop saying *we're* the ones who lack a sense of humor!"

Later, in the early 1980s, when I was working on *The Amazon's Brother*, I had tried to find a copy in various local libraries in order to quote from it, but none ever had it on their shelves. I couldn't even obtain it via inter-library loan!

Now I held the elusive little volume in my hands. It was only about 26 pages plus some unnumbered pages with publishing information and so on. I spoke to the person at the service counter: "Is it okay to make a copy of this? It's out of print and I can't get it anywhere else."

"For personal use only? Well...there's a xerox machine against the wall over there. It's coin operated. You aren't restricted from using it. If you break any copyright laws with what you do with materials you copy, that's your responsibility."

I took that as sufficient permission and made change from a five dollar bill and photocopied the pamphlet.

I performed various office tasks and other types of repetitive work as the summer progressed, sometimes typing, more often organizing and culling data.

I never felt particularly comfortable in Carol's home. I had been given a room upstairs and occasionally, mostly on evenings when Carol's children were elsewhere, would be invited to join her and Reggie for dinner. Reggie would occasionally direct a comment or question to me; Carol never did, except during working hours, and then only narrowly constrained to issuing me tasks or finding out how far I'd gotten or whether I was able to do what had been asked of me. When her boys were present in the house, she interacted with them exclusively, tuning out anyone else.

I spent several lonely evenings upstairs reading. I missed Jenna intensely. I could see that she was going through a phase in her life where she needed to feel emotionally self-reliant, and that getting close to me had threatened that. And I hadn't handled it well. I could understand why she felt like she had to push away. But I, too, was a person with emotional deficits and needs. I craved intimacy, a sense of belonging, an awareness of being understood and loved for who I was.

In mid-July I asked if it were okay to visit the shelter facility, and Carol told me that I was welcome to do so. It was institutional but a lot more hands-off and less constrained than the homeless shelter and RCCA environments I'd been in up in New York. Homeless people were designated a bed which was theirs for the duration of their need if they didn't violate any rules. They had a small bedside table and a particle-board wooden wardrobe to use as an all-purpose storage space. I was given a tour by a homeless resident who had a volunteer role within the shelter. Our New York facilities had not delegated any such roles to the residents.

After a few days of pondering the idea, I asked Carol if she had any objections to me taking a bed in the facility and then coming back to the house in the mornings to do whatever work CCNV had for me. She shrugged and said that would be fine if it was what I wanted to do.

After the first couple of days, she began not having any work and suggesting I come back the next day, or telling me in advance that she'd be out of the house and not to bother coming by.

I made some phone calls to the Financial Aid department back at Old Brookville and ascertained that they could find a work-study position for me which would pay a meager amount. I wasn't sure where I could sleep, but figured at worst I could take up residence in Creedmoor Building 25 again and commute.

I called Reggie Thompson. I apologized. He apologized, too: "I'm sorry I didn't take a more active role in making this work out." Then I bought a train ticket back to New York.

PART THREE: GRADUATE STUDENT

I leaned back in my five-wheeled office chair and for the fifth or sixth time reread Dr. Aaronsen's comments on my first real, for-credit feminist theory term paper. In my three years as a Women's Studies student at Old Brookville, I had often turned in papers that I regarded as feminist theory in some sense of the word, but only now, in graduate school, had I been in a class actually *titled* "Feminist Theory" and where the assignment was for me to write *about* feminist theory as subject matter. I was finally getting to participate in the discussions I wanted to be a part of.

Dr. Aaronsen's prominent "A" at the top, coupled with the comments that followed, was both an invitation and a thrown gauntlet. I was being challenged to elaborate on my assertions and defend my perspective—

> *"Your paper is as superb as it is frustrating. I found the effort at applying what was useful to you in each theory to a particular topic to be provocative, entertaining, and carefully developed. As you wrote about each theory, you adopted its style as well as presented its content. But you are pretty transparent in your endorsement of radical feminist theory. I don't believe that radical feminism is inimical to sociology, that one can't do sociology if one is doing radical feminist theory. I believe that radical feminism is simply BAD sociology. You should take a serious look at socialist feminist theory. I think you'll find it more useful and appropriate for your work as a practitioner of sociology."*

Diane and Rafe walked in together, chatting about their duties as teaching assistants to Dr. Sanger. Eight of us occupied this office, a comfortable long stretch of floor space interspersed with grad students' desks with a couch and a coffee maker at the back.

I nodded and waved. On some days that might have been the extent of interaction but today they meandered over in my direction. "Hey. I heard through the grapevine that you're boycotting stats next semester and that you told them it's because they can't teach," Rafe said. "We've all been focused on Collier and his political bullshit, but you're right, the teaching isn't very good."

Diane moved behind me to better read over my shoulder. "Aaronsen's class?"

"Yeah, I'm thinking maybe I could do a theory track paper out of this."

"You're already doing a track paper? You're disgusting! I never figured you for the Type A nose-to-the-grindstone type."

Rafe shook his head. "Derek is totally grindstone. He's deceptive. Watch him for a while, though. He may look like a hippie but he's like 'You don't let me work hard enough around here'. His idea of relaxation is to write papers that nobody assigned, just to stay in practice."

The Sociology Department here at Setauket University operated differently from a lot of academic departments. Instead of oral examinations, grad students were supposed to submit three self-assigned papers, called "track papers," one delving into theory, one into reviewing all the relevant literature in a given topic area, and one describing research that they'd done. Each one was kind of like a third of a dissertation, and we were allowed to reuse two out of the three in our actual dissertation when the time came.

I was thinking I could reply to Aaronsen's comments, addressing the concerns that had been voiced, and do it as my theory track paper, diving deeper into radical feminist theory.

The paper that had received these comments was my term paper from last fall's seminar, "Feminist Theory," and the paper I had written was titled "The Socialization and Education of Children." In it, I had looked at how children are shaped into gender-specific identities and fitted into social roles that perpetuate the social system called patriarchy, drawing upon multiple different types of feminist theory both as a way of showing Dr. Aaronsen that I understood the different versions as taught to us and to highlight my preference for radical feminist theory as the most useful theory type.

The subject matter, meanwhile, was inspired by a different course that I had also taken, titled "Socialization and the Self," which had presented an in-depth overview of how the field of sociology thinks of the process, as reflected in sociological theory.

Loosely speaking, sociology tended to think of individuals as blank slates, fully formed by the social processes that teach them who to be, how to be, what things in life matter, what things mean. I saw a problem with that. If the contents of people's heads (and hearts) were always determined by society—social determinism—then by what mechanism could people arrive at a critical perspective on the society of which they were a part?

Basically, they *wouldn't*. If some glitch in the institutional behaviors somehow evoked that kind of rebelliousness, the institutions would modify until a stable situation arose that didn't and it would cease to happen.

And this would have nothing to do with being a free or perfect or fair society, that was the more important point, really: if the contents of people's heads were just a passive consequence of socialization, that— by definition—included any conceivable *notions* of fairness or equality or justice or freedom, or even more fundamentally the *notion* that such things were desirable characteristics in the first place. For a stable system to arise that didn't inherently program people to be rebellious, all that would need to evolve would be a sufficient internal consistency of ideology.

This social determinism was far more socially conservative than it might appear on the surface. It wasn't merely that it couldn't explain the process by which individuals would ever come to question the norms with which they were raised. That was of legitimate but passing concern. The real problem was that it left no space for anyone to say that any social situation was *better* than any other.

In essence it not only said that if you had switched the infants Martin Luther King and Adolf Hitler at birth, the identical social experiences would have produced a tyrannical genocidal dictator out of King and a social justice leader of Hitler; it *also* said *to you*, the observer (or sociologist) studying any of this, *you* could not anchor the claim that the social justice efforts of Martin Luther King were better for society than the control-seizing efforts of Adolf Hitler. You could not value liberty and equality and individual freedom over authoritarianism, coercion, and complete subservience of the individual to the state.

Instead your own theoretical matrix would prompt you to study the specific elements of your own socialization and education that had led you to *think of* those first set of attributes as somehow superior and to consider them as no more than the outcome of how you yourself had been socialized.

I saw that the Marx-inspired kinds of analysis that I'd encountered at Old Brookville—including the "socialist feminism" that Heidi Hartmann had praised in that article that Dr. Baxwood had given me to read—didn't deal with any of this. It ignored the problem. It, too, treated individuals as passive puppets of their social environment and didn't delve into how "class consciousness," to use the socialist-marxist term for it, could ever happen.

But radical feminist theory did. And I intended to write about that.

FALL 1987—SENIOR YEAR

I returned to Old Brookville campus from my Washington DC adventures to find a letter waiting for me from the APEL committee. After reviewing my portfolio and reading *The Amazon's Brother,* they were awarding me four credits in feminist theory, four credits in autobiographical writing, and four credits in creative writing for a total of twelve, definitely sufficient for me to graduate this year.

My internship at the Coalition Against Domestic Violence was a lot more pleasant and productive than the attempted summer internship at Center for Creative Nonviolence had been. Like Carol down in Washington, Molly and Joan had a backlog of unfiled paperwork, and beyond that, they had a well-stuffed four-drawer file cabinet that had not been maintained in an orderly fashion, so I began my stint there by pulling everything out, making notes about what was in each folder and which cabinet each folder was in, and then alphabetizing everything. I also generated an index which cross-referenced every file by several other titles or descriptions that someone might be looking for it by. The people at the Coalition were appreciative and made me feel like I was making a useful contribution.

Then I was handed a provocative article by McNeely and Robinson-Simpson titled "The Truth About Domestic Violence," and asked to read it and to make suggestions for a rebuttal argument. I chased down all the referenced citations and read other comments on the research and then wrote a response which the organization could use as the basis of a reply article. They ended up using large chunks of what I'd written with just minor grammatical modifications, added some statements, and exchanged some correspondence with an academic in Wisconsin, Daniel Saunders, who had already penned a rebuttal article.

Meanwhile, I worked with Psychology professor Dr. Dixon to

do my first research project. I wanted to interview heterosexual sissy guys and heterosexual butch gals about whether they had been made to feel like they had to choose between their sissy or butch expression of themselves and heterosexual viability, and the ways in which they'd found it complicated to negotiate heterosexual connections in their lives.

I ran ads in the *Catalyst* and announcements were made in psychology and women's studies classrooms, and I ended up with about fourteen interested people. Some did not complete the interviews or else turned out to have misunderstood the description of what I was looking for, but I did open-ended interviews with follow-up questions with eight subjects and wrote it up for the Psychology Research special seminars class.

It wasn't enough, I needed a hundred times that many people to be able to describe a population I could call "us," or to draw many conclusions, but it was good to make the initial attempt and to have dipped my toe in the water of this kind of research at least.

I dropped in on Cowboy and Mary, who were now living in Section 8 housing in Spanish Harlem, 116th Street off Lexington Avenue in Manhattan. Cowboy was trying to get a license to drive a cab, and they'd bought an old used car which they showed me and drove me around in. Except for their friend Jay Richardson, they weren't really in contact with anyone from the shelter / RCCA days. We reminisced about people we'd once known and things we'd done.

In the upstairs halls of Academic Village the various departments had their departmental offices. Heading back from the American Studies offices, I was greeted by a student I remembered from one of the courses in American Studies that I'd taken. It was someone I had a good impression of but I couldn't conjure up the name and admitted this to her. "Donna Mason," she said and shook my hand. "There's no reason you'd necessarily remember me, because I don't often say very much in class. Unlike you. I knew who you were immediately. We were in American People I and II together and you always had interesting comments and good questions." I told her I definitely remembered her, I was just awfully bad with names and faces; but I remembered her with positive associations from class.

I mentioned that I had come up looking for Ros Baxwood to ask her something about my internship, and Donna asked where I was doing it, and when I said I was at the Coalition Against Domestic Violence, her face lit up in amazement, "What a coincidence! That's where I work! Of course, you're probably at the coalition office, with Joan Cucina?" I confirmed that. "I work in the shelter itself, with the battered women who have left their situation and need a place to be safe while they sort their life out." We stood there talking for maybe half an hour, about patriarchy and the family, about relationships, about physical violence and how women's supportive emotional strengths and their role lays the foundation for the inclination to feel responsible for one's batterer and to try to "fix" him instead of leaving him, and SUNY in general and American Studies in general.

"Hey," she suggested. "I'm really starving, do you...I hope I'm not being too forward but would you join me for lunch?" She indicated that she had her car with her and that she had a place in mind in Roslyn, a nice cozy little tavern with a good menu. I was happy to accept and continue the conversation, and I was thoroughly enjoying being with her. On arrival we got a table and kept going, comparing notes and going over our respective past histories.

We had some drinks with our meal and were both kind of effusive and well cheered and our faces flushed when it came time to leave, and she asked if she could show me where she lived, in Glen Cove. As long as we were pretty close to it from where we were and all. And upon arrival invited me in, up the outside steps that went to a second story entrance and then into the big open room that constituted her apartment. "Umm, I...I'm really enjoying being with you a lot, and, umm, I want you to know that I'd ideally want the connection to continue and to keep on getting to know you...," I blathered awkwardly.

Donna grinned a wicked mocking sort of grin, "Are you asking whether I'll respect you in the morning if you sleep with me?" I blushed and we both laughed. "Umm yeah actually." She stepped up to me. "You guess right. That's why I brought you here. And I love it that you said that." And she put her arms around me and I reciprocated and we kissed and she led me over to her bed.

Donna was interested in my research project. She said she'd reached conclusions of her own about the politics of personality and gender. "I hate the way for men, for lots of men anyway, that their whole sense of personal identity is all about proving they are *not* women. Afraid of being like us, of having the same characteristics as us, of being seen by other men as being like a woman."

I nodded, "Like y'all have cooties or something?"

She laughed, "Exactly! I think it is such a good thing when a guy is cool with his, I hate to call it 'feminine side,' I mean the part of who he is that is associated with women, though."

I began going to the library and investigating graduate schools where I could continue my work in women's studies. What I found was discouraging. There were a handful of masters degree programs, but they didn't provide any funding. I had no source of income and at a minimum would need some kind of financial aid and preferably funding. Doctoral programs were more inclined to fund their students but there were even fewer of those: University of California at Santa Cruz had some kind of academic department called "History of Consciousness" which specifically had a feminist studies concentration, and that looked like the most promising one; then there was Case Western Reserve University which had an American Studies department offering a women's studies concentration for the PhD, and that looked worth applying for; then there was the Ohio State University, which was mentioned as a possibility because they had an option for creating your own personalized course of study; so even though they didn't specifically offer a PhD in feminist studies or women's studies, an individual student could create one there.

I applied to all three, sending in college transcripts and high school transcripts and paying application fees and writing essays and statements of purpose. I thought I would look good on paper myself, being one of presumably only a few male students who wanted to pursue a trajectory in women's studies and had already done well in that field at the undergraduate level, and because I had a specific social justice agenda and could put it into words. That I wanted to make an academic career on the social experience of the heterosexual sissy.

In late May, the Ohio State University said that my application process had been discontinued because something they had requested— an official transcript from the first college I'd attended but from which I'd withdrawn during my first semester, the University of Mississippi— had not been provided. I wasn't too concerned, as I had been thinking of them as the backup to the backup plan, a place to go if for some reason neither of the other two took me on. But I really wanted to attend a school where I would be in a women's studies graduate curriculum, not just a place where I could pursue it on my own. I wanted the connections with other people doing women's studies.

Then in early June, I got correspondence from Case Western Reserve University explaining that the former American Studies department was being absorbed into the History department. I had been accepted as a graduate student into American Studies, but now it no longer existed, and I was hereby informed that I could still attend and still pursue the course of study for which I had been accepted, and could obtain my PhD within those legacy parameters, but there would be no funding, as the History department could only fund those grad students who had applied as History PhD seekers.

My parents came out to see me graduate. I was hugged and praised, and told that I had made them both proud. Donna, who would be graduating a year behind me, sat with us and cheered our class on. I introduced Donna as a new friend. We hadn't discussed exactly what it was that we had, but had continued to spent time together. Jenna came to see me graduate as well. I was happy to see her again but felt awkward, not knowing what was appropriate any more. She told me she was glad I had been in her life and I deserved my moment of triumph and more to come. I introduced her to Donna and my parents but that felt a little awkward too.

My folks invited me to join them for a couple weeks in Hilton Head for summer vacation. I asked if they'd buy me a bus ticket that would let me go out to Santa Cruz, departing from Hilton Head but coming back to Old Brookville, and they said they'd be happy to. I spent a week on the beach, occasionally doing a turn in the kitchen, insisting on showing my parents some meals different from what they'd taught me to cook, and my mom in particular praised chicken parmesan as a very lovely dish. Then I hopped on the bus and rode westward.

I was unable to meet with any of the students in the Santa Cruz PhD program. The departmental secretary said most of them lived in their own homes and only came to campus to turn in materials or to lecture. "Almost nobody gets in unless they already have at least one PhD in some other field, you know. This is a very exclusive program.

They only admit maybe five or six new people each semester." I still thought I was a sufficiently rare prospect overall that I stood a chance.

"Oh, well, have you read some of the materials by our professors? I recommend that you take a look at the books by Teresa de Lauretis, she's the professor most responsible for the program's existence," the departmental secretary told me.

So I went to the library and found a copy of *Alice Doesn't* by Teresa de Lauretis and found myself confronting something unrecognizably different from anything I'd previously encountered that identified itself as feminist theory.

I read some other materials written *about* de Lauretis. She was being called a "semiotics" or "poststructuralist" feminist firebrand, a leader in a new form of feminist theory that was all about ripping apart established concepts as a means of challenging the prevailing patriarchal and hegemonic discourse. I kept looking for some sense of what she believed or was asserting to be true. *Alice Doesn't* began with a parable about people chasing a woman's elusive spectral form and not catching it, and then building a city where they'd seen it, in which she herself didn't reside, and this was somehow significant, somehow symbolic of how things were about being a woman. I didn't have hours and hours to keep trying to parse it, but I found the whole experience offputting and I didn't have a good feeling when my time was up and I had to leave for the east coast.

Donna suggested that I spend the rest of the summer with her in her apartment in Glen Cove, since once again I had no place to go when classes let out.

"If you can chip in for rent, that would be good, but don't worry about it, you being there isn't going to cost me anything. If you can split the cost of food, that would make more difference."

"Okay, let me see what I can find. I haven't done the job search thing in a while, but I'm a college graduate now."

I applied for a job with Greenpeace but it turned out to be door to door fundraising, and not something for which I had a talent. There were limited opportunities to get office jobs in Glen Cove where I could leverage my typing and organizing skills.

I saw a sign that an Italian restaurant close to campus was looking for a dishwasher, and told them I'd worked kitchens in the past, and they took me on. So all summer Donna would drop me off on her way to her own job, and pick me up in the evening.

Sure enough, University of Cal at Santa Cruz declined my application for admission to the program, and in midsummer I faced the worrisome prospect of nowhere to go.

Dr. Rosencranz was in the American Studies office that summer and asked how I was doing and I told her. "Let me do some investigation, and get back to you," she told me.

Later, she said "Apply to become a PhD student in Sociology at SUNY Setauket. They won't fund you because the time frame for selecting funded students has passed. But apply for the joint program in Sociology and Social Work. The Social Work department will fund you for your first year within the joint program, and the next year you can get funding from Sociology. I think you'll probably get in."

So I did, writing the essays and statements and arranging for my transcripts to be sent in, and in late July, SUNY's Setauket University accepted me into the special joint program of Sociology and Social Work, where I would be a joint major and would receive both a PhD in Sociology and an MSW in Social Work, assuming I completed all of my courses of study.

"But I want to do women's studies," I whimpered to Dr. Rosencranz. "I don't know anything about sociology!"

"Sociology is pretty open to any kind of social theory," she said. "And there's a man on the faculty, Dr. George Aaronsen, who has made a name for himself as one of the leading male voices supporting feminism and the advancement of feminist theory."

Oh really?!

Well, that would address the concern I had about being a male pursuing feminist studies. If there were a male faculty member there doing feminist material, that ground had already been broken. And I'd have an ally. This was going to be all right.

"Hello?"

"Hello," I said. "I got this number from off campus housing...I'll be starting in the fall. You're looking for another student to split the rent?"

"We are. Would you like to come by and look at it? Could you come tomorrow evening after seven? My name is Padma. I can meet you then."

I confirmed the arrangements and the next day drove my decrepitated, recently purchased used Toyota, out east to Cedar Beach.

"Hi Derek," Padma greeted me from the driveway. "Park over here on this side, the neighbors down there hate it if we block their part of the driveway. We have this house rented until next summer." She aimed a thumb back over her shoulder at the boyish-looking fellow who had followed her out. "This is Chris. And Sachi is inside. Each of us has a room."

Chris nodded in my direction. "There's a fourth person, Amy, who is taking a room at the top of the stairs, but she isn't here yet. She's an undergraduate. She won't be moving in until later in the semester, she said."

Padma added, "Your room is also upstairs. Come on in and we'll show you around."

The house was cute, all blond wood and nautical trimmings, and the setting was utterly gorgeous: from the front of the house, the driveway led to Harbor Beach Road and, directly across it, there was a bay full of driftwood and birds and little pools of water. The back yard sloped down to the beach with Long Island Sound lapping at the sand's edge and, way off in the distance, the shoreline cliffs of Connecticut.

The room that would be mine was outfitted as some kid's room, with kitschy cartoon ceramic tschochkes of fishermen and commercially embroidered throw pillows with airplanes and foam footballs on the shelves. The bed looked comfortable; I tried it and it was solid and supportive.

I really liked the idea of living with other grad students. We'd live together and be our own little community and cook together and discuss our respective studies. It would be great!

I met Sachi. "Sabyasachi Puthenveedu," he told me. He and Padma Sikhar were from India. Chris Weber was from here but had met Padma while an exchange student and the three of them had become a solid friendship during his stay in India, and now they had come back to the US to pursue their studies at Setauket University. Sachi was pursing an engineering degree. Chris and Padma were both English majors.

I said I was definitely interested and they said they had to discuss it amongst themselves and that they had at least one more person who wanted to come see the room, but they'd get back to me shortly.

Later that evening Padma called me and said the room was mine.

My courses were a mixture of required courses from the Department of Social Welfare and a required course from the Department of Sociology plus two electives, for which I picked Feminist Theory with Dr. Aaronsen and Socialization and the Self with Dr. Felthauser. I also had a field placement in social work with the Sayville Project, a psychiatric-rights-oriented program for people with a history of psychiatric incarceration.

I came in to meet with the folks at Sayville Project and they were enthusiastic about having an intern who identified as a militant schizophrenic and escaped mental patient.

Along with the other PAR (program planning, administration, and research) social work first year students, I was in Lynne Slocumb's seminar, which quickly shaped up to be a brainstorming and mutual support group for interns to discuss our field placements and what we were trying to accomplish there.

If there was a class that felt designed to weed people out, a deliberately difficult course set up to test us from the outset, it was Statistics and Methods, the required Sociology class.

It didn't start off too bad, although it began with a formal and somewhat stuffy tone. We had two instructors, Dr. Collier and Dr. Holcombe, with Collier clearly in charge. We were seated at a long table, with students on either side, all arrayed face to face, with the professors down at one end next to the chalkboard.

Dr. Collier introduced himself and Dr. Holcombe, then narrated, "Look around you. This is your cohort. You are in for some difficult years, but we hope rewarding years, and you will come to think of your cohort as your team. You will be passing through some of the same experiences at roughly the same time. I still maintain contact with members of my own cohort and it's been, well never mind how many years it's been. I don't like to dwell on that. But I still correspond with people who were in my cohort, and so I imagine does Dr. Holcombe." Dr. Holcombe gave a nod. "So," continued Dr. Collier, "I'd like to go around the table and have each of you introduce yourselves, and since this is Research Methods, to identify any sociology research study that you particularly admire or that you feel had a significant impact in the field." He pointed to the person at the far end of my side of the table and indicates that she should begin.

"Hi, everyone. My name is Lee Chase, umm, Leona Chase, and I was at Dowling for my BA. My favorite, well one of my most admired research projects I guess, was Dr. Barbara Ehrenreich's 'For Her Own Good' about women and the medical health system."

Collier scowled. "And what was it that you liked about Dr. Ehrenreich's...research?"

Leona Chase spread her hands to the side expansively. "She showed how our assumptions about medicine need to be challenged, and the role of the 'male expert' and how authority, like medical authority, needs to be rethought and questioned."

"If you ask me, this is a good example of what good sociological research is *not,"* Dr. Collier replied, glaring. "A good sociological research project should not be a polemic, an invocation to take up a viewpoint that is supported by a thin sprinkling of data that is not sufficient to derive the conclusions that the author states. But I'm glad to have this so quickly on the table for us to discuss because I did want to discuss that, and I'll circle back to that point in a bit. I apologize, Ms. Chase, and welcome to the class. I put you on the spot and I didn't mean to attack you. It's not easy being the one who goes first. And you sir?" he said, indicating the student to my left.

"Hi, I'm Rafe, Rafael Ortiz. I was here at Setauket as an undergrad. It's nice to meet you," he said, glancing around the table with a smile. "I'm going to say, for my favorite piece of research in sociology, I admire Mark Fenstermacher's study on weak social ties."

Dr. Collier nodded his assent. "Dr. Fenstermacher is a colleague of ours here on the faculty. It's a good choice. It focuses on a specific question and assesses the matter strictly from an empirical research perspective. I'm sure he would be pleased to hear his paper mentioned in this context."

Dr. Collier glanced in my direction. I was next. "Hi," I said, "my name's Derek Turner. I'm a women's studies graduate from the SUNY Old Brookville campus here on the island, and I'm interested in feminist theory. I haven't devoted all that much attention to research, at least so far, but I loved that, who was it, umm, Rosencranz?...who did that

'Being Insane...I mean 'Being Sane in Insane Places' article."

"A classic. You're referring to Rosenhan's 'Being Sane in Insane Places'. Welcome, Mr. Turner. Good choice."

Good, because it's the only thing I could think of.

"Hello. I'm Jerry Wiesenthal. I did my undergrad at Kansas State. Umm, I'll go with the Asch conformity study."

"I'm Diane Kuhl, that's 'K U H L,' not 'C O O L,' I got my degree in Anthropology and Social Psychology at Five Towns College. I'm sorry but I can't think of any sociological research study that has stuck in my mind."

The round robin continued down our side of the table and up the other side. An older woman across from me kept me from being the only person in our cohort who didn't appear to be in their twenties. She introduced herself as Tess Lautenburg and described returning to school after her children were born. She named a research project on voting behavior that I wasn't familiar with.

I wasn't required to take the Classical and Contemporary Sociological Theory courses in my first year. The rest of my cohort had to, but because I was in the joint program that was waived until the following year.

But I was very happily signed up for Dr. Aaaronsen's class, "Feminist Theory." It was the first time it was being offered, and it was of course central to my interests. So not only had I managed to get myself (however belatedly) into an academic program where a male professor had established that male people could participate in feminist thought—and that feminist thought in turn was significant and relevant to social analysis—I was also getting to kick off my career as a grad student by being in his feminist theory course.

"We are going to study the many different kinds of feminist theory over the course of this year," Aaronsen told us on the first day. "So I'm dividing this semester's course into units, one on each of the several subtypes of theory that feminists have used to analyze women's situation in society. We will start with liberal feminism, then psychoanalytic feminism. We'll finish the first half of the semester with a unit on Marxist feminism. After midterms we'll do socialist feminism, and then to complete our tour we will do a unit at the end on poststructuralist feminism."

I approached him after class. "Hi, I'm Derek Turner, and I was a women's studies major at Old Brookville, and I'm very happy to finally be in a feminist theory class. And I came here specifically to do feminist studies as my focus in sociology. Hey, listen, I notice you didn't mention radical feminism. Are you leaving that out? It seems like an important theory type..."

Dr. Aaronsen rocked back on his heels a bit, then nodded. "You are right. That is an omission. I think I'm going to have to modify my course structure, that's an important viewpoint that should be covered. Thanks for bringing that to my attention, and hey, it's great to have you in my class."

"I'm really getting tired of Dr. Collier's cranky 'Uncle Bruce' act, that whole 'I know better than you young people' thing he's got going," Diane announced as she led the way into our grad student office. We'd just finished another session in Stats & Methods.

"Yeah," Rob agreed, dropping his books on his desk and then turning around and sitting on it to face us. "He's really toxic. Every time any of us says anything about feminism or race issues, he jumps in and tries to prove we're wrong and we don't know what we're talking about."

"He's the guy on the corner who yells at the kids for walking on his lawn," Rafe said.

"I'm getting tired of it too," I said as I slipped into my seat. "It's not a level playing field. He's supposed to be teaching research methods, not lecturing about beliefs and attitudes, and if he's going to introduce *his* viewpoints it isn't fair for him to shut down people who disagree with him on it."

"He's got an attitude about economic inequality too," Rafe observed. "He's said a lot of things that basically add up to saying anyone could get ahead if they just tried."

"He's not all that stodgy about race and ethnicity," Jerry remarked.

"True, but it's feminists who really got his panties in a knot," Rob replied.

"I'm tired of being spoken to like I'm a misbehaving child," Diane said.

"You think we should go as a group to the department chair and complain about it?" I asked.

The others shook their heads unhappily. "Dr. Tomlin? He isn't going to do anything. Collier has been here forever and Tomlin's not going to cross him," Rob said.

Diane nodded. "The other faculty know how he is, but their attitude is, 'He's paid his dues and he gets to be that way. We haven't, and we have to put up with it'."

Donna came out to spend the weekend with me about once a month, and I'd go to her place in Glen Cove about that often. As of the time I had first started up at Setauket, we hadn't really discussed "us." I belatedly realized from things she said later that she'd sort of expected me to move on with my life once I started attending there, but she was happy that I still wanted to see her even without the convenience factor. Nevertheless, she sometimes felt that once she was out of my sight, she was out of my mind and that I would forget about her for long stretches and then expect to pick up where we left off when we did get together.

I wasn't clear on what she wanted, what she would like to change. We were both busy and we no longer lived together where we'd be in proximity very often with no effort.

I thought I called her more or less as often as she called me...I thought about it...maybe that wasn't really true. Did I tend to wait long enough that she would often end up calling me before I got around to calling her? I vowed to call her more often. Still, I did reach out to her often enough that it wasn't a huge disparity.

And we had spoken a few times about commitments and expectations and she'd always said she did not need or expect a traditional commitment. But it seemed like she still felt underappreciated in some sense though.

Dr. Kevin Holcombe was at the blackboard; Dr. Collier sat passively at the table with us while Holcombe went over the statistical methodology we were covering in this chapter.

"Okay now the nice thing about chi square is you have to remember that the, hum chalk is missing, why don't they ever put chalk over here on this blackboard? ...dependencies can exist, if you read the chapter seven, did everyone read chapter seven? Mark Ewling did that study, he was an associate of a friend of mine, actually, did you know you could get grants from Dept of Health and Human Services for studies like that? Anyway, on this axis, if you...reconsider your grant proposals if you haven't applied to public, oh here's the chalk, *divide* this, I know I did assign chapter seven, please students, read what has been assigned before coming to class, okay see how..."

Dr. Holcombe turned his back to us and drew some equations in chalk on the blackboard

"...and that tells you it's statistically relevant. Yes, Mr. Turner, you have a question?"

"I'm sorry," I apologized. "I'm lost here again. What's the difference between chi square and that gamma thing you were talking about earlier? Why would you use one and not the other?"

Dr. Holcombe looked perplexed, as if I'd asked him why you'd cook your bacon but wouldn't cook your ice cream. "Well, you don't use gamma in situations where your model has a null hypothesis and you're not concerned with the order. Or actually you *could* but it depends on what your purpose is. Listen, I'm sorry if you're getting lost here, but if you need to study more in order to keep up, I suggest you do, I really need to move on since I have the whole class here that I have to teach."

Dr. Collier nodded his approval. I sighed.

Tess came alongside me in the hallway as I left. "It's not just you. My eyes are glazing over. I don't feel like I'm understanding more than about half of this stuff, and it feels like numerology, not science."

Rob joined us. "Hey Derek, thanks for speaking up. I was wondering the same thing. I gotta say, Collier is offensive and annoying but Holcombe is incomprehensible. It's like we're all scared to admit we don't understand this stuff because we don't want to look stupid."

During that first semester, I was exposed to how the academic field of sociology thinks of the learning process, the process by which people are brought into membership in the society, learning the language and concepts and, along with it, the attitudes and belief systems of their culture. I got that from Dr. Felthauser's "Socialization and the Self" class, which presented a wide range of viewpoints, but the "blank slate" perspective definitely seemed to predominate, both in conservative and more politicized theories.

There was another set of theories that were far less inclined to treat people as empty receptacles into which culture gets inserted. These were dubbed the "interactionist" sociological theories. They tended to focus on small-level processes, paying attention to step by step situational dynamics so as to dissect out how, exactly, socialization occurs.

All the while, I was in Aaronsen's class, of course, where all the flavors of feminist theory had to explain patriarchy and women's oppression. All of them dealt with the notion that there had been (and still were) a lot of taken-for-granted notions about how women and men were different, which included men's "natural" qualifications for being in charge and occupying positions of social authority.

Those old notions were also chockfull of attitudes about personality characteristics and behavior considered typical and appropriate for each sex, and these were the things I would have to delve into in order to pursue my interest in doing an academic career about the identity of the sissy, the male feminine person who violated those assumptions.

Aaronsen's presentation of Marxist feminism clarified my sense that it didn't contain useful tools for explaining how a sex role nonconformist would come to exist. Like the other big structural theories, it treated all individuals as passive receptacles of their socialization. It also wasn't interested in them. It was all about classes of people in relationship to other classes of people.

Only the psychoanalytic feminism unit paid a lot of attention to exactly how individuals came to be constituted. But like the interactionist sociological theories I was encountering in Felthauser's class, these psychoanalytic theories didn't tend to address social structures except in a vague way at the end, where they'd say things like "In order for the relationship between the sexes, including the power inequality between men and women, to be addressed, the centrality of the mother figure would have to be altered in people's individual lives."

When Dr. Aaronsen got to the unit he had shoehorned in on radical feminism, he used Susan Griffin and Mary Field Belenkey and basically portrayed radical feminists as people who believed women had a different, and inherently better, nature than men did. So everything associated with men, including their values and priorities and personality characteristics, were The Enemy, definitely bad, and to be done away with. Aaronsen acknowledged that radical feminists didn't all think that men were as they were by nature. He said radical feminists believed culture was evil and that male nature was created by culture, but that women had been kept out of culture and were more akin to a natural state, which was morally superior. I got other more nuanced things out of the Belenkey material than he was teaching, and would have chosen other texts to begin with.

Laura Wahlberg scowled at me. "I don't get it. I thought you cared about these issues. And now you've got a field placement at Sayville Project, this is a chance to really make a difference! But it sounds to me like you're just phoning it in!"

"Look, I'm frustrated with the situation myself," I retorted. "I was so fired up to be able to be a social work intern at a place where they use phrases like 'psychiatric oppression' and 'patients' rights' and they're already on the same page with us about the right to refuse treatment..."

"And the lies that the psychiatric and pharmaceutical establishments tell about so-called 'chemical imbalances,' it's not just right to refuse, it's the right to not be lied to when the liars are designated as medical experts, don't forget that!"

"...and yeah, informed consent, all that, listen, I do care and I was very excited. The social workers that run Sayville Project really care, too. But the clients who come in are nearly all over sixty, most of them were kept locked up and drugged up in Pilgrim State or King's Park for years and years, and now they're in community housing."

"Well, gee, I hope when I get to be sixty, I don't get written off as too old to be worth caring about."

"You know that's not what I mean!" I glared back at her, taking a moment to assemble what I wanted to say, what I was trying to explain, in my head before speaking again. Laura waited, scowling, arms crossed.

"Okay...imagine a meeting, a regularly scheduled meeting of the Sayville clients, what they call the 'psychosocial club,' all right? So Karen welcomes them in and gets them all to sign in, and then she tells everyone there was a new court case that says judges can't combine whether or not you're dangerous with whether or not you lack capacity to make your own medical decisions, and isn't that great news for the psychiatric survivors' community? And then Nancy makes a presentation about how if anyone in the group ever gets threatened with eviction for not taking whatever meds have been prescribed, Sayville Project will go with them to court and try to get a lawyer. Then they have *me* go up and talk about my own experiences with my rights being taken away in psychiatric institutions and how I've gone to demonstrations and spoken out at Department of Health public meetings.

"So everyone is quiet for a while. And Nancy asks if anyone else wants to say anything. And after a moment Marty says 'How about them Mets, huh?' And Agnes tells us all about going shopping at Grand Union and how selfish this other woman was, for not getting her shopping cart out of the aisle.

"The clients show up to socialize with each other. They talk with each other about their week, what's been happening, who they saw doing what with whom, what they ate, and so on. They don't come to Sayville Project to organize and defend their rights. That's *our* agenda. We present as much of that as we can, but at some point we have to let them have their meeting, I mean it *is* their meeting. They wouldn't keep coming if we insisted on force-feeding them three hours per week of anti-psychiatric radical politics, and even if we did, that's not empowerment.

"For most of them, whatever they felt when they first got locked up and labeled with a psych diagnosis, that happened years ago, decades ago, and they've had the stuffing beaten out of them, you know that, the system punishes you for getting angry, until you learn not to care, or not to expect it to be any different.

"And they *don't*. I mean, they don't contradict us and say 'Oh no, you got it all wrong, my psychiatrist helps me,' or 'Oh no, I need my drugs, they help me'. They say 'Well you're right but if I don't take them they'll lock me up,' which is *true*, and Sayville Project doesn't have a team of free lawyers ready to jump in. We have social workers who are willing to go to court with them or even carry protest signs and walk around outside.

"And we are willing to. I'm willing to get arrested and try to get the newspapers and TV to pay attention. But as long as they're saying, I mean as long as the clients are saying 'I just want to keep my head down, I can't afford to get in any trouble,' we can't do much.

"And there's a limited, umm, you know, a limit on how appropriate it is to tell them they *should* be taking those risks, make a stand, make a difference for psychiatric rights for everyone, when they'd rather play games and listen to 'Sing Along With Mitch' on the record player. It *would* put them at risk to stand up to this."

Laura had let me monologue without interrupting. Now she said, "If that's how it is, then you need to attract a different population. If the people who are outraged and want to fight aren't coming to the meeting, you need to go out and *find* them."

I nodded. "I know. I've been trying to push for that in our agency meetings. But the social workers don't want to abandon the clients we have, and the Mental Health Association funding doesn't give us a budget for outreach beyond the housing area these folks come from. And it's basically an old dumping ground for discharged long-term psych patients, so that's who we've got."

Lynne Slocumb's seminar on Program Planning and Development met on Tuesdays. She encouraged us to talk about our frustrations and concerns at our field placements, and to let this seminar function as a combination of strategizing and mutual emotional support and gripe sessioning for those of us in our first year as social work students.

"I've rewritten this grant proposal three times," Cindy complained, "and he still says it doesn't look professional! But he won't say specifically what he thinks is wrong with it."

"Bring it in," Slocumb replied. "I'll look at it and we can have other faculty take a look and if necessary we'll write a letter if we don't see any shortcomings."

"I can't get a straight answer about my hours! They don't have me coming in enough to meet the minimum required for getting credit for the field placement, and I don't know what to do!" Mark complained.

"Put it in writing," Donna suggested. "Then you've documented that you've made every effort on your end. Keep a copy for your file."

"Yeah, good idea," Irene added. "And make sure the school here is officially informed. Get them to either say on paper that you'll still get credit if it's not your fault, or else assign you a different field placement."

"I have an issue," I told the group. "The funding sources have a measure for whether we're serving the clients as described in the proposal, but it's basically getting an attendance signature. We're not really doing what the proposal originally said, advocacy and empowerment work. Instead, a team of social workers goes out to each supported living facility and they bring refreshments, and the clients sign an attendance form before they can get any. They're supposed to discuss whether the facility where they live is stepping on their rights as tenants, but that's not happening, so we're collecting signatures for Kool-Aid pouring. I mean that's what it amounts to. Here, sign your name and today's date and we'll let you have cookies and fruit punch. The people at the agency feel like we can't stop doing that or the funding sources will say it's breach of contract, and that they won't pay us to go out and try to find clients who actually want to know about their rights and get help with that, because the looking process and advertising it and all that won't collect any signatures to prove we're doing stuff."

"Yeah, I hear you," Slocumb said. She smiled sadly. "Kool-Aid pouring. I think I'm going to use that phrase for it from now on. Anyway, there's a lot of that in social work. Of doing the things that can be measured which aren't the real work, because the people paying for it want to see something measurable, something that looks like progress or involvement, in exchange for their money. I think there's an art, a skill at finding ways of doing the real work even when it can't be measured, and finding ways of getting the measured and counted stuff done without letting it take up all your time and energy. You have to find that. Do your Kool-Aid pouring but get it over with and don't let it get in your way. Don't let Kool-Aid pouring become a priority to the point that you aren't doing the real work."

The Department of Sociology occupied the fourth floor of a grey and coldly functional building known as the Social Behavioral Sciences building. I came back to our office after one more Collier and Holcombe class in which we were again subjected to editorial essays about how a lot of socially progressive notions that purported to be 'social science' were nothing but unanchored frothy opinion, and that real social science was empirical and firmly founded on facts. I took a piece of goldenrod-colored construction paper and a batch of ink pens and colored highlighters and made a poster, the left side of which stated "YOU ARE NOW LEAVING THE CENTER FOR SOCIAL-BEHAVIORAL SCIENCES" in authoritative-looking chunky capital letters, and to its right, in an eclectic mix of angular and curvy and artsy mixed-case deco lettering, "and entering the Antisocial, Misbehavioral *Periphery* of the Social Arts." Then I taped it to our office door.

On the following Thursday, Tess followed me out of Collier's classroom and asked if I'd been the one to create the poster, and, when I nodded, said, "I wanted to tell you I like it, it really nails the unquestioned assumptions that often get made here about normativity and mainstream experiences and what constitutes science."

I thanked her, then told her, "We had a really arrogant teacher for public speaking when I was an undergrad. Collier does the same thing that guy used to do, which is to use countercultural or socially progressive authors whenever he wants to make a point about the technique not being right. In Collier's class, saying that the research design has flaws. Then when someone in the class replies to defend the purpose or the social importance of what those authors were trying to say, he gets to say 'that's off topic, we're only discussing research methodology'. It's deliberate. He never picks some stuffy boring study like whether the switch from paper address books to computer contact databases has an effect on the size of people's professional social network when he wants to hold up an example of the wrong way to set up our research. He always picks something he disagrees with."

When the time came for us to sign up for the classes we were taking in the next semester, I didn't sign up for part two of the year-long required Statistics and Methods course. Dr. Tomlin, the current head of the Sociology Department, waved me over and mentioned that I'd apparently neglected to do so and that I should rectify that.

"I didn't forget. I've decided not to take it. I know it's a requirement of the program that I take Statistics and Methods, but there's no requirement that I take them during my first year, and I've decided to postpone it until at least next year."

Tomlin stared back at me in surprise. After a couple beats, he said, "Would you mind writing a memo to the department explaining your decision, for your file?"

So I said that I would.

Attn: Department of Sociology
Subject: Statistics and Methods / Derek Turner / Spring 1990

When I applied to be accepted by the Department of Sociology as a graduate student in pursuit of the PhD, it was made clear to me that I needed to take and pass the year-long course "Statistics and Methods," because this course laid a foundation, providing a set of understandings and skills that a person would need in order to pursue a professional academic career in Sociology.

Hence I can see why the departmental faculty may have some concerns occasioned by my decision not to take Part II of this course of instruction along with the rest of my cohort this spring.

Briefly, although I am maintaining an A minus average at the end of Part I, I understand no more than a smattering of what is being taught. I am able, in a limited sense, to follow procedural recipes to analyze a dataset and obtain assorted statistical values. But I seldom know what they mean, nor do I often understand a reason for making any given one of these assessments.

My attempts to have this more clearly explained to me in the classroom have not met with any success.

My A minus grade is less a product of my success as a student than it is a reflection of the instructor's technique of grading on the curve, of providing a passing grade on any given test to at least the upper half of the scores that the students attained on it. So while that mark does not reassure me in any way that I'm actually learning the material at an acceptable rate and to a sufficient degree, it does support my contention that the problem lies not with my unwillingness to apply myself as a student but with the inability of the professors to teach the material. While I am sure that professors Collier and Holcombe have many qualifications and skills that make them an asset to the Department of Sociology, I doubt that their primary expertise lies with their performance as educators.

If this coursework is fundamental to my future in Sociology, I see no purpose in continuing in coursework from which I'm not gaining that foundation, and to that end I am suspending my attendance in Statistics and Methods until such time as it is offered by personnel who are able to teach the material.

Toward the end of the semester I started pulling together two papers. The really formidable one I titled "Coercion"; it was about non-mutual socialization processes. This socialization wasn't designed to let children (or other individuals) affect their social environment but were designed to bring children (and other individuals) into compliance with social expectations. Then a more specialized one I titled "The Socialization and Education of Children," specifically in fulfillment of the class assignment for the Feminist Theory class, using each of the different theory types to make certain points about the subject matter. This let me demonstrate that I'd understood each of those separate feminist theory approaches while leveraging their best insights to make points I myself wanted to make.

"Coercion" sprawled, but Dr. Felthauser accepted it as my term paper and wrote comments in the margins and praised the scope, if not the tightness, of my thinking.

Aaronsen also gave me an "A" and a lot of praise, but wrote comments indicating that he thought I was on the wrong track and should embrace socialist feminism instead.

SPRING 1990—INTO THE TRACK

I had been so immersed in proving myself in various ways as A Mind To Be Reckoned With at the grad school level that I didn't take conscious notice of it at first. I'd park my rusty old car and come into the shared grad student house on Cedar Beach and smell the most phenomenal smell of Indian style potatoes and greet Chris and Sachi as I came in. Or I'd come downstairs to be less isolated while working on one of my papers, and do my typing in the living room, glancing up from time to time to tune in and perhaps participate in the conversations.

But Padma would apologize and say "Sorry, I only cooked for the three of us, if I had known, but really we only have enough for us." Or Chris would say "We're going out to Chi Chi's, see you later" and they'd leave together, not asking me if I'd like to join them.

They tended to do their grocery shopping together on the way home from campus, and would come in and mark their acquisitions with CPS—Chris, Padma, Sachi—and stash them in the kitchen cabinets as their joint property.

Sometimes I'd come in with groceries and start cooking, and Padma would wince when she saw me preparing things. "How much longer will you be?"

"Hi! I have ingredients for pork chops and mustard greens and cornbread. Come on in, I'll make room. You want to eat together?"

"Oh, umm...I think we'll wait until you're done, just...how long do you think before you'll be out of the kitchen?"

The mysterious Amy had postponed her arrival several times, so it was the four of us in the house.

I lost my temper about it one evening when they were unpacking food supplies. "Look, why don't you simplify what you write on your boxes and cans? Just write 'Not Derek, Not Derek'. That's what it amounts to! I don't feel like I live here. You all have your backs turned to me. I thought this would be like a community of graduate students but I come in and walk past the three of you sharing space and socializing and I go up to my little upstairs room and I feel totally left out!"

Sachi said, "We didn't mean it to be that way, but we already know each other and we ride together, and we haven't really gotten to know you."

Padma said, "You should find your own friends. This is a room to rent. We didn't promise you a family."

Chris apologized. "I can see where that wouldn't feel very good. I'm sorry, like Sachi says, we didn't set out to keep you out, but Padma's right, you know, it's...originally there were four of us, and one empty room and Amy said she would rent it. She wasn't going to try to be in our lives. Then Jeremy dropped out. So we had another empty room we had to fill. I guess we just thought of you like Amy, we weren't trying to set up a new community. We already know each other, and we didn't talk about it, we just assumed we'd remain a unit by ourselves."

Dr. Felthauser said he'd be pleased to be the second advisor for my theoretical track paper. He had ploughed his way though my longwinded "Coercion" paper and since I was drawing in part upon the socialization concepts he had taught, he seemed like a good choice.

But the paper was aimed at Dr. Aaronsen primarily, as a continuation of our dialog, because of his response to my "Socialization and Education of Children" paper. Although he'd given that paper a lot of praise, he'd ultimately made an issue of my embrace of radical feminist theory, and I wanted to make my theory paper a reply to that.

I typed and printed, corrected, and rewrote for days on end (eliciting complaints from Padma about the constant noise, although Chris defended me) and eventually felt like I had a good initial effort, although—as with "Coercion"—it was a bit on the longwinded and sprawly side.

This is the structure of the paper I turned in, as divided up by chapter:

1. Introduction—an introduction of myself, a women's studies student (not a sociology student) prior to being in graduate school.

That I was pursuing a graduate career intending to follow a feminist course of study.

2. Until All the Children At Last Shall Be Free—the "Socialization and Education of Children" paper, reiterated verbatim, as the subject of discussion

3. Until These Assertions are Grounded in Reality—A summary of the objections raised by Dr. Aaronsen, and the general background of axioms and postulates and assumptions in sociology, arrayed as a critical assault on radical feminism as "pre-sociological" or otherwise inappropriate.

4. We Feel Truth While You Rationalize Patriarchy—A counter-summary of the indictments made *by* radical feminist theorists about conventional mainstream academic disciplines, including but not limited to sociology; in particular, the claim that radical feminist theorists are not allowed to make initial assumptions in the same way that other theorists are given unimpeded authority to make; that other theorists are given nearly free rein to begin with assumptions that they don't have to defend, but when radical feminists do it they are held to a different standard, accused of making ungrounded assertions.

5. Metaphysics of Social Reality—The real core of the paper, an examination of how individuals in a society process social information as participants, including the tools at their disposal for making a critique of the society in which they live. Comparing the assertions made by radical feminist theory to the contrasting assertions made by structuralist and conflict theories in general use within sociology, and also to those made by the other type of feminism called "socialist feminism."   6. Summary and Conclusion—Discussing the impact of radical feminist theory within sociology.

With the references included at the end, this paper—which I titled "The Radical Feminist Perspective in (and/or on) the Field of Sociology: a metatheoretical excursion"—came to 141 pages. It was too thick to staple. I put one copy each in the inter-office mailbox of Dr. Aaronsen and Dr. Felthauser, putting the loose sheafs of paper into accordion folders and rubber-banding them with a note.

This was the kind of stuff I'd been wanting to sink my teeth into during my entire time at Old Brookville. Now I was a grad student and I was ready to unleash my concepts.

My second year field placement was *supposed* to have been with a sexual identity support organization aimed at helping teenagers and young adults deal with questions of their sexual identity and have someone to talk with to explore such questions. It sounded even more perfectly matched to my interests than Sayville Project had sounded. But then it turned out that they didn't have a qualified MSW to supervise me, so I was told I'd have to choose a different agency. The field placement supervisor in the social work program, Dr. Bleu, said he knew of one he thought I'd be good for and gave me contact information for the Community Service Program of Suffolk County. They dealt with people convicted of crimes who did community service instead of doing time in jail or prison. I spoke with them on the phone. The director was Ellie Sayorno. I'd be working in part with her but reporting on a more daily basis to Robert Paulo, her main assistant.

I had become obsessively focused on my writing. What I'd come here to do. I actually thought I'd written something pretty powerful, in and of itself, even though it was originally conceived of as setting the foreground for being able to talk about being a militant sissy or sex role nonconformist or whatever term I felt like sticking on it.

I definitely wanted to use radical feminist theory because socialist feminist and other so-called feminist theories gave no room to understand why a male person would find the male role horribly confining. Radical feminism didn't assume power was delicious. It didn't assume male people were *getting away with* oppression and living a wonderful life as oppressors. Instead it looked at interactions and negotiations between people and examined the ones that involved domination and oppression and considered them pathological, considered the ones doing the dominating to be distorted, stunted personalities with twisted emotional scopes, persons with damaged senses of priority and value.

But in defending it, I'd written some good stuff. I'd elaborated on what radical feminist theorists themselves had had to say. I had followed the lead of theorists such as Robin Morgan and Marilyn French who had seen where to borrow some thoughts elsewhere that patched in nicely, and had also added my own contributions. I had *theorized*. I was a participant in theory.

And that, too, was in keeping with radical feminist theory, which embraced a demystification of how theory is produced. Feminist theory had come from consciousness-raising groups, of ordinary women coming together to talk about their situation and speak from their own experience and build on connections they made with the other women in their groups. That's what Dr. Baxwood had taught me, had shown me, had introduced me to in the assigned readings.

I knew it needed work. It needed tightening, the paragraphs needed to be clearer, the structure of the piece perhaps reorganized to make its points more effectively. I was looking forward to the feedback from my professors. .

Padma sighed and gave me a wry smile. "I have not been fair to you. Chris and I have been working on personal matters and I have not been a good companion for anyone, because of it. I wanted to retreat and be in a cocoon of people I know and love and sometimes hate, people who know me already, do you know what I mean? Don't you sometimes want the world to go away so that you can think, and make a plan for your life? I didn't want new people. You seem like someone that in different times I could have been a friend. To have acted like a friend. I don't think I can right now, but I want to apologize."

I smiled back. "Is there any way I can con you into showing me someday when you have time how you make those potatoes?"

Robert at the Community Service Program showed me the listings that had been sent in for agency after agency in the state of New York, describing their alternative to incarceration program for convicted people. "You said you had some computer experience. We were thinking that if there were some way to make a directory and print it without having to pay a typesetter at a printer's office...is that something you think you could do?"

"Yeah, let me play with it. I think I want to start by typing this all up in a spreadsheet so that the pieces of information are all in the same columns. Some of these agencies provide more information than others but they're all answers to the same questions. Then we can format it somehow. I have some ideas." Which I did. If I couldn't come up with anything better, I could write a macro that could methodically copy each column and paste it with a label for each row into MacWrite, the word processor I was accustomed to using, the same one we used for the *Catalyst*. I had recently learned macros, and you could do amazing things with them so that you could automate complicated procedures. But there might be something better. .

Dr. Felthauser's letter was in my inter-office mailbox. He said he thought I had coalesced some of the ideas from "Coercion," talking about how oppression works on a cognitive level, and that while he didn't necessarily *agree*, I had taken on a large project and demonstrated an ability to write theory. He said he was not directly familiar with feminist theorists but that even without that familiarity, I had made some good observations about the limitations of assumptions within sociological theory and that from the outside, as a person without any familiarity with radical feminist theory, he felt that I'd made a good case for why he should read it. He said there was room for improvement but that he was willing to sign off on my theory track paper now if I so wished.

I went back to my desk in the grad student office and read his letter a few times, glowing. Rob and Rafe wandered in. I waved and they waved back. "I may be on course to nail down my first track paper before the end of the semester," I announced smugly.

"Way to go," Rafe said, extending his hand for a high-five.

Rob read Dr. Felthauser's comments and nodded. "I haven't had Felthauser yet. I've heard he's a good lecturer but he assigns a lot of reading."

"He does," I acknowledged. "A lot of it is xeroxed articles but it's like five or six papers for each class. But he's willing to read long papers from students and comment on every page, so it's kind of mutual."

"Better than Dr. Harrison. I got a paper back from him with a B+ on it. No comments at all, just a letter grade."

"Yeah, that sucks," Rafe noted. "I want to know why I get the grade that I'm getting."

"I think he's lazy as shit," Rob said. "I bet he doesn't even read them, he just looks to see who we have in references."

I received Dr. Aaronsen's reply and comments the next day. He, too, said that he would sign off on my paper if I wanted him too, but he encouraged me to deal with its deficits first. "I think it's self-indulgent on your part to position the field of sociology as foil. However much you may enjoy playing the role of rebel and outsider, it is a role that has its intrinsic limits. I think you have overstated the opposition case that you attribute to me. I don't think radical feminism cannot be an accepted theory within sociology, but I do think it constitutes bad sociology.

"You go on to embark on a tangent about meaning and psychological processes but you don't address the primary concerns that you voice in your chapter that purports to be the 'voice of sociology,' and since these are points that you bring up, your failure to address them directly weakens your position.

"Also, in your radical feminism chapter where you issue a reply, you go off on yet another tangent, this theory of origin myth about the birth of patriarchy, which is a set of assertions for which you have no evidence. Either you need those assertions, in which case I think you're in trouble, or you don't, in which case they don't contribute to your paper.

"I'd like to see a revised version if you're willing to put some more work into it."

I was amenable. It definitely felt like a first draft, although a good one, and I thought there was a better paper lurking within it if I gave it some polish and revamp. .

"I'm sorry," I said. "I haven't said this well, and I may not say it well right now. But not even trying seems to be worse. I was in love with Jenna. I'm not saying she was objectively a good match or that I still wish I was with her instead, but we can't talk about us if I can't talk about the situation I was in when we first started out. I was reboundy, not like 'Oh I need to go out and get a new girlfriend and get my mind off Jenna,' but in the sense of still having the after-effects, kind of like withdrawal symptoms if you want to think of it that way. Anyway, you acted like I could just do a casual one night stand and that would be okay, or we could be friends with benefits and that would be okay, or we could go all in.

"I definitely wanted to get to know you, and we had a good couple months together in Glen Cove, you took me in and took care of me. I hope I was decent company for you too. I think I'm not as open, not because I'm wishing I was with Jenna, but just because I'm still recovering from how that went. Meanwhile, though, it's like you want me to be the one to say I want more. You leave yourself room to only want it casual, or no big deal, no strings, but then you get mad at me."

Donna opened a couple beers and solemnly extended one to me. She sighed. "You know I was working with the Coalition Against Domestic Violence. I had an abusive boyfriend, that's how I got connected with them originally. I know I'm not emotionally consistent, it's part of my baggage, okay?

"Things seem good, and I don't want to lean on them, crush them with a bunch of expectations, you know? We have a good time and I like being with you. You're nice, and it's fun, and we're good together.

"But then it gets into my head that maybe you're not good for me, that I'm being blind to how toxic you are, because it's been like that for me before, see? I can't even think about it without worrying about it, but if I don't think about it, it could be happening again.

"Anyway, yeah, you're pretty stuck on yourself, in your own head, you like being the absent minded professor. You care about people when they come to your attention but a lot of time they don't. A lot of time I don't. Maybe I want more. You're right, I didn't go in saying I wanted more. Maybe I don't. I might run the other way if you tried to make it more. This isn't easy, is it? This whole 'being a person' thing. They should give us better instruction manuals."

REHABILITATION

The short-term rental arrangement that Chris, Padma and Sachi had arranged with the house owners was over, and the owner was coming in to inspect and prepare for moving in with his family.

I wanted the shared living experience I thought I was opting for when I moved in, so I decided to ask around.

While sipping frozen vodka shots with Sheldon Isaacs and reminiscing about our *Catalyst* days, I described my disappointments with the Cedar Beach household.

"Hey, I got an idea," Sheldon told me. "There's this lady, Ruth, I know her from the Art Department, she bought this piece of land across from the shopping center in case more shops wanted to move in, expand, or put in a parking lot, you know? So, well, it's got this old house on it, a little run-down but not too shabby, and she wants to rent it. Maybe you and some other students could combine forces and make a go of it!"

I visited Donna and ran the idea past her. She was starting at Stony Brook herself, enrolling in the same social work program (but not the sociology) and Glen Cove was too far to commute. "Wanna live together, along with a bunch of other college folks? Eat meals, hang out and have chats over coffee and discuss stuff in the living room, split the bills and all that?"

"Oh, I'd love that. Make up our own little collective. Sure, I'm in! Who else do you know who might want a part of that? I should call Cindy and see if she knows any possibilities."

"I was thinking I'd run an ad, like the one Padma and them did, with off campus housing, list it as rooms to rent, house to share, that should get us some possibilities too."

Ruth had agreed in principle and named a reasonable amount for taking the house for the year, and we agreed that I'd let her know by the end of next week if we could get a group together.

We got a firm commitment from David Eaton, a student who would be coming in from California to do Anthropology at Stony Brook, and a local guy, Mike Monsecco. That left us with just one extra room to fill, so we told Ruth we wanted to proceed.

I brought a diskette with me into the Community Service Program, containing a Macintosh application I'd discovered called FileMaker II. It was a database, similar to the database module in the Microsoft Works application I'd been using since the *Catalyst* days, but it was more versatile. One thing it did that the Works database couldn't do was print as many records on a page as would fit without splitting them. That meant that for agencies that had submitted just a short little blurb, perhaps three or four would go on a single page, instead of leaving a huge empty blank space; then other agencies that had turned in a lengthier description could take up all of that space for themselves if their entry required that much room.

I had to get the information from the spreadsheet into the database, but I had discovered that the spreadsheet would let me do a "Save As" and save the document in a different format called "SYLK," and FileMaker could convert SYLK documents.

Like other database programs of this type, FileMaker let me design how the data fields would display. Each record showed up like a single page or card, at least until you printed it. So I dragged the fields into a visually attractive arrangement and formatted them with good font typefaces and sizes, so that it looked like they'd been carefully typed out in a page layout.

I showed Ellie Sayorno and Bob Paulo. "Oh, that's nice! And all we have to do is print it and take it to be run off and stapled at the printers?"

I nodded.

The year-long Statistics and Methods course was being taught again, this time by the team of Bess Tavin and Reggie Sharp. I signed up for it, retaking the semester one material since I didn't feel I'd understood it very well, and would take semester two in the spring.

Instead of being with my original cohort of doctoral students who'd started at the same time I had, I was now with the cohort starting new this fall. This cohort was larger and had more women in it, many of whom said they were interested in feminism when we went around the table introducing ourselves. There was Debra Gimson, who wanted to explore anorexia and body image as feminist issues, and Rebecca Animas who was interested in the depiction of women's sexuality and the female body as social currency, and Maria Kelas, planning on focusing on women in Eastern Europe.

Rafe, Diane, Rob and Tess told me at various times that they wish they'd done what I'd done. "I didn't really want to do quantitative research anyway, but I wish I understood it better," Rob had told me. And Tess had said, "They put us all together and expected us to all herd nicely down the cattle chute, doing exactly what we're told. You pushed back. And the rest of us watched you do it and realized, yeah, if we're smart enough to be pursuing doctorate degrees and we believe in social equality and social justice, what are we so scared of? The faculty doesn't threaten us, but we all internalize this sense of 'Gee, we need their blessing to become professionals, don't make waves' and the faculty, I think they're just used to that."

Tavin and Sharp were a lot less offputting and a lot more skilled at presenting the methods and the mathematics of statistical analysis. Like Rob, I didn't gravitate toward it, particularly, but I was happy to be feeling like I had some comprehension of it. Tavin and Sharp had a teaching assistant, another grad student, Leslie Vissom, who was about our age. She promised to work with us in the computer lab and set up our analyses.

Having thrown away the long protracted back-and-forth sequence of radical feminist chapters and sociology chapters, and eliminated the "origins of patriarchy" subsection, I arranged the sections of "The Radical Feminist Perspective In (and/or On) The Field of Sociology" so that it now began with a brief introduction of myself and how I had come to the field from outside. Then came a long middle section that introduced radical feminism and then explained it as a form of what sociologists call "conflict theory." I followed that with the piece I'd written on radical feminist theory as a radical interactionist theory that could answer questions about oppression and consciousness. Finally, at the end, I summed up the relationship between the radical feminist perspective and the discipline of sociology, emphasizing the positive contributions rather than highlighting a history of opposition.

This new version of the paper was barely half the size of its predecessor. Writing it the second time around, now that I had a clear sense of what I wanted to say, was easier and my writing was tighter.

After a week's worth of additional passes to clean up awkward sentences and look for errors and confusing paragraphs, I ran off copies and put them in Dr. Aaronsen's and Dr. Felthauser's inter-office mailboxes.

"Hey, Derek, you got a minute?"

"Hi, Leona! Sure! What's up?"

"Have you used email much yet?"

I shrugged. "I get messages from Tavin and Sharp, and sometimes other people in our class send out group emails too."

She shook her head. "You can use email to write to people outside of class, people attending other universities. The reason I was asking is, well, there's this email list I joined, for people who want to work in women's studies. And there are these...a couple of men who joined and they're always posting how feminists are biased and women's studies doesn't belong in college, I thought it might be good to have some male voices in support of feminism. So it wouldn't be so men versus women."

"Well, I doubt they'd pay me any more attention than they do to women, but it sounds like something I'd like to be a part of. That was my major as an undergrad and it's pretty central to my thinking."

"Yeah, I know, that's why I decided to ask you. Anyway it's called 'W M S T dash L,' Women's Studies List. I'll send you an email with the instructions for how to join."

Bob Paulo said, "Hey, Ellie was really impressed with the work you did on the NYAASP brochure. We've gotten a lot of compliments from the statewide agencies."

"Thanks! I learned some new things about database software myself."

"I was wondering if you had any ideas of your own about projects you'd like to do here. We can definitely find useful things for you to do but I don't want your internship to be all support staff and drudgery stuff."

"Well, thank you. I really appreciate that. Not that I mind doing office work, and it's not really drudgery, but yeah, my social work concentration is program planning and administration and research, so I do daydream about doing things on an actual policy level! So...the main thing that would make a difference as far as getting more support and funding for alternatives to incarceration would be if we could show that the alternatives do a better job of dealing with criminal violators than locking them up in a cage does, right?"

"Do a better job how? A lot of the people who oppose alternative programming want the experience to be as bad as possible, to be a deterrent and to get their pound of flesh."

I laughed, nodding. "Yeah, I hear you. But how about recidivism? That's one of the main things most people care about, whether or not people learn their lessons and stay out of trouble from then on, or however you want to put it. Whether it's rehabilitation or vengeance, it's all about getting them to change their ways, right?"

Bob nodded. "At least in theory. I think some people would want their pound of flesh even if it didn't have any effect. They think people have it coming to them for what they did, and they want to make sure they get it. But you're right, it's the main argument, or at least that plus incapacitation, where if they're locked up they're prevented from doing any more damage at least for as long as they're kept there."

"Okay, so I'm thinking we could compare people who are otherwise statistically identical and see if the ones who get alternative sentencing are more likely or less likely to commit more crimes later than people who are locked up for what they did."

"That would be a pretty ambitious project. Let me think. We have our own records here, if you wanted to use those for the alternative sentencing. You'd need to get information from the state to find out what they did later on. How would you compare it to people who got incarcerated?"

"I think I'd need that from the state somehow too. I'd need to pick a random sample of people who got convicted and sentenced to jail or prison time."

We agreed that I'd write a proposal to the NYS Division of Criminal Justice Services outlining the proposed research and asking for access to the state records of a selected population of Community Service Program participants and a batch of randomly selected records of incarcerated people to use as a control group. The letter would go out on Community Service Program stationery with a cover letter from Ellie, and we'd see if they'd go for it.

WMST-L, the email-based community that Leona Chase had hooked me up with, came into my computer account's mailbox once a day as a "Digest" that contained everything that anyone had written to the list. Many of the individual emails were replies to previous emails, so it was an ongoing dialog. I found it very entertaining and was soon shooting off my own thoughts and notions.

The question of men's position (or lack thereof) in women's studies was one of the ongoing discussion topics. Most of the objections were tied to misbehaviors and disruptions, much of it at the student level. What to do about young men taking the class and making it unpleasant for the group. What if they're sincere and really wrestling with these issues but they come from a different situation and background than the women and the women sit quietly not talking and the guys take over? Is it reasonable to have separatist space, women-only space in women's studies? Is it unreasonable that women's studies should be women-only space in its entirety?

Meanwhile, some of the discussion took place on a more philosophical plane. Some participants were appalled at the idea of keeping men out, saying the problem was getting them in, getting them to listen, getting men to take women's thoughts seriously. Almost no one seemed to think males had an inherently different nature that made us unwanted participants. But what about the university's tendency to hire and promote men preferentially? Shouldn't women's studies be a space where women's careers would not have to be in head to head competition with male academics?

I said I could see how it could be problematic for me, pursuing an academic career based on women's studies, to try to get hired as a professor in a Department of Women's Studies or a Department of Feminist Studies or whatnot. What I was more inclined to try to do was to seek to get hired in a more conventional department, such as Anthropology or Sociology or Social Psych, specifically as a professor whose reputation was as a feminist theorist and a person who studied gender and maleness and sissyhood.

By the time I had signed on to the list, the males who had been harassing and belittling the purpose of the group had mostly been kicked out by the person managing the list, Joan Korenman, but I got to participate in some of the final exchanges, adding my voice to the others telling the men that if their sole purpose was to trash the purpose of the list, we had no interest in hearing it.

One of the recurrent types of posts in the WMST-L Digest was a "call for papers." One academic journal or another would be seeking academic papers from feminist authors on a specific subject. "Call For Papers," the email would read, "The experience of women in police and military settings will be the focus of our fall issue. If you have research, theory, or other relevant contributions please submit papers for peer review by this coming July..."; I often read these, daydreaming of a time when I could submit my own research or pen a significant article.

"When I was a child," Aaronsen wrote, beginning in his comments on my latest version of my theory track paper, "I spoke and thought and reasoned as a child. But when I grew up, I put away childish things."

He said that there was some improvement but he still saw a lot of work before this paper was ready to stand as a professional paper. I had cited an array of standard "Intro to Sociology" textbooks to establish that, generally speaking, sociology textbooks taught that sociological theory was divided into structuralist-functionalists, conflict theorists, and interactionist theorists. He didn't like my use of the textbooks and said I should strip that out of there.

Then he raised some objections to my introduction of radical feminist theory in general, saying that I should constrain my focus to the specific ones whose theories I was interested in, name them by name, and describe what they had in common as a group.

He made very few direct comments about the whole radical interactionist theory idea, but instead wrote two full paragraphs about how I would be painting myself into a corner if I continued down this road, because I, as a male, lacking a womb and therefore the magic centerpiece granting me connection to nature, would never be able to participate in radical feminism, which could be analyzed from the outside but should not be something I persist in trying to defend from the inside.

Some of his requested changes were easy enough to implement, although I didn't agree with most of them. I didn't see a problem with how I'd structured the paper. But more to the point, he didn't seem to be open to any of the things I was trying to say, which didn't bode well for doing a dissertation with him on my committee. It might be true that the theory part of a dissertation that contained research on the sissy experience wouldn't be the hard part to get past the committee people, but on a different level, if he was this inflexible overall, it was raising a lot of warning signals for me.

One of the loudest warning bells was the fact that feminist topics were considered to be Aaronsen's turf in this department. He was the first and, so far, *only* person on the faculty who had expressed interest in that area. There were several women faculty members in Sociology, including our Stats & Methods teacher, Dr. Tavin, and Dr. Barthes who taught Contemporary Sociological Theory, but feminism wasn't their topic area or the lens through which they viewed things.

Meanwhile, though, since Aaronsen had already told me he'd sign off on it if I wished—he'd said that in response to the first version—I shrugged and wrote him a note indicating that instead of continuing to try to tailor this indefinitely to address all of his concerns, I'd like to go ahead and get my theory paper marked as accepted.

Within a few hours I had a reply in my mailbox informing me that Dr. Aaronsen was no longer willing to sign off and required me to make further changes to my paper first.

I was annoyed. I thought Aaronsen's objections were way over the top. I knew it was a good paper. It could be polished more, it could be improved, but Aaronsen was really complaining about the substance of it, not the lack of polish, and I just didn't agree with him.

I looked up the addresses for Sheila Ruth, author of *Issues in Feminism*, our first-year women's studies reader, and for Verta Taylor, a prominent sociologist who definitely wrote as a feminist. I wrote to them explaining why I was seeking feedback on a feminist theory paper I'd written.

I also wrote to the WMST-L list, titling my email "Paper for Calls," and explaining that I was hungry for feedback on the quality and relevance of a paper I'd written, and described how the paper had come about and what it attempted to say, all in the course of a couple paragraphs.

By the next day, I had received a dozen requests to see the paper, with promises to provide me with some feedback.

The computer on which I managed my email was a PC deployed as a dumb terminal in the computer lab of the Social-Behavioral Sciences building. The terminal interacted with the school's IBM mainframe, a model 3090. The interface was primitive compared to the Mac I was used to. To email a file attachment, I had to convert it to an all-text format called "binhex" on my Mac, then put it on a PC formatted diskette and upload it to my account on the mainframe. Then I had to invoke the file from the command line to append it to the email, where it appeared as row after row of gobbledegoop coded text. The person on the other end would have to save the email and then decode the file. Somehow it all worked.

In addition to requests for a copy of my paper, I received a handful of replies to my WMST-L posting that recommended some email lists for male people who wanted to discuss feminism or gender issues. I read the descriptions and signed up for "MAIL-MEN" and began receiving a daily email Digest from the participants.

"I am all for women's equality," wrote DavidCM@cs.utexas.edu. "It's just fair. And when Joe (jwilladr@umw.edu) says feminists are not fair to men, I think that just displays his patriarchal indoctrination."

Farther down in the Digest, Joe replied, stating, "What about unjust accusations of rape? Feminists are starting to use the word 'rape' metaphorically. They're pretty much calling all men rapists by defining everything male people do as 'rape.' Meanwhile, they consistently ignore any real rape that was not done by a *man* to a *woman*. Women rape people too, and men can be raped."

Not all the MAIL-MEN posts were focused on the pro-feminism versus anti-feminism argument. There were John Bly fans who wrote about men's drumming weekend retreats and the importance of getting in touch with our primal masculinity.

"I'm not sure I have a primal masculinity to get in touch with," I wrote. "All through childhood I was told I behaved like a girl and had a girl's sense of priorities. I was really hoping to find some other male people who have had it up to here with this whole 'masculinity' thing."

Someone named David Thorpe (thorpe@boeing.hsv.com) wrote back to me, "I think you'd like the PROFEM list better. Those guys are real fire-eaters and totally on-board with feminism," and he sent me the subscribe link.

Sometimes our grad student office devolved into a gripe and complaint session, and this was one of those days. I was one of the people making it so. "I can't believe he's jerking me around like this!" I stated, waving Aaronsen's litany of critical remarks about my paper in my hand. "I thought it would be so cool to come to a space where there's a guy doing feminism and feminist theory."

Rob passed me the plastic cup full of bourbon and told us, "The rumor is, he's got some pretty hot pants, Mr. Feminist. They say he's getting it on with at least one of the female grad students, which is not exactly the message I think he oughta be sending. Assuming just for the sake of argument that it's true."

"Well, wait now, are we talking consenting adults?" Jerry dissented. "I think Aaronsen's got an ego on him a mile wide but he's not that bad a guy really, and as long as it's consensual..."

"No way," I disagreed, passing the cup onwards. "It's not the effect that it has on her, whoever she is, whoever she might be. It's the rest of the women grad students, if they get to thinking 'Oh, so I guess *that's* how you get ahead around here?' ...I'm sorry, but professors have no business getting involved with grad students, it sets up all kinds of conflict of interest stuff."

Debra, who didn't have a desk in our office but was hanging out, added, "It's power. When there's a power difference, consent is always affected, it can't be freely given."

"Well, Aaronsen's not the only problem around here," Diane said. "I've been trying to work with Dr. Barthes, I've got a paper I've been hoping to get into AJS, and you'd think she'd be helping me, right? But she really hasn't been. And yesterday there were a bunch of us hanging out around her desk as class was letting out and she said some student wanted her to be on his committee, and she looked at us like this and said 'So why would I want to help him if he's not referencing any of my articles in his work? What's in it for me?' And we all looked at each other like 'Oh seriously, is that how it is?'"

Tess shook her head. "You don't think she was making a joke?"

Diane shrugged. "Was she? I don't think it was in very good taste if it was."

Rob added, "Then there's Harrison. I'm TA'ing for his Race and Economics class this semester and I write the study materials, I grade all the papers, and I proctor the exams. What does he do besides show up and do the same lecture he always does?"

Tess took the bourbon cup and poured more into it. "I think what's sad is that I thought they were going to mentor us and be interested in our ideas. But it really doesn't feel like that. It's like working for Citibank. Or State Farm Insurance or something. I dreamed of this for a long time and it's not like how I thought it would be."

In conjunction with Steve and Joel in the Social Welfare school, I had developed a master's thesis that was essentially a course design around teaching an alternative and critical perspective on the mental health system. By the design of the joint social work / sociology program, it was supposed to be allowed to *also* count as one of my three required sociology track papers, and I had focused it on review of literature, because I was bringing together the course materials for teaching the course. I had not found time to go hang out with Laura Wahl, but I had her notes and lots of materials she had given or loaned out to me over the years, and I'd done my own research. Dr. Felthauser and another socio professor, Dr. Oxford, signed off on it for sociology and in early March it became my first official approved track paper and also brought me a major step closer to graduation from the social work program.

I pulled my rusty blue Toyota into the gravel drive and clambered up the steps and into the yellow house. The new person, Stephanie, waved to me from the living room couch, where she was perched with her cat.

"Hi, Steph, hi Oedipus!" I greeted.

Mike stuck his head out from the kitchen, beer in hand. "That's a great name for a cat. You know," he said, approaching the cat with his skritching fingers extended, "your *real* name is Edward. Edward E. Puss."

I nodded to him and stepped close enough to the kitchen to wave to Donna and David who were sharing cooking tonight. "Hi folks."

"We're doing rice and beans and flour tortillas," Donna informed me, "with cabbage to go with it."

This was more like it; this was the way I wanted it to feel coming home from a day at the university, not shunted aside and feeling like a visitor in somebody else's household.

INTO THE VOID

Rebecca and Debra came by my desk in the grad student office. They drew up chairs. "What's up?" I asked.

"I wasn't sure you knew," Debra said , "but there's a cluster of faculty from several different departments coming together to kick off a women's studies certificate program."

Rebecca nodded. "They're going to crosslist some courses that are already being taught but also teach some directly out of the certificate program, with a feminist approach, and maybe later on down the road, they could offer an independent graduate degree, like an interdisciplinary women's studies doctorate."

I had been reading printouts of my emails, which included several responses to my "Radical Feminist Perspective in Sociology" paper. These other academics from other campuses had had nice things to say about my paper, and I was wishing I was in a more supportive environment. "How do I get connected to this? You're right, I'm definitely interested!"

"All you have to do is email Dr. Munchen. She's 'amunchen' here on campus. She'll send you an invite when they schedule an orientation."

Debra added, "Were you serious about wanting to read my eating disorders paper? Well, if you want to. Here's a copy of it."

I had enrolled in the Women's Studies Graduate Certificate Program and after going to orientation, signed up for their colloquium for designing a women's studies course as if we were the teachers, and also an interdisciplinary course in Feminist Politics and Theory. I had it in my head, in a half-formed sort of way, that with the way things were going between me and Dr. Aaronsen in particular, maybe an alternative pathway to doing my dissertation would become available through this new program. Perhaps it would be possible for my committee chair to be someone from the Certificate Program but from outside the Sociology Department.

I had another thought about my stalled theory track paper though. Dr. Barthes might be willing to take Aaronsen's place since she taught the Contemporary Theory course, and feminist theory was sort of in that category.

I knocked on her door.

"Oh, hi, Mr. Turner, come on in, what can I do for you?"

"I don't know if this would be appropriate or not, but I have a disagreement with Dr. Aaronsen over some theoretical content in this paper, which I've been trying to submit as my theory track paper for over a year now. I thought maybe a different set of eyes would be a good idea."

"Well, leave a copy of it for me to look at. We don't have any policy or rule against switching to a different advisor for a track paper. I can't make you any promises but I'll make some notes."

The Department of Criminal Justice Services was willing to send penal system records for a submitted sample of Community Service Program clients, and was willing to do likewise for a specified batch of New York State ID (NYSID) numbers of whatever control group I wanted, but I would have to select my own control group and, furthermore, for confidentiality reasons, would have to do so in person at the DCJS facility out in Yaphank. They sent a mass of paperwork, guarantees of our respect for privacy that had to be signed by Bob and Ellie and me.

Once the final official permission was in place, I made an appointment with the Yaphank facility. I spent six hours staring at a DOS screen and doing searches that each matched demographic parameters of our own clients and then jotting down the NYSID numbers of ten individuals in each demographic category to use as a matching control group.

It was time-consuming and I had to come back several times before I had the set of ID numbers, carefully copied into my spiral notebook.

Finally, these were sent in to the state office, along with the NYSID numbers of our own randomly selected clients. We would receive a diskette in the mail with a tab delimited text file containing the criminal justice records associated with those NYSID numbers.

Several people on the PROFEM email list informed me that I was incorrect in referring to myself as a feminist or defining any of my political activities as part of feminism.

"Our role is to be supportive of feminism, to examine our own behavior as males and to challenge the behavior of other males when we see it as problematic," one Ronald DiPietranntonito wrote.

Mark the Shark (Marcus Rivera) told me "Some feminist women don't accept that men can be feminists, and as long as some of them feel that way about it, I don't think we should be claiming that label for ourselves. Let the women lead—it's their movement, and men have led enough things on this planet, do us good to be followers for a change."

"If I lift feminist women's ideas and concepts and don't acknowledge where they came from," I posted, "that's appropriating their work. They *are* feminist perspectives. And when I theorize, I'm doing so within that tradition. I don't need to call myself a feminist, but I'm definitely a theorist within my own right and speaking from my own concerns. I'm not trying to do a chivalrous thing and come to women's rescue. I'm acting from my own needs with my own voice. It just happens to fit in with what feminist women have been saying, and not so much with what men have insisted are their needs and concerns."

"Oh I see," wrote David Johnson. "So you have to make it all about you. How manly of you."

There was a lot of discussion about male sexuality, but rather than coming from a personal place of "here is what it is like for me," the focus was on whether this or that aspect of sexual nature is tolerable and permissible for pro-feminist men.

One person began a reply with, "Let me be the first to acknowledge that feminists are right when they say we, as males, eroticize domination." In my head I could hear someone replying, "Oh no, let *me* be the first!"

Dr. Meg Barthes had a note for me in my mailbox. "I find your description and identification of the 'fluid essential radical feminists' interesting, and would welcome a paper focusing on them as subject matter. However, you appear to be adopting their assertions as your own, according them a status that in contemporary theory we reserve for theorists whose work is published in academic journals. I would suggest that you look for theories that you like within the pages of *Signs*, the *American Journal of Sociology*, *Gender and Society*, and the like. The authors you are embracing would be regarded as popular book authors and they don't have any academic status."

"I'm sure Sheila Ruth would not be at all surprised to hear that Robin Morgan, Sonia Johnson, and Marilyn French don't count as social theorists in the academic classroom," I muttered. "She did warn us of that attitude. Toxic expertosis. You can't just have an opinion or a viewpoint and put it into words, you have to be qualified."

From the first version of my track paper:

> "Ruth, for example, claims that 'The feminist challenge is met with all the anger and resistance one would expect from a company of threatened warriors trying to preserve their own territory...Weapon 1: Methodolatry -- You can't (or did not) fit your experience into a verifiable proposition deductible from general principles and that's what you must do according to the rules of the game.'"

I shrugged. "I may as well rip out the stuff that Aaronsen doesn't like. It's ruining the piece but I guess I'm not supposed to care about that. It's not like I won't still have my own version to work on. Maybe I'll get the real version published some day and stick it under his arrogant nose. But I need to get this project over and done with."

I spent the weekend rewriting "The Radical Feminist Perspective In (and/or On) the Field of Sociology," addressing Aaronsen's concerns and quibbles. After an additional day to fix typos and repair badly worded sentences, I dropped off the revised version in his mailbox with a copy to Dr. Felthauser.

I got a note from Dr. Aaronsen almost immediately, asking "So, this is a paper you're writing for Dr. Barthes and Dr. Felthauser, I take it? Do you just want my comments on it?"

I ran back to my office and checked my own copy and, sure enough, I had left Dr. Barthes' name on it. It seemed likely that he already knew

I'd asked Dr. Barthes to look at it. I had no idea whether he resented that or was needling me for failing to change the name back, or what. I wrote a note explaining that, no, I was still trying to move forward with the track paper, with him as designated advisor.

Three days later he left a note saying that if I'd tighten the section discussing socialization and expand the analysis of competing theories of power and hegemony, add a disclaimer about other feminist theory types that were embraced by sociology, and get rid of the personal preface about how I had come to write this, he'd probably sign off on it at this point.

The interdisciplinary Women's Studies Graduate Certificate Program's course on designing the kind of women's studies course you'd teach if you were to be hired somewhere as a women's studies teacher was quickly shaping up to be one of my favorite courses.

Like Lynne Slocumb's social work class, this one functioned as a sort of mutual support and gripe-session class for feminist students to discuss their headaches in their traditional disciplines. The instructor, Dr. Mendocino, didn't see that as being off-topic or irrelevant, but as consistent with the consciousness-raising roots of feminist praxis.

Cheryl Bascombe and Suzanne Jackson were refugees from the English department where one of the big feminist issues was the "canon" in literature, the body of literature that lit students were expected to read, study, be familiar with, use as a basis of comparison when reading other works, and so on. The canon was very much composed of "dead white European men" and the standards of excellence were notions that had been derived by analyzing what those dead white European fellows had done when they wrote.

"Dr. Munchen is pushing us to use poststructuralist feminist theorists as a tool for prying open the canon," Cheryl said, "but I really hate that stuff. It's just not very accessible, and the way I write isn't going to blend with that at all."

Suzanne said, "Well, it's very useful, if you look at how it's been used in the past."

Vivian Herzog, from History, scowled. "We have perfectly good feminist theory without cozying up to pretentious Frenchmen who think Freud is a demigod."

I nodded. "I ran into that stuff back when I was looking for a grad school to attend. I think it's not just opaque but deliberately opaque, that they're trying to intimidate readers. Also, the arguments that they use, yeah, you can use that kind of argument to say that Toni Morrison or Alice Walker are as good as Norman Mailer or Ernest Hemingway, but you could use the same argument to say that a Bazooka Joe bubble gum comic is just as good as Toni Morrison's best work."

I had briefly described my frustration with the Sociology theory track paper, and how they were making me eviscerate it. "I think you should bring it in," Cheryl Bascombe said. "It might not be good material for an intro to women's studies but you might be able to use it for a more advanced course."

Leslie Vissom helped me in the computer lab, showing me the obscure command line instructions to type to get the SAS program on the mainframe to import the data from the DCJS floppy disk and convert it to a database table.

I worked for weeks in the evening, learning how to weight my control group to account for minor demographic differences from my study population, and how to run regression analyses to see how much of the variance in recidivism outcome could be explained by other variables and how much seemed genuinely due to whether or not a person had been sentenced to community service or to a jail term. We had information on the legal classification of the severity of their crime and the specific statute violated, and their prior criminal history, as well as age, sex, race, ethnicity, education level. We didn't have socio-economic status directly but we had zip code and the presence or absence of court appointed attorney, in combination with the other factors mentioned, and it would have to do.

I found that for people convicted of felonies, their recidivism rate was lower, all other things being equal, if they were sentenced to community service than if given jail time. For people convicted of misdemeanors, the difference wasn't statistically significant.

It wasn't likely to be a study that changed the world but it might be useful for the Community Service Program and other alternatives to incarceration. And for me it was going to be my empirical research track paper. A quantitative analysis paper, no less.

I sat at a Mac computer in the computer lab and wrote my paper, making graphs and tables and pasting them in to the word processor.

"I really like this," Vivian said, indicating my paper. I'd continued to work on my *own* version of "Radical Feminism in (and/or on) Sociology," separate from the watered-down and scope-limited version I'd turned in to Aaronsen. And this was the version I'd brought to the colloquium. Vivian continued, "I took sociology as an undergrad. You're saying to think of feminist theory as a conflict theory, like Marx or Weber. That makes all kinds of sense."

That analysis was in the early pages of the paper. I was glad she liked how it began, and I was looking forward to her thoughts and feedback about the radical interactionist theory notion that the paper developed farther in.

Donna lifted a six-pack onto the table and offered me a beer. "I need to talk to you about something. It's important. You're important to me and I don't want to hurt you. You know David has been talking to me and hanging out with me a lot since he came in from California. Well, he asked me if I would go out with him. And I told him I would have to talk to you about how you feel about it. Derek, I need to know how you feel."

I held hands with her, both hands. "I love you, and you're important to me too. I think I haven't always acted like it. I'm kind of immersed in my stuff these days and I'm sorry about that. I need to make a distinction between being sexually possessive and wanting to have you in my life. Because I'm very happy to have you in my life. But I've never been a sexually possessive person, never saw a reason for sexual exclusivity. Do you like him? If you knew it was okay with me, would you like to?"

Donna nodded. "Yes, yes I would. He's nice. And what you're saying...that's consistent with what you've said before about not believing in sexual possessiveness. So it's not like I need your permission," she added with a wry smile, "but I wanted to get a sense for how you'd handle it in real life. It seems to me...like you care about me and want me to be happy. And I am," she added, with a warmer smile.

The email from the latest WMST-L Digest contained a call for papers from a journal called *Feminism and Psychology*, explaining that they were going to do a special issue on "Heterosexuality" and wanted feminist papers submitted that would explore heterosexuality, problematising it the way that gay and lesbian identities were conventionally problematised: What causes heterosexuality? How did you discover that you were heterosexual? Did traumatic events in your life make you that way? What expectations get foisted onto you when people discover that you're heterosexual? And so forth.

Something powerful clicked. This was a wonderful opportunity to write about being a heterosexual sissy. My take on the institution of heterosexuality was from the outside despite being attracted to female people as a male person, because I was a sissy. I could write about my most central stuff!

I made sure to save a copy of the email to my local drive, and to print out a copy and take it home with me with all the contact information on it.

I was busy these days but now I had another paper to write. An important one.

Vivian's praise for my 'Feminist Perspective on Sociology' paper didn't last until the next grad certificate group session. When we met next, she held it out in one hand and said to the group, "It's just like a man to write all this pompous claptrap. I don't know who you think you're going to impress, Derek, but seriously I don't have time for this shit. Can we move on to materials that women wrote?"

I had another note from Dr. Aaronsen in my mailbox. It was an acceptance letter, indicating that he'd sign off on my theory track paper at this point. But he went on to write, "Since this is obviously the way you intend to write your papers, I have no interest in trying to push you to write or think in different ways and challenge the ways you've come to see the world."

I was trembling and breathing in shallow breaths. "Really?" I muttered. "Could have fooled me. With those four complete rewrites and the way you tore it apart..."

He went on to say I keep on stringing quotes together without any critical elaboration or reason, make wild and unsubstantiated assertions that seem to come from a personal sense of being threatened. He chided me for saying previous versions of the paper had been "rejected"—"We don't work on a submission / rejection model, we work on a tutorial / advisory model, to which you have poorly availed yourself," he wrote.

He went on for five full paragraphs explaining my shortcomings as a student and as a writer, and the shortcomings of radical feminist theory, all this in the process of finally accepting the paper for academic credit, apparently with great reluctance.

I ran into Aaronsen in the hallway on my way out of the mailroom and lit into him for being unsupportive, harshly and abrasively critical. "This has been a nightmare. I can't believe you claim this isn't a submission-rejection model, I feel like I've been jumping through hoops since I began this project."

"Well I'm sorry you see it that way, but I've done everything I can to be a mentor and colleague. You're the one who has rejected the mentoring opportunity."

"A mentor is supposed to help someone go in the direction they want to go. It feels like you've done everything you can to change my choices or keep me from getting there."

"Okay, I think we're done here. I'd prefer that you don't ever speak to me or contact me again."

"I just finished reading your paper, 'The Radical Feminist Perspective in (and/or on) the Field of Sociology,'" Dr. Sheila Ruth wrote in her letter. "I must say I was fascinated. I had not meant to read all of the paper as promptly as I did, because I am so busy and struggling with some deadlines, but once I picked it up, I had difficulty putting it down."

That brought an immediate glowing grin to my face. She went on to say that my twin perspectives as a radical feminist, on the one hand, as outsider (sociologist, male) on the other, put me in a position to make a very valuable critique and theoretical contribution. "I cannot say very much about the technical aspects of interactionist sociological theory because a good deal of that is outside of my range, but as to the feminist theory, I believe that you are right on target. I agree completely with your definition of the essence of radical feminism and with your reading of its epistemology."

Dr. Verta Taylor's letter came a day later. She also had praise for the piece. "I agree that radical feminist thought can be understood as a kind of 'marriage of conflict and interactionist social theory,'" she wrote. "I enjoyed in addition your reflections about the state of sociology as a discipline. Certainly this piece is much more than a paper—perhaps the beginning of a book-length project—and much would be lost if you had to reduce it to sociology journal format."

I hadn't sought out the external opinions in order to stick them under Dr. Aaronsen's nose. I just wanted some feedback. I had dared to think I'd written a powerful theory piece, and yet my primary advisor had cut me down repeatedly and made me wonder if I just had an outsized ego and couldn't see the weaknesses and limitations of my work. I was not a person easily convinced that my intellectual work lacked merit, but I had really started to doubt myself. Having Vivian turn on a dime from saying supportive things about it to dismissing it as pompous male claptrap had also stung. So these two reviews made me feel much better about myself.

Even so, why was I—and my paper—provoking so much hostility and attitude?

I continued: "...and then the next time our group met, she said it was pretentious male garbage. And that's after all the headaches I've had with getting Aaronsen to sign off on it. I don't know if there's something in the paper that's hitting a real nerve, or what!?" I concluded with a sigh.

Tess Lautenberg gave me a long level appraisal, then replied, "I think there's something you need to understand. Most of us come into programs like this, hoping to end up teaching college or doing research somewhere. And we get assigned to read sociological theory, so we read it and study it. And in class, we manage to say or write something about it that sounds intelligent, that sounds like we actually understood it.

"*You* glance at it and...I've seen you do this, I've watched you do it in classroom discussions...you read through it once and then you look up and you say 'Well this person is dead wrong about this thing, because if this was true about stratification look at how that would affect what Merton says about sense of identity, and it's really like this instead'...

"You can hold an entire theory in your head like it's a noun and think about another one at the same time, and you start talking about how this first theory bends in this place over here if you accept the ideas of this second theory, and how that lets the modified first theory reshape the second theory's analyses and do these other things to it. Or how if you remove or discredit some critical piece of a theory it means this part of it over here can get reshaped to make some different point."

Tess looked to her left and to her right like watching invisible diagrams in the air around us. "Two thirds of the time I can't follow what you're talking about, but maybe one third of the time I can see what you're saying. Just often enough that it's obvious that you don't just throw out any old crap trying to make yourself sound smart, you know? And when I can follow it, it's like you just wrote a publishable quality analysis paper, except you did it all off the top of your head the way someone else might say 'If you take the LIE instead of the Northern State you have to get off at this exit instead of that exit,'" She leaned forward and spoke more softly now. "Vivian is older than you, she's my age, and she's a woman, and she is in the university to do feminism and women's studies. That paper you wrote is probably threatening to her, not because something you wrote about hit a nerve, but just because you can spin that stuff and she probably can't. And it's not just her. George Aaronsen isn't stupid or dense. He's made a name for himself, male sociologist studying how feminism and sexism affects men. But you don't see any books or articles of his being called feminist theory classics. And all of a sudden there's a guy in our women's studies class and he writes stuff like this," she said, pointing to the copy of my paper on the corner of my desk. "You need to realize how the way you think and write can affect people."

The letters confirming departmental funding for graduate students were out, but I hadn't received one. I dropped in on the departmental administration office. "Hi! Hey listen, I didn't get a funding letter for the fall."

"Oh. Well you don't get any more, do you? Hold on...yeah, right, you started in spring of eighty-eight so this was your last year for funding."

Well *that* was frightening. I had misunderstood something. I thought I'd get as many years of funding from sociology as other sociology grad students, *plus* the funding I got from my first year as a social work student due to being in the joint program. But I wasn't going to get the extra year.

I was nowhere close to finishing up. I'd completed most of my coursework, and I had two track papers completed and one more nearly done, but I didn't even have a dissertation proposal, not a rough draft, nothing. I didn't have a dissertation committee. Working with Aaronsen was firmly off the table. And even if I had a committee and an accepted proposal, a dissertation takes time.

What did I want to do for my dissertation? Well, I still wanted to do something exploratory, open-ended qualitative research about the experience of sissy males who didn't feel described by "gay male." That was one possibility for sure. Then there was the possibility of doing a theory dissertation. That would be rare and unusual, students nearly always focus on a research project for their dissertation. But I'd written a real, solid theoretical contribution to my subfield, and Tess was right, I was first and foremost a theoretical thinker. So if it were all up to me, that, too, was a possibility, to flesh out the paper into a larger theoretical monograph.

But I'd burned more bridges than I'd crossed since starting my studies at Setauket University.

I had a lot weighing on me, between the impending end of financial support, the rift with Dr. Aaronsen, the need to tie up remaining loose ends for my social work master's degree program, the question of my dissertation...superficially I suppose it might have looked like an additional stressor to dive into the "special heterosexuality issue" call for papers project and see if I could write an article to submit.

But actually it was an escape dive. I hadn't written directly about the sissy experience since *The Amazon's Brother*, and I was itching to get into it, writing for people outside the Setauket environment so that I could blot those people from my mind for a bit.

I had the computer lab nearly to myself and it was quiet. I sat down at 5:30 in the afternoon and began typing, freehanding what I wanted to say as if I were writing a letter, using plain language and explaining things in the most direct way possible. I made notes to myself where I wanted to insert a quotation or cite a reference—in most cases I knew what they'd said but would need to look up the exact words they'd used. I was using my citations to illustrate a point, not to be a source of data. Nearly everything I was saying was rearranging the elements of conventional wisdom about the sexes in a different pattern. All the pieces were "truths" that were socially acknowledged (whether as literal fact or as widely shared beliefs) and had been spoken of and sung about and depicted in film and so on. They were used so widely that I could reference them as everyday familiarities without having to demonstrate with formal references that they form a part of our shared mental landscape. That we all tend to rely on them when it comes to thinking about gender, thinking about maleness, thinking about heterosexuality and the male role within it.

At 11:45 a bell sounded and the public address said the computer lab was closing for the evening. I'd worked for six hours straight and basically banged out the piece in one setting.

And I knew it was good. It was very very good.

I would go home and look for the Marge Piercy poem and the snippet from *The Women's Room* where Myra talks about the disconcerting need for physical touch and how disruptive that is at puberty, and whatever it was that Mae West had said about you can't rape the willing...and I'd clean up some individual sentences and paragraphs, no doubt, and fix typos for sure.

But I had a paper. I gave it a title: "Same Closet, Different Door: A Heterosexual Sissy's Coming-Out Party." Yeah. That was good.

Dr. Oxford was a good Sociology person to chat with, since he had been a nominal advisor on my review-of-lit alternative psychiatry perspective track paper, where the real advisors had been my social work professors, and he had been cooperative and flexible in ways that not all Sociology personnel tended to be.

"I wanted to do a research project on the notion of the 'sissy,'" I explained. "Select people who identify as considering themselves more like women, or one of the girls, or feminine, you know, rather than conventionally identified with the rest of the male folks as men. Then do qualitative research, open-ended interviews, to get a sense of their experience, especially those that don't identify as gay, because that's already an identity that's offered up to feminine or sissy males."

Oxford nodded, but then said, "The problem from a conventional research model standpoint is that all of your variables depend on personal testimony. There's no outside indicator for what it means to be a sissy. If it were a research project on people who are male and have sex with other males, that's an objective identifying factor, even if the only way we have of knowing it is their own statement that they've done so. If it were a research project on people who are male and have dressed in women's underwear, that's objective in the same way. But trying to identify a study population by whether or not they *think of themselves...*," Oxford said, making air quotes, "as being more like girls and women than boys or men, now you're not using an objective category, you're asking subjects to classify themselves, so it's focused on how they think of themselves. Then your research would focus on other aspects of how they think of themselves. I'm not saying that's not valid or that it's not interesting, but it may be hard to define it as sociology."

"Well, I also thought about doing a theoretical dissertation, but mostly I think I'd have more impact if I could put some light on the experiences of people like myself, and then wrap that in a political analysis of how patriarchy and sexist expectations shape our lives and experiences kind of similar to how they shape those of women."

"Well," grinned Oxford, "nobody cares what you think. It's all about what you can get into print and get others to cite. That's what gets you ahead in academia. But no one is going to read anything you write and give any consideration to what you're trying to say. It's just whether or not they can use your paper to support what *they* want to say."

I knew he meant well, and was trying to be both honest and supportive, but what he'd just said shocked me, not because I wasn't cynical enough to believe it to be true, but because it really encapsulated my sense that nobody ensconced in the ivory tower of academia here at Setauket seemed to care about ideas and concepts for their own merit. All the focus was on advancing one's professional career as an academic. Some of the other students seemed to be passionate about what they believed and cared about, but the professors? This was not an idealistic environment. Felthauser seemed genuinely enchanted with his area of study, but he wasn't trying to change anything, just fascinated by the processes of socialization and theories about it. Holcombe, Collier, and Barthes all seemed like corporate office-holders, trying to look competent and thoughtful and chock-full of expertise, but mostly concerned about continuing to be established professionals, not people who cared about social issues, not people for whom academia was a means to an end. And that seemed true for Aaronsen as well. Feminism as a career ticket. Not as cause.

I still didn't know if my cause would be relevant to enough people to matter. I'd been expecting to light the world on fire with this issue since well over a decade ago and it hadn't happened yet. Maybe I was clinging desperately to a set of flimsy notions simply because they seemed to give *my* life meaning, and it would turn out that they didn't offer anything like that to anyone but me.

But be that as it may, the entire notion of an academic career had been all about getting an opportunity to put my thoughts into words, and be heard. And that, yeah, people would care about what I had to say.

The email from Sue Wilkinson, co-editor of *Feminism and Psychology*, said that my submitted article, "Same Closet, Different Door," had evoked a lot of discussion, with arguments breaking out among the reviewers, and that it had generated a lot of subsequent debate. All of which meant that I'd created a piece that stirred the pot and stimulated thought, which is exactly what they'd been hoping for in this special issue, and they'd very much like to include my article. Enclosed, she added, were scans of the written feedback from the delegated peer reviewers, who had some concerns and some issues with my piece, and could I please address those in the weeks before final copy needed to be received prior to publication deadline?

I opened the TIFF files that were scans of the reviewers' comments. They were academics in various institutions scattered around the globe. I printed them out on the computer lab's laser printer and took them back to my desk to read.

A gay activist took strong exception to my article's title. "'Same Closet Different Door' implies to me that heterosexual sissies such as the author are in the same situation as gay males but that a different door to get out of it is available for all of us, if we choose to take it. Suggest change to 'Same Door Different Closet,' because otherwise this is offensive." I nodded. Okay, I could live with that.

Several reviewers wanted more engagement with existing theory, including psychoanalytic, poststructuralist, symbolic matrix, other stuff. Some challenged my assertion that these notions were "already out there" as common social currency. A couple wanted to know why I said "male" and "female" instead of "man" and "woman" in various places and wanted me to explain my terminology. Two reviewers wanted me to address the question of my participation as a male in feminist discourse, and whether or not that was politically intrusive.

I spent two days trying to shoehorn responses to these questions and concerns into the body of the article without ruining its flow. As per instructions, I printed out the revised article and took it to a place where it could be FAXed to England, the locale where *Feminism and Psychology* was printed.

Two days later, Sue Wilkinson wrote back to say she'd modified my new additions, accepted the article name's change, and would I look over what she'd done and give a final okay? I printed out the attachment and found that she'd mostly removed all the verbose replies to the reviewers and restored the article to its original format, with just a brief additional line early on about how not everyone would understand why I hadn't engaged with contemporary theorists in the gender field but to hold those concerns in abeyance. So my article was going to go into print in its native elegance.

I emailed my enthusiastic confirmation.

The Special Issue on Heterosexuality would go to print in October of 1992. I was going to be in print. My words were going to be embraced by a genuine academic peer-reviewed journal and would echo in university corridors as a published authority. For a rebellious nonconformist troublemaker, maybe I wasn't doing too badly after all.

On April 12, my grad student mailbox contained the signed approval for my empirical research track paper, the recidivism study I had done for the Community Service Program. So I now had all my track papers finished. I was mostly finished with my coursework as well. If I had anything remotely approximating a dissertation proposal, and a committee of faculty members inclined to work with me, I'd be closing in on the status called "ABD"—"all but dissertation."

Drs. Tavin and Sharp had been my stats and methods teachers, and the advisors on my recidivism track paper. I liked them and liked working with them, but they had not mentored me, I had not developed a close relationship with them in which they'd shaped my research and helped me pursue my interests overall. The "tutorial / advisor" model relationship that Aaronsen had alluded to was something the department believed in, and what it meant was that faculty members were somewhat reluctant to participate on dissertation committees of students who were not their protégés, or whose dissertations weren't focused in areas that they themselves were familiar with, preferably including a familiarity with the actual studies and methodologies at the core of them. So they said they would consider being on my committee if I intended on doing a dissertation focused on the recidivism study, but not if I was going to do a dissertation that involved interviewing sissy males or a theoretical dissertation delving into the relationship of radical feminist theory to the field of sociology.

Unfortunately, the empirical research involved in that project was not of sufficient scope to anchor a dissertation. It would have to be linked to a more protracted research project, perhaps one to look into why community service has a different recidivism outcome for felons but not for misdemeanants. As I was no longer attending a field placement at the Community Service Program, that would be somewhat complicated although they'd probably be willing to cooperate.

A bigger problem was that I was no longer going to be funded and needed to go out and find a job to support myself, and whatever new research would have to be fit around the margins of that, including the time constraints. If whatever job I managed to land tied me up working during normal business hours, that would mean I'd be attempting to do research in criminal justice environments after hours when many of their facility offices were not open.

But the biggest problem was that this simply wasn't my topic area. I opted to become a college student in order to pursue women's studies and to engage with others who wanted to study patriarchal sexism and sex roles and how they affected sissy males. I didn't have any compelling interest in doing further research on criminal justice and recidivism and even less in becoming "branded" by that research as a sociologist whose specialty was in that area.

At the end of May, Donna and I graduated from the School of Social Welfare with our Master of Social Work (MSW) degrees. I'd started a year before her, but had taken longer because of the sociology coursework.

Donna's long-term friend Cindy Samuels came to watch her get her diploma, and after the ceremony she joined me and David and Donna and we piled into Chi Chi's Mexican Restaurant nearby.

"I'm so happy that we ended up graduating together," Donna told me. "You believed in me. I'm with the people I love the most on a day of triumph!"

My own feelings of triumph were somewhat more muted, because of the messy situation with my PhD program, but I had a professional degree now that should make me employable, a nontrivial accomplishment considering that I'd been in a homeless shelter six years earlier. And I was going to have an article published! Seeing the glow on Donna's face brought me into the spirit of the celebration.

David was in the midst of his own PhD program, in Anthropology. "I've got a research advisor," he told us, "and I may be getting my name on a published journal article too, as one of three researchers studying the body mechanics involved in chiropractic adjustment."

David had come here because Setauket University was one of a small handful of schools that had a physical anthropology program. It was a very different subject from the cultural anthropology that most people think of when they think about anthropology.

"Yeah, a lot of my courses are crosslisted with the MD program at the Health Sciences Center."

Cindy poured us refills on our margaritas from the big icy pitcher. "So, how do you like having an office?" she asked Donna.

"I like being listened to, and treated like I know what I'm doing and what I'm talking about," Donna replied. "Now Joan wants my opinion and discusses ideas with me about the program. But to tell you the truth, I kind of miss the days when I was just the house manager at the shelter, just me and the women and their kids. You know, I don't see why the policy makers and the people who work directly with the clients need to be two different groups of people. It kind of treats the people who do the real counseling as if they aren't as smart, or the work they do doesn't matter as much as the paper and computer-screen stuff."

After we ate dessert, Cindy headed back home and the rest of us drove back to the yellow house. Donna gave David a long hug and a kiss out in the hallway and then came to bed with me. "I have to pinch myself sometimes. I have two very nice men in my life and you're both okay with that." She perched on her elbows and leaned forward on the mattress and began kissing my face, radiating joy and delight.

Maria, the quiet student who was interested in studying women's situation in eastern Europe, smiled and came over to me while I was examining my inter-office mail in the mail room. "Hey, Derek, I don't know if you've heard about this. Dr. Aaronsen is very unhappy with the Women's Studies Certificate Program. They're promoting a type of feminist theory that he doesn't like, and they aren't inviting him to participate in the program. I thought you'd appreciate that situation."

Sure enough, Dr. Munchen and Dr. Amy Cornier, who taught in the English Department, were addressing the Certificate Program participants about the Feminist Theory course. I went with the others to hear.

That they weren't embracing the socialist feminism of which Aaronsen was so fond was the good news.

"With her extensive background in women's literature and art, Dr. Cornier will be taking the lead for the feminist theory symposium. Women in the academy have learned that in order to wage an attack on the master's fortress, we need to be able to raid the master's shed and use his tools. Poststructuralist feminist theory is the result of that raid for tools, and will be our focus in presenting and teaching feminist theory."

As participating graduate students, we were invited to write our thoughts and make contributing comments and recommendations.

I wrote that I was concerned that the poststructuralist viewpoint, like the old structuralist sociological perspectives about socialization and learning, put so much emphasis on social determinism that it left no space within which individuals could arrive at any possible critique; their critical opinions, like any other opinions they might hold, were entirely the byproduct of their accidental location in culture and time and specific experience, leaving no room to argue that anyone's notions of social justice or social ideals of any sort were correct or better than anyone else's.

I also noted that if we were to be teaching feminist theory to undergraduate students, using a form of it that was notoriously opaque and difficult to parse was more likely to antagonize students who weren't already feminist-leaning, and might even push away many who were.

"Radical feminist theory is feminism's *own* theory. It didn't grow in the hothouse of academic intellectualism, it came from the women in the sixties and seventies who started off caring about racial equality and economic equality and ran head-on into sexual inequality and began to find their own terms and their own concepts to discuss it. It blossomed in consciousness-raising groups. Here in the sociology department, I had a professor tell me that the theories of people like Sonia Johnson and Marilyn French and Shulamith Firestone didn't count because they hadn't published their feminism in peer-reviewed academic journals. But that's exactly their strength. This is real revolutionary theory. Which of these paragraphs are going to resonate and explain the social situation of women to a roomful of nineteen year old first-year students?—

Discursive fields overlap, influence, and compete with one another; they appeal to one another's "truths" for authority and legitimation. These truths are assumed to be outside human invention, either already known and self-evident or discoverable through scientific inquiry. Precisely because they are assigned the status of objective knowledge, they seem to be beyond dispute and thus serve a powerful legitimating function. (Joan Scott)

Western thought is profoundly dual, which is to say that in the West difference is more important than similarity. Put another way, distinction is more important than equivalence, division than solidarity. Such a valorization is a necessary component of a morality that exists to confer superiority on one group or caste of humans; their superiority rests upon their difference from other humans. (Marilyn French)

I went on to say that poststructuralism-based theories dismantle all meanings *except* power, leaving power and its desirability unquestioned. "I don't mean it's not a great tool for stripping away the excuses for unequal power. For exposing the ideologies that support it. But it provides very few tools for peoples of any social identities whose marginalization isn't primarily a removal from the exercise of power. And by leaving power centralized, in the final analysis it endorses raw power grabs by whoever is in a position to do the grabbing, since with all other values dismantled, it's the only show in town. And that's actually a conservative ideology. The people in charge may prefer to dress up their hegemony in prettier clothing but when pushed to it will resort to defending their right to power on the grounds that they have it."

I urged the program to consider embracing and teaching multiple types of feminist theory and not just the poststructuralist variety.

Leona and Tess looked at each other and then back to me, simultaneously shaking their heads. Leona said, "So when they asked us to let them know what we thought about what they said they were doing, you actually believed they wanted to hear what we thought?"

Tess said, "Dr. Cornier is lit crit. Poststructuralist postmodern feminist literary theory is what she does. And Dr. Munchen is putting her in charge of feminist theory development within the certificate program. That's an appointment. A woman's career is being enhanced. A lot of women academics are in English literature. So when you pull together a pool of feminist women, you get a lot of English lit types. They're a bloc, a faction. If you want your certificate program to be a success, you're going to want to please your largest faction. Look around you. It isn't radical feminists."

I nodded. "Point taken."

Leona handed back my copy of what I'd sent them. "I agree with nearly everything you've said here. Most of us hate that stuff. All that Freud and Lacan and Derrida. You say a lot of what many of the students feel. But you know, there's a reason we aren't saying it."

The reply I had received had suggested that, as a male student deigning to participate in the certificate program, I obviously had very little experience being marginalized and had probably never been deprived of power and opportunity in my life of comfort and privilege, and should therefore strongly consider silencing myself as an exercise and a learning experience.

"The participatory possibilities for a male in feminist scholarship is problematic," Dr. Munchen wrote. "If you are seriously contemplating writing a paper or making a contribution to feminist theory, I would suggest you focus on that, and whether or not a male, even one whose beliefs, viewpoints, and attitudes are fully aligned with the feminist endeavor, can speak and write 'as a feminist' without coopting feminism the moment he begins to do so."

I shook my head, thinking about that. If that's the sole subject that's deemed appropriate for a male feminist...or a, let's see how to put this...a nomenclaturally problematic participant in the social struggle against patriarchy that is known as 'feminism'...if that's the sole subject that male participants can theorize about, we aren't participating. We're always already not talking about anything except whether we can talk about the things we're not supposed to talk about.

Yeesh. You spend enough time reading poststructuralist feminist theorists and you start to talk like them yourself.

In October of 1992, the *Feminism and Psychology* special issue on Heterosexuality came out. Not only was my article included, but it was mentioned several times in the editor's introduction, juxtaposing my insights with those of other theorists or using things I'd said in my article as examples of the growing feminist understanding of the components of the institution of heterosexuality.

Other graduate students offered me congratulations, and Dr. Tavin and Dr. Oxford did likewise, but generally speaking the faculty of the Department of Sociology passed me in the hallways with averted eyes.

One the one hand, I'd done it. I set out to go to college and be in women's studies in order to talk about the sissy experience, and to see it spoken of, testified about, put on people's map of identities and possibilities. And now my paper was out there. People would read it. All throughout the academic world, there would be some people who would read *Feminism and Psychology*. My thoughts would dance in institutional hallways.

But did that mean that I should regard the viewpoint of Dr. Munchen and Dr. Cornier as just another barrier I needed to hurdle? Did I even now have a potential career as a feminist in academia?

Leona Chase wandered by about five months later . She saw me from the hallway, packing up some papers and materials in manila folders from my desk in the grad student office, and came over to where I was sitting. "Hi. Haven't seen you around much lately. Are you *leaving*?"

"Well...yes and no. I'm feeling like a chestnut tree lately. Do you know about the chestnut trees in America? Basically there aren't any, the blight fungus killed them all a hundred years ago or thereabouts, but they're actually still alive. They put out new shoots from the old stumps, and they grow for a couple years and put out leaves, but then the fungus gets to those, too. So technically they're alive but they're never going to become trees again. Well, I'm technically still enrolled in the program. If I could get a committee together and get a dissertation proposal accepted and do a dissertation, I could get my degree. But I work in the Bronx now. I'm a social worker. I work with senior citizens who are victims of elder abuse. I wake up at five-thirty in the morning and I get in at nine thirty at night. The rest of my time is spent commuting on the train and then working at my job. When I get home, I drink a few beers with my housemates and unwind, and then I go to sleep."

Leona nodded. "Congratulations again on your article. I miss seeing you post things to the women's studies email list. Do you think you'll eventually come back and do a career in women's studies and do feminist theory work?"

I shook my head. "I don't agree with the perspective that Dr. Munchen and the poststructural feminists have. I think they're wrong, and that includes the participation of males and whether or not we benefit from dismantling patriarchy more than we benefit from keeping it around. But I've come to realize that even if they're wrong, they're right."

I looked off into the distance for a moment, then continued. "Feminism is women's voice. It's also the voice of activists with a certain perspective on patriarchy, but nearly all of those voices are women's voices. If there had ever been hordes and hordes of male people also being politically active with those same politics...maybe it would have different name, I don't know, but there isn't, they didn't.

"Feminism can have a male voice here and there that mainly adds or contributes, but there can't be a situation where in a room where there's dissention, everyone decides that the feminist who should be listened to is the male. If the authoritative feminist voice can be male, then men can take over feminism. That kind of thing has happened before, like with the midwives who used to do all the medicine, and men took over medicine.

"I don't mean it would automatically happen but since there's no safeguard against it, feminist women have to consider women to be the authority on feminism. And because it's that way, I can't make a career out of trying to say what I came to college to say, and do the things I wanted to do, from a feminist platform. Because at any step, if my ...if my priorities or perceptions depart from what a lot of feminist women say or how they see it, I can't be the authority on the matter so I will always be at risk of being shut down and considered an intruder.

"I think I need to find my own voice somehow, sissy libber or whatever you want to call it, but that I can't do what I set out to do 'as a feminist,'" I concluded, "and I can't use women's studies as a platform. It's not my platform to use."

Leona nodded. "It's interesting you should say that. I was thinking about you just the other day while I was reading some of the women's studies list posts. Somebody was writing about some new programs that are calling themselves 'Queer Studies,' and they have people in them who are gay men and lesbians and transsexual people. And I was wondering if that would be a better fit for you."

"I don't see why it would," I answered. "I'm not gay or transsexual, so they'd just say the same thing, that I don't have the relevant background of being mistreated and marginalized the way they are, so I have no business stealing their platform."

"Well, that's what I was going to explain. Some of the people who are doing the Queer Studies are saying they don't identify as gay or as transsexual, and they were arguing about what to call it. And that reminded me of things you've said in class and I thought 'You know, it's a shame that Derek isn't a part of this conversation.'"

My article "Same Door, Different Closet" was republished when *Feminism and Psychology* released an expanded volume in 1993, a full-sized Reader on Heterosexuality that contained all the original articles and a handful of additional ones as well. Nearly a decade later, in 2002, I was again reprinted, this time in Heasley & Crane's *Sexual Lives* textbook. Over time, my article was cited and referenced by other academics.

I released "The Feminist Perspective in (and/or On) The Field of Sociology" to an early precursor of "digital commons"—giving people anywhere the right to copy and distribute it as long as they left it intact and acknowledged me as the author. I occasionally got emails about it over the years. In 2006, it was selected and included in *Readings in Feminist Theory,* edited by Subhadra Channa; and therefore it, too, was eventually published.

I never returned to complete my degree.

READERS GUIDE

1. What are your thoughts about a male student being in a women's studies classroom? What did you think about Derek's participation? How do you feel about the representation of feminism and women's studies within this book? Did you learn anything about either? Were they presented in a respectful and accurate manner?

2. To pursue an academic course in women's studies, Derek careened through hitchhiking, heroin dens, and homelessness. Did you read his tale as being about someone who couldn't be dissuaded from doing what he wanted to do, or did you see Derek more as an impractical person who didn't plan well and brought many of his problems upon himself?

3. Derek is an intellectual, and a lot of his narrative is about the abstract thoughts going on in his head while things are happening. In what ways did he incorporate self-awareness and intellectual analysis into his everyday life? Did the book manage to strike a balance between action and events and dry intellectual theory?

4. One ongoing theme in the story is the distinction between the specific feminist theory type that Derek likes and other forms that he is less fond of. Can you name these and distinguish between them? Did it strike you as a meaningful difference, or did it seem to you that Derek was obsessing about tiny unimportant details?

5. Another major theme in the story is marginalization and the intersectionality of different oppressions and privileges. What different types of power differentials did you take notice of? Did you feel that

any identities or forms of marginalized experience were misrepresented or distorted? Were there any described experiences that you feel you learned from?

6. Domestic violence also plays a recurring role in the story. Along with rape and other forms of male violence against women, it creates a backdrop for interactions between male and female people. How does this affect their romantic and sexual relationships? How can individual people cope with this in their romantic strategies? Did you find Derek oblivious and/or part of the problem when he was reluctant to let go of his relationship with Jenna?

7. The narrative describes some polyamorous relationships, although that term was not yet in vogue in the 1980s. Polyamory refers to ongoing emotionally involved sexual relationships that don't incorporate sexual exclusivity. Had you been exposed to the notion of polyamory or known or read about polyamorous people before this book? Do you feel the descriptions of polyamorous relationships here can challenge some reader's assumptions? Is it, or is it not, compatible with feminism, and for what reasons and in what ways?

8. Throughout the book there are several would-be change agents, including individuals (Derek himself; Cowboy and Mary; Laura; Jay; Sharon; Tom Duffman, the homeless people's advocate who forced RCCA to open their doors to all homeless people) and organization and institutions (Project Release; Identity House; Coalition Against Domestic Violence; Center for Creative Nonviolence; Sayville Project; the Community Service Program). What did their various approaches to social change have in common, and how did they differ? Do you perceive tensions between being radical, being pragmatic, and being effective at producing social change? What about the relationship between feminism and the academy? In this story, and in the wider world, is feminism invading and changing academia or being coopted by it?

9. Yet another theme in the story was the conflict between sex positivity and critical takes on sexual objectification and subject-object sexual dynamics. How did the political concerns about unequal power

and boundaries and unfair social structuring of sexuality play out in interpersonal relationships and interactions in this book?

10. The psychiatric patients' rights community and its politics plays a prominent role in this tale. Were you familiar with this as a social issue before reading this book? Were these notions provocative to you? Did you find the presentation of these issues unfair either to mainstream medical-model psychiatry or to other views pertaining to counseling and therapy, or to cognitive/emotional disabilities and impairments?

11. Have you read the author's previous book (of which this book is a storyline continuation), *GenderQueer: A Story From a Different Closet?* If so, in what ways did their focus differ and in what ways did it feel like it picked up where the other book left off? How did Derek himself change over the course of this extended story arc?

GenderQueer: A Story From a Different Closet is available from Amazon, and other major booksellers.

There were also two academic articles whose creation played a role in the "Graduate Student" section of this book: "Same Door, Different Closet: A Heterosexual Sissy's Coming-out Story" and "The Radical Feminist Perspective in (and/or on) the Field of Sociology." Did the description of them in this book inspire any interest in reading the articles? These are both available on the author's website: https://www.genderkitten.com

www.ingramcontent.com/pod-product-compliance
Lightning Source LLC
Chambersburg PA
CBHW010113270326
41927CB00018B/3368